# THE RISE AND FALL OF MARKS & SPENCER

# THE RISE AND FALL
## OF
# MARKS & SPENCER

JUDI BEVAN

**P**

PROFILE BOOKS

First published in Great Britain in 2001 by
Profile Books Ltd
58A Hatton Garden
London EC1N 8LX
www.profilebooks.co.uk

*Grateful thanks is expressed to Marks & Spencer and George Davies
for use of the photographs.*

3 5 7 9 10 8 6 4 2

Typeset in Minion by MacGuru
info@macguru.org.uk

Printed and bound in Great Britain by
Clays, Bungay, Suffolk

The moral right of the author has been asserted.

A CIP catalogue record for this book is available from the British Library.

ISBN 1 86197 289 X

To John and Josephine

# Contents

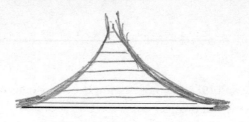

# List of illustrations

between 1972 and 1984. During that time he showed his passion for 'good human relations' but profits growth was pedestrian.

11  Derek, Lord Rayner, who chaired M&S from 1984 to 1991 was the first non-family director to run the company. A brilliant, irritable, chain-smoking homosexual, Rayner was a great moderniser and visionary.

12  Sir Richard Greenbury, the last of Simon Marks's protégés, was a brilliant instinctive merchant but one of his boardroom critics said, 'he could not innovate his way out of a paper bag'.

13  'The Arch', M&S's flagship store on the corner of Oxford Street and Orchard Street was viewed as a great gamble when Simon Marks opened it in 1930, at the depths of the 'Great Depression'.

14  Boulevard Haussmann, sadly the only consistently profitable store overseas, but not profitable enough to prevent M&S announcing its closure in 2001, producing demonstrations in Baker Street.

15  Peter Salsbury, chief executive from early 1999 until 2000. A protégé of Sir Richard Greenbury, he turned on his mentor. In his revolutionary fervour 'he ripped the heart out of the business' and earned himself the sobriquet Pol Pot.

16  Clara Freeman, the Oxford blue stocking who became M&S's first woman executive director as head of personnel.

17  Keith Oates, deputy chairman from 1994 to 1998: his attempted boardroom coup was the catalyst for M&S's fall from grace.

18  Luc Vandevelde, the olive oil pressing Belgian brought in to chair M&S following Greenbury's departure after the company's profits and share price collapsed. He earned himself the nickname 'cool hand Luc' but his regular predictions of recovery proved over optimistic.

19  Roger Holmes, the man from McKinsey, who came into head M&S's UK retail operations and went back to basics, daring to ask the customers what they thought of the company's products.

20  M&S's new look: Greenbury's immediate successors produced redesign after redesign but failed to revive the profits.

21  (Example from new Per Una collection) In his incarnation as founder of Next, George Davies saw M&S as his role model. Then after his success with the George range at Asda, his old adversary turned to him in its hour of need. The result was the Per Una range of women's fashion clothing on which M&S pinned high hopes for the early years of the twenty-first century.

# *Acknowledgements*

In the course of writing this book I have talked to a vast number of people connected with Marks & Spencer, all of whom have helped me to piece together the final picture. Most have worked for the company in the past or work for it now, others supplied goods to it while still more worked for competitive retailers. And there have been myriad contributions from almost every person I have met socially, for to mention the name Marks & Spencer in virtually any situation in Britain today is to evoke an opinion. The majority of people who have helped me would prefer to remain anonymous, but to everyone who has contributed I offer my heartfelt thanks.

In particular I would like to mention the former chairman, Sir Richard Greenbury, who gave generously of his time despite the almost certain knowledge that he would disagree with some of my conclusions. Undeterred by major surgery, two former directors, Henry Lewis and Clinton Silver, both spent several hours giving me a flavour of life under Lord Marks and Lord Sieff. Sir David Sieff helped patiently with the founding families' perspective while Brian Baldock and Sir Michael Perry spoke eloquently for the non-executive directors. Paul Smith gave insight into the Far East operations. Tony Good, a former long-term advisor, took me painstakingly through parts of the background, while Bill Green described life at the coal face running a provincial store in the 1950s and 1960s. Sundeep Bahanda of Deutsche Bank gave me the benefit of access to his hard-won research.

Of the suppliers, past and present, I would especially like to mention Sir Harry Solomon, Lord Haskins, Sir Harry Djanogly, Martin Taylor and David Suddens. Cheri Lofland and her team at the Marks & Spencer press office eased my path to the current chairman, Luc Vandevelde, and to directors such as Roger Holmes, David Norgrove, Alan McWalter and Robert Colvill as well as two former executives, Hugh Walker and Brian Godbold.

Finally, I would like to thank Andrew Franklin, Stephen Brough and Penny Daniel at Profile Books for their patience and professionalism, my copy editor Trevor Horwood for his thoroughness and my husband John for his unwavering help and support through what have sometimes seemed dark days.

# *Chronology*

| | |
|---|---|
| 1863 | Assumed year of birth of Michael Marks, the founder, at Slonim in Russian Poland (as quoted by his son, Simon. Michael himself stated 1859 on his British naturalisation papers though his wedding certificate implies 1864.). |
| 1882 | Marks arrives in England, meets wholesaler Isaac Dewhirst who lends him £5 to set up as a pedlar. |
| 1884 | Marks sets up his first stall at Kirkgate open market in Leeds. |
| 1886 | Marks marries Hannah Cohen. |
| 1888 | Birth of their son Simon. |
| 1894 | Marks forms partnership with Tom Spencer, Dewhirst's cashier. |
| 1902 | Simon Marks forms schoolboy friendship with Israel Sieff. |
| 1903 | Marks & Spencer becomes limited company with capital of £30,000. |
| | Profits £6,800 from thirty-six bazaars and shops. |
| 1907 | Tom Spencer dies. |
| 1907 | Michael Marks dies at Christmas. |
| 1908 | William Chapman becomes chairman of the company. |
| 1911 | Simon Marks becomes a director. |
| 1916 | Simon Marks becomes chairman. |
| 1924 | Simon makes first business trip to America. |
| 1926 | Israel Sieff joins Simon. |
| | June: Company floats on the stock market capitalised at £500,000. |
| 1927 | Year to March shows profits of £74,938 12s 9d from 135 stores. |
| 1931 | New food department opens selling fresh fruit and vegetables. |
| 1932 | Queen Mary visits Oxford Street store. |
| 1935 | Profits exceed £1m for the first time. |
| 1939 | Number of stores rises to 234. |
| 1939–45 | Sixteen stores destroyed and one hundred damaged by bombing. |

| | |
|---|---|
| 1956 | Operation Simplification to cut bureaucracy and cut staff. Profits exceed £10m. |
| 1964 | Simon, Lord Marks dies at work; Israel, Lord Sieff becomes chairman. Profits hit £25m. |
| 1966 | All shareholders are given full voting rights. |
| 1967 | Edward Sieff (Teddy) becomes chairman. |
| 1972 | Marcus, later Lord Sieff of Brimpton becomes chairman. |
| 1974 | M&S acquires 55 per cent of Peoples' Department Stores, Canada. |
| 1975 | First M&S store in Europe is opened, on Boulevard Haussmann in Paris. |
| 1976 | Chilled Chicken Kiev on sale, birth of recipe dish business. |
| 1982 | Scandal over directors' housing arrangements. |
| 1984 | Sir Derek Rayner, later Lord Rayner of Crowborough, becomes chairman. |
| 1984 | Formation of financial services arm in Chester. |
| 1985 | Launch of M&S charge card. |
| 1988 | February: First out-of-town M&S store opens near Cheshunt. M&S buys Brooks Brothers menswear chain in US for $750m. Profits exceed £500m for first time. |
| 1990 | Food sales reach more than £2bn. |
| 1990 | First M&S store in South East Asia opens in Hong Kong. |
| 1991 | Richard Greenbury, later Sir Richard, becomes chairman. |
| 1993 | *Sunday Times* carries fashion spread on M&S clothes. |
| 1994 | Greenbury creates four managing directors reporting to him. |
| 1995 | July: Greenbury Report published. |
| 1997 | Profits exceed £1bn for first time. July: Acquisition of nineteen stores from Littlewoods. September: £2bn expansion plan announced. |
| 1998 | November 3: Half-year profits fall by 23 per cent. November 5: Keith Oates attempts boardroom coup. December: Peter Salsbury appointed chief executive, Greenbury to be non-executive. |
| 1999 | January: Shares fall 23 per cent on profits warning. May: Profits collapse by 50 per cent. June: Greenbury resigns as chairman. |

—Brian Baldock becomes interim chairman.

October: Salsbury terminates contract with William Baird.

December: Philip Green confirms interest in bidding for M&S.

2000    January: Luc Vandevelde becomes chairman.

February: Philip Green abandons bid plan for M&S.

—Launch of Autograph range.

September: Salsbury resigns as chief executive. Vandevelde chairman and chief executive.

—Roger Holmes appointed head of UK retail.

2001    February: George Davies appointed to create Per Una brand for M&S.

March: Continental store closures announced at cost of 4,400 jobs.

May: Announcement that the headquarters are to move from Baker Street to Paddington Basin.

# *Prologue*

Springtime 1998 and 13 million shoppers a week were pouring through the doors of Marks & Spencer's 286 British stores. More important, those customers were pouring out again laden with bright green shiny plastic bags bulging with M&S clothes, food and homeware. That May, one of the sunniest and driest on record, directors and store managers alike were bedazzled by the figures. Business had rarely been better for Britain's largest and most trusted retailer.

Sir Richard Greenbury – the second chairman in the company's 114-year history to come from outside the founding families – would sit in his study in his Berkshire home on Sunday afternoons examining his weekly board summaries. Until 1980 these had come in the form of the old 'checking lists' created by the remarkable Simon Marks, son of the founder who had built Marks & Spencer from a string of penny bazaars into a national institution. Originally they had been handwritten, then typed. Now the lists of figures came from the company's computer systems, but they gave much the same information as the old checking lists – sales, stock position and commitments with suppliers – plus the balance of the season's sales estimate.

Like Marks, Greenbury's mentor and role model, Greenbury could 'read' the figures faster and more accurately than anyone else in the business – or so his admirers believed. To Greenbury, an instinctive retailer who had joined M&S straight from school at 17, they gave a snapshot of how the company was doing. They showed just what Mr and Mrs Average Shopper were buying fastest and, equally important, what they were leaving behind on the rails.

Greenbury was known for his almost feminine intuition as to where the problems lay. He could pick them out in seconds, ringing each figure that concerned him in red for further investigation. But for weeks that spring the news had been better than even he could have hoped. That unnaturally sunny May, the figures showed clothing sales up by 10 per cent on the same month the previous year – compared with a national increase of 5 per cent – while some lines were a staggering 20 per cent higher. 'We couldn't believe it,' said Greenbury. 'We thought we were geniuses.'

On Monday mornings Greenbury would hand copies of the lists with the circled items to his personal assistant – at the time an energetic M&S lifer called Nigel Robertson – and send him off to distribute them to the various relevant executive and divisional directors. Answers were expected sharpish from the individual departments and sometimes individual stores. The information from the computers was vital but the credo laid down by Lord Marks was always to probe beyond the figures. Back in 1956 following 'Operation Simplification' – a drastic streamlining of the business Marks had written: 'Both the executives and merchandisers of the department should probe into the goods in the stores with seeing eyes and a critical mind … To depend on statistics is to asphyxiate the dynamic spirit of the business.' Even though technology had improved the quality of the statistics, Greenbury still lived by his mentor's philosophy – or so he believed.

A powerfully built 6ft 2in sports enthusiast, Greenbury had worshipped the diminutive Marks, who was just 5ft 6in. Marks had singled him out on one of his store visits, giving him the nickname 'Big Fellah' and moving him to the flagship Marble Arch store – known simply in the business as 'The Arch'. But his chairman also took him on visits round the departments, where Marks was famous for asking, 'What's new?' of the managers, and for throwing garments that did not please him on the floor, declaring 'you are ruining my business'.

Once he became chairman, Greenbury, like Marks, visited 'The Arch' more frequently than other stores, simply because it was both the flagship and just ten minutes' walk from headquarters. Greenbury's style with the store staff was more benign but, even in his final years as chairman, he visited the stores at least twice a week and expected all senior personnel to do the same, though unlike the founding family chairmen before him he rarely asked 'what's new?'

The May 1998 figures were supported by reports from the stores. M&S clothes were flying off the rails. Even so, the atmosphere at the weekly executive directors meeting – EDM for short – was far from euphoric. 'We didn't sit around congratulating each other,' recalled Greenbury. Those Monday meetings, which took place in the boardroom under the gaze of Simon

Marks and the former chairmen, whose portraits decked the walls, started at 10 a.m. and ended at 12 noon. But although main board directors were expected to attend if available, they could send deputies, and the meetings were sharply different in style from the formal board meetings that took place once a month with all six non-executive directors present. The EDM each Monday was to thrash out operational problems and to discuss the immediate future – not just for clothing, but food, finance, home furnishings and the overseas operations.

Greenbury invariably dominated the proceedings, setting the agenda, ostensibly inviting other views while making it all too plain what his were. Only a few directors dared oppose or question him, fearing the harangue that could ensue. One of Greenbury's former aides said: 'The thing about Rick is he never understood the impact he had on people – people were just too scared to say what they thought. I remember one meeting we had to discuss a new policy and two or three directors got me on one side beforehand and said they were really unhappy about it. Then Rick made his presentation and asked for views. There was total silence until one said, "Chairman we are all 100 per cent behind you on this one." And that was the end of the meeting.'

Under Greenbury Marks & Spencer had prospered as never before. In the year to March 1998 profits before tax hit £1.2bn, almost double the £640m made in 1992, Greenbury's first full year after succeeding Lord Rayner as chairman in 1991. During the previous twelve months the retail giant had expanded its store space by another half a million square feet to nearly 11 million. It had taken on 2,500 new people, bringing the total number of M&S employees to 68,000 around the world. Any director who dared to criticise policy would be met with the riposte from Greenbury: 'If we are getting it so wrong, why are we making more than £1bn a year?' One former director said: 'It was hard to argue with Rick. He said he wanted our views but he is a physically intimidating man and he did not respond well to criticism.'

Despite the success it was becoming evident to Greenbury, his fifteen executive directors and the six non-executive directors too, that the purchase of nineteen Littlewoods stores in July 1997 for £192.5m, masterminded by the deputy chairman Keith Oates, was, in retrospect, looking expensive in the light of the unforeseen work that had to be done on the stores. And the £2bn expansion programme, including a new push into Europe, embarked on in a blaze of euphoric press coverage in late 1997, was going to hit profits harder than they had previously thought.

More important, there were signs of discontent among customers, although they continued to buy the spring and summer ranges. The company credo – quality, value and service – was under siege – and had even been dropped after decades from the front cover of the annual report. For some time the in-house research had shown customer satisfaction starting to wobble. 'It became volatile,' said David Norgrove, who conducted a survey in 1997 and became a director in 2000. 'For years it had been absolutely rock solid, but it had become extremely volatile. Customers were less satisfied that we were giving them value, quality and service.'

By 1998 M&S's return on sales had risen to 14 per cent – the highest of any retailer in the world apart from WalMart – but such a margin could not be sustained. Simon Marks, in his day, had wisely put a ceiling of 10 per cent on this figure.

Something had to give. Peter Salsbury, the director in charge of store operations, had under Greenbury's instructions been taking a scythe to staffing costs. Staff numbers had been rising overall, but that was because the retail footage was rising. In 1991 there had been 61,685 UK staff (excuding those who worked in head office) servicing 9.5m square feet of retail space. By the end of 1998 there were 62,425 staff servicing 12m square feet. In other words, one employee looked after 165 square feet in 1991 but 205 square feet by 1998.

The result was a theoretically more productive workforce – but in practice one that was increasingly alienated and discontented. Training suffered as budgets were nibbled away at each year. 'They cut costs, cut costs and cut costs,' recalled one former store manager in the west of England. 'And they put up prices, and put up prices.'

Customers began to notice not only the lack of sales staff but a surliness creeping into the service. Yet visiting executives, who were usually expected, would always be surrounded by eager, smiling faces. Shoppers began to feel M&S had become pricey and increasingly complained that they could not get an item on display in their size or the colour they wanted. The male non-executive directors reported a growing stream of complaints from their wives, but they were batted off by Greenbury. 'Rick dismissed these as unfortunate one-off incidents – he refused to take us seriously,' reported one.

Customers also complained that the older high-street stores had become shabby and down-at-heel – worthy of 'Moscow in the 1960s' according to one. Under Greenbury, M&S spent as little as possible on the older, smaller, high-street stores, which were nearly all freehold. Greenbury's rationale for this was quite clear: 'The twenty-two out-of-town stores plus the top twenty big city-centre stores take about £4bn a year between them,' he explained. 'Then there are fifty or so second-tier stores in places like Peterborough and Stoke with sales of £1.5bn. Then you had the 200 medium to small high-street stores with sales of £1billion between them. We tried every conceivable mix of product with those stores, but it was impossible for them to make money.'

So Greenbury preferred to spend money on big new stores, which made oodles of profit. Some of the problem high-street stores were converted to food only, but most were too big. And because of the nation's perception of M&S as a quasi-public service, attempts to close them had always been met with furious campaigns via the local press and letters to MPs. So, while customers flocked to the new Marks & Spencer edge-of-town and big city-centre stores, which carried a full range of goods in airy well-designed surroundings, they increasingly avoided the high-street stores, which looked ever more dismal. Meanwhile, lighter, brighter more fashionable shops sprang up near by.

The competition had reinvented itself since the recession of the early 1990s, but Greenbury and his team barely noticed. Next was doing well, but Marks & Spencer had seen off Next before in 1990. The Gap, too, was making waves, but to M&S directors it looked like a tiny niche business with a narrow, narrow range. As for Matalan – the successful discount store run by a renegade M&S executive, Angus Monro – it was too downmarket to count. The competition, they felt, was too fragmented and narrowly focused to merit concern.

Marks & Spencer, 114 years old and the second most profitable retailer in the world, the subject of three Harvard Business School case studies, five times winner of the Queen's Award for Export Achievement and with cupboards groaning with trophies for managerial excellence, steamed on full-throttle towards the iceberg.

The report and accounts for the financial year ending 31 March 1998 trumpeted the expansionary mood on the very first page, where a summary of a three year capital investment plan spelled out future plans. 'From 13.3

million square feet to 16.3 million square feet – 23 per cent more space', it declared. The timing could not have been worse. Within months it had become clear that 23 per cent more space was the last thing M&S needed.

Back in the directors' offices on the first and second floors of Michael House – a vast rabbit warren of a building of four linked blocks running from 27 to 67 Baker Street – it seemed entirely reasonable for the directors to budget for a continued growth in sales of 10 per cent. The word went down from the chairman, through the executive directors, the divisional directors and the executives to the selectors and merchandisers in the buying departments: place your orders with suppliers accordingly.

A little further down the ranks ambition took a hand. Some ambitious young selectors decided the way to become stars was to beat their budgets. They ordered certain lines from suppliers, 20 per cent up on the previous year. 'There was a huge increase in our order books,' remembered David Suddens at the garment maker William Baird.

Then in July and August 1998 the great British public started buying fewer clothes. Not only that, customers were unimpressed with the M&S autumn ranges, which hit the shops in early September. An attempt to woo the younger customer with a predominance of synthetic fabrics in offbeat colours misfired, while the more mature ranges were mainly black and grey. Although grey was indeed the fashion colour that autumn, the clothes looked drab and drear displayed in the vast, unbroken retail floors of the bigger M&S stores.

Regular customers who had sworn by M&S for a decade could suddenly find nothing new or exciting to buy. In November 1998 Vicki Woods, former editor of *Harpers & Queen* and a devotee of M&S, wrote in the *Sunday Telegraph* of her disillusionment.

'In those days [the early 1990s] I browsed in Marks & Spencer nearly every single day. Spending a month's wages on a gold-buttoned display jacket was one thing but chucking good money after bad on the basics and the underpinnings was quite another; and why bother, when the M&S quality was unrivalled? Knickers, tights, blouses, boots, jumpers, T-shirts, those curious garments called "bodies" that fastened under the crotch for neatness at the waistline – all from M&S.' Woods went on to describe how her young staff on *Harpers* would spend whole afternoons in M&S, 'rootling through every garment in the store, looking for the M&S star purchases: the things that looked as though they came from Bond Street but which sold for a tenth of the Bond Street mark up.' And they were proud of them. 'They'd display them in the office, marvelling at the quality of the fabric (look – it's pure cashmere; look – it's silk and wool) and the skilful cut (skinny white linen shirts, just like Donna Karan; perfect navy blazers, just like Ralph Lauren; floaty viscose tunics, just like Ghost).'

But by 1998, how all that had changed. She wrote: 'I nipped into the Newbury M&S … and found myself drifting around the clothing racks out of habit. There was nothing. Nothing. Aubergine blouses, skimpily-cut in satin look viscose. Horrible little suits in cheap fabric, in funny colours like rusty brown. Hordes of acrylic polo-necks in puzzling pastel shades. Devore velvet "evening tops" in Hawaiian Tropic colours.'

There were management problems too. In early 1998 Greenbury had decided to swap his managing directors around. Greenbury and the non-executive directors of M&S, headed by Sir Martin Jacomb, at the time chairman of the Prudential, and Brian Baldock, a former Guinness director, had been wrestling with the problem of who would be the man to take over from Greenbury. There were four managing directors: Keith Oates, also deputy chairman, Andrew Stone, Guy McCracken and Peter Salsbury – one of whom it had been hoped, would have shown himself clearly as the leader. But by 1998, still undecided, the non-executives asked Greenbury to put the most likely candidate for chief executive into the toughest job – that of heading the clothing business.

At that time Andrew Stone, viewed as a merchant of great flair and talent, had been running clothing. Quirky and eccentric, Stone was an old-style merchant who had started his career on a market stall, a creative force for good bursting with whacky ideas that the customers often loved. 'Andrew had his finger on the pulse of what "she" wanted,' said one supplier, using the company shorthand to describe the M&S core customer. He also worked well with the design team headed by Brian Godbold, which had scooped up the fashion plaudits in 1994 and 1995. 'Andrew allowed you to get on and develop ideas,' Godbold said later.

But the non-executive directors urged Greenbury to put Peter Salsbury into the major role of running clothing so they could assess his abilities. Greenbury did so and put Stone, who had received a working peerage the previous summer, in charge of food, about which he knew relatively little and which in any case was run by the divisional director Mike Taylor and his team.

By accepting the peerage Stone had effectively ruled himself out of the race to become chief executive – because he would have to attend all the major debates in the House of Lords. Guy McCracken – who had been running food and now went to head personnel and store operations, had not come through as chief executive material, which left Greenbury and his team of non-executives with just two candidates to choose from: Keith Oates, the deputy chairman in charge of international operations and financial services, and Peter Salsbury, the personnel supremo.

Salsbury had the reputation of being an able manager but he lacked Stone's flair. That autumn, women customers voted with their account cards and took their custom elsewhere. Instead of sales growing by the anticipated 10 per cent they fell by 2 per cent, leaving a small mountain of unsold stock at a cost of £150m. When the 1998 first half-year figures were announced on 3 November, the disaster was plain for all to see. In the first serious fall since the Second World War, profits were down by 23 per cent. Greenbury reported: 'It's a bloodbath out there on the clothing front … business has fallen off a cliff.' Prophetically he continued, 'We all thought that sales would recover in September and October and in fact they have gone further south. The entire high street is on sale.'

Just six months earlier there had been little sign of such a precipitous downturn although, with the mysterious prescience for which the stock market is famous, the share price had already started to fall from its peak of 664½p in October 1997. Insiders had picked up the tensions bubbling beneath the surface. Behind the smiling directors' faces that gazed out from the annual report each year, frustrations were building. The succession dominated everyone's thinking. Greenbury had been chief executive since 1988 and chairman since 1991. His retirement had already been deferred twice because of his and the non-executive directors' indecision over who would succeed him. Someone would have to take over soon but, whereas previously the anointed candidate had always been plain to see, in 1998 there was no one obvious.

The succession issue took up more of the directors' mental energy than any other, including trading. Ultimately it was to gouge a hole in the side of the ship so wide it may yet sink. Greenbury had begun to regret his decision made back in 1994 to create four managing directors and let them fight it out and he began to talk to friends of his concerns about the candidates. 'They are not coming through fast enough,' he said of the four. 'There still is not an obvious successor.'

Yet Keith Oates, the deputy chairman, felt it was all too obvious that he alone of the candidates had the qualities to lead M&S into the twenty-first century. His consequent bid for power, made two days after the 1998 results announcement in November, provided one of the more spectacular corporate dramas seen in British business. More seriously, his attempted coup destabilised the business, acting as the catalyst for the undoing of an icon – the fall from grace of a company that for the previous half century had been held up as a benchmark of excellence around the world.

Who could have guessed that within two short years the company's reputation would be smashed, perhaps irretrievably, or that all but one of the sixteen executive directors would have gone, consigned to the dustbin of corporate history? Who would have believed that branding experts would compare the name of Marks & Spencer to Rover as an example of a British brand that had lost all credibility? And who could have foreseen that learned commentators would be dismissing Marks & Spencer, along with the Tory Party, the Monarchy and the Church of England, as one of those national institutions that had ceased to have any relevance to life in modern Britain?

# CHAPTER ONE

# In the beginning

On 18 March 1932 Queen Mary visited the largest Marks & Spencer store, which had been opened two years before in Oxford Street. She went, 'to see specimens of goods made in England' as she wrote in her private diary. Not only did she see the goods, she bought some as well. According to the next day's *Times*, she purchased an Axminster rug for five shillings, a leather handbag for 1s 11d, a willow-pattern teapot for 1s and a 21-piece tea service for 6s. In the days that followed, the public flocked to buy willow-pattern teapots and Axminster rugs.

If one event marked the transformation of Marks & Spencer from a simple chain of shops into a national institution, this was it. Simon Marks, the chairman and son of the founder, squired the Queen around the store during her half-hour visit. She is reputed to have told her host that it was the most successful shopping she had ever done. After bidding her and her entourage farewell, Simon turned with shining eyes to one of his executives, Willie Jacobson, and said: 'Well, Willie, that wasn't bad for the son of a pedlar!'

Exactly fifty years before, in 1882, Simon's father Michael Marks had arrived in England, fleeing the anti-Semitic pogroms that followed the 1881 assassination of Tsar Alexander II in Russia where whole villages were torched. He went first, the story goes, to Leeds, but according to the historian Asa Briggs he more probably went to Stockton-on-Tees.

The details of his arrival are swathed in the mists of legend but we do know that, when he was just 20, he met Isaac Dewhirst, an equally youthful man who had already built up a modest wholesale business in Leeds. According to the former M&S archivist the late Paul Bookbinder in his biography of Simon Marks, Dewhirst was approached by a slightly built, bearded young man who kept repeating one word: 'Barrans'. The young Michael Marks could speak little English but luckily Dewhirst's manager spoke some Yiddish and ascertained that Michael, who was looking for work, had been told to go to Barrans, a tailoring factory employing many immigrant Russian Jews.

The two men, barely out of their teens, clicked. Instead of giving him the directions and thinking no more about it, Isaac Dewhirst invited Michael Marks back to his warehouse. It seems likely, in view of what then happened, that Michael told Isaac Dewhirst that he had been a pedlar in Russia. 'My grandfather was fascinated by the stranger,' recalled Alistair Dewhirst, grandson of Isaac. 'He offered to lend him five pounds. Michael Marks asked if he might use it to buy goods from the warehouse. My grandfather agreed and as Michael Marks paid off the debt, he was allowed to make further purchases to the same amount.'

And so Michael Marks became a pedlar servicing the villages around Leeds. Unable to speak English he attached a sign to his tray that read 'Don't ask the price, it's a penny'. This cut out all the haggling usually conducted with pedlars, and because Michael chose his cotton reels, buttons, soap, candles and other items carefully and seemed, even then, to have an eye for what attracted customers, he did well.

There the story might have ended, or it might have ended at the open market trestle table he went on to rent, or the covered market stall that followed. The various accounts of Michael Marks outline bare events – portrayed almost as a string of coincidences that could have happened to anyone. We know tantalisingly little of Michael's personality, although his many obituaries speak of a generous benefactor to the poor as well as of a remarkable businessman.

Michael's early childhood was of the kind that creates great men out of the few not crushed by it. Born in the town of Slonim in the Russian–Polish province of Grodno, Michael was the youngest of five children. His mother Rebecca died shortly after his birth. His father Mordechai, a biblical-looking figure with a luxuriant white beard, was a tailor and part owner of a grain mill and Michael was brought up by one of his elder sisters. As the baby of the family he was probably spoiled and fussed over by all four of his older siblings while at the same time suffering the insecurity of a motherless child.

To be a successful pedlar and stallholder he must have possessed some charm. He certainly had tenacity and an ability to think laterally. Right from the beginning, with his penny-price no-haggling policy he broke the mould. And from the moment he arrived in Britain he revealed himself to be a driven personality constantly looking for the next opportunity to increase his fortunes. From a pedlar's tray he moved to open market stall to covered market stall to penny bazaars in the high streets of his adopted country.

Peddling was hard physical work in northern English winters. Even then, the man who was to die at 47 of overwork and 'twofahs disease' (from smoking cheap cigars that were two-for-a penny) had uncertain health and within two years, as soon as he saved enough money, hired a pitch in Leeds' Kirkgate open-air market, setting up a trestle table just six feet by three. The market traded only two days a week, on Tuesdays and Saturdays, so on the other days he would travel to other market towns such as Castleford and Wakefield to sell his goods. Nearly every day he would collect new stock from Dewhirst's warehouse near the market and there he met Tom Spencer, the Dewhirst cashier. The two men hit it off, although it was some years before their names would be joined above a shopfront.

If Michael was lucky in his chance encounters with future business partners he was also fortunate in finding a wife. The story goes that while visiting Stockton-on-Tees on business he started chatting to a stranger as he sheltered from a sudden downpour. The stranger, whose name was Cohen and who was also a refugee from Russia, invited Michael home and introduced him to his daughter Hannah, with whom he fell in love. They were married less than a year later on 19 November 1886 in Leeds' Belgrave Street synagogue when he was 22 and she was 21. Michael described himself as a 'licensed hawker' on the marriage certificate. Hannah would help him, counting up the money and working into the night assembling little sewing kits and supervising the stock of simple household items such as cotton reels, nails, screws, pins, needles, buttons, soaps, sponges and egg cups.

Israel Sieff, who formed a lifelong partnership with Hannah's son Simon and married her daughter Rebecca, described her thus in his memoirs: 'a wonderful woman ... a rare creature, small, slight, delicate, devoted. She was in spite of being small, immensely energetic, a dominating little lady who ruled her husband and her family.' She was by all accounts, a pretty typical Jewish mother who bound her family together with love, good food and discipline.

Michael and Hannah's happiness was blighted by the loss of their first child, a boy, at birth, but the business prospered and in 1888 they moved from a poor area of Leeds to a terraced house in the slightly more salubrious Trafalgar Street. Not long afterwards their son Simon was born to much celebration.

Meanwhile Michael had begun to employ other people, initially using two girls from Dewhirst's to run stalls so that he could operate in two towns on one day. He graduated from the outdoor market to Leeds' indoor market where he changed the sign above his stall from 'Don't ask the price, it's a penny' to 'M Marks: the original Penny Bazaar' and then to 'Marks Penny Bazaar'. Within two years he had opened up penny bazaars in covered market halls in several towns in Yorkshire and Lancashire.

Michael believed in making life easy for his customers. He had cut out the haggling over price and he was more than happy for customers to have a good look at and handle the goods. As his English improved and the range of goods expanded he had penny items on one side of the stall and variously priced objects on the other. He also pared his own profit margins in order to boost sales, producing the value proposition that became so crucial to the later success of Marks & Spencer.

The birth of his son and then his first daughter, Rebecca, changed Michael's attitude to Leeds, which had more than its share of social problems – 'a hotbed of drunkenness and immorality, the haunt of criminals' was how one chronicler of the time described it. He looked for a better place in which to bring up a family and in 1891 they moved to Wigan, a smaller, poorer town but within a short rail journey to places such as Warrington, Birkenhead and Bolton where he could expand.

Michael's children grew up in a matriarchal atmosphere because their father was mostly away working and achievement went with the decor. His son Simon later wrote: '... my first memory is of a little house in Wigan at the age of four ... We lived in modest though comfortable circumstances and conditions and our happiest times seemed to be when father spent the Sunday with us. He was the most lovable of persons and seemed to be away a great deal. He was, of course, pre-occupied with the building up of his business to which he devoted all of his energies.'

By this time Michael had maybe a dozen market stalls. He then made the leap that so many small businessmen fail to make and thus stay small businessmen. Michael decided he needed two things if he was to expand – credit and a partner. Until then Dewhirst had bankrolled him as well as providing him with goods and staff. He had several discussions with fellow stallholders about going into partnership but nothing came of it. So he asked Isaac Dewhirst to go into partnership with him. 'What better partnership than a wholesaler and retailer?' he argued. We do not know exactly why Isaac said no. Ostensibly it was because he was committed to his own business, but possibly he sensed that he would inevitably become the junior partner. Or did he realise that Michael had his eye on Dewhirst's chief cashier, Tom Spencer, who was getting restless and muttering about setting up on his own? Michael and Tom Spencer had got on well for some time and Spencer's second wife, Agnes, had tutored Michael in English, recalling in her diary her pleasure when he wrote his first cheque in English. Spencer was a details man, a meticulous accountant with the kind of administrative abilities a growing business needs. A thrifty Yorkshireman with a love of cricket and drinking, he provided the nitty-gritty business skills that Michael lacked.

Thus in September 1894 Tom Spencer put his life savings of £300 into buying a half share in Michael Marks's penny bazaars – and so the Jew and the Gentile formed a partnership from which grew the most successful retailing dynasty in British history.

That same month, Michael moved his family to the more cosmopolitan Manchester, where, unlike Wigan, there was a thriving Jewish community. They moved to Cheetham Hill Road, where he opened what was effectively the first Marks & Spencer shop on the ground floor, while the family lived in the six rooms above. 'Marks & Spencer Penny Bazaar' read the sign – the first time the names had been linked – and on the doorframe were the words 'admission free'. Once again Michael Marks was breaking the mould. The public was invited in to browse – the goods were on display as they were in market stalls – all in sharp contrast to the other shops of the time where the products were kept under the counter. By this time, although he was still buying from Dewhirst and other British suppliers, he found many goods cheaper in Germany, Austria, Czechoslovakia and France.

From there the business flew. In 1903, when the net profit was £6,800, there were thirty-six market bazaars and shops, including three in London. That year they formed a limited company with capital of £30,000 in £1 ordinary shares. Michael Marks and Thomas Spencer were both allotted 14,996 each while one share apiece went to the seven other signatories of the Memorandum and Articles of Association. Three shares were never allotted. The agreement stated that if the two partners, or those who subsequently replaced them, should disagree, control of the company could pass to the owners of the few loose shares.

It was an agreement that was to jeopardise the future of the business. If

Michael had been lucky in his choice of partner, he was unlucky in the way events unfolded. In 1905 Tom Spencer decided to retire to take up gentleman farming, attending only monthly board meetings yet still drawing his half of the profits. It was an almost stereotypical parting of the ways. The Anglo-Saxon Spencer retired to enjoy his money in the countryside while the Jewish immigrant worked increasingly long hours to achieve as much as possible and to leave as much wealth as possible to his family.

In practical terms, Spencer's decision left Michael without a working partner, which put huge additional strain on him. The name that became famous throughout the world as a model for retailing was based on a partnership of just eleven years.

Desperately in need of a partner to share the workload, Michael once again approached Isaac Dewhirst, who once again turned him down – an event that evidently displeased Spencer, for he replaced Dewhirst as his executor with a handkerchief manufacturer called William Chapman, who would cause Simon Marks a great deal of trouble in the years ahead.

The company continued to prosper. Marks & Spencer was fast becoming a household name, certainly in the north of England. By the turn of the century Asa Briggs wrote that there was evidence of penny bazaars in twenty-three market halls and 'branch establishments' in eleven other places. The halls included Hartlepool, Huddersfield, Middlesbrough, Rotherham, St Helens, Scarborough, Sheffield, Southport, Stalybridge, Warrington and Wolverhampton. There were also inroads south with halls in Bath and other towns. But as the century wore on, the partners realised that shops in high streets were more profitable. Liverpool was one of the first in 1903, followed by Douglas, Isle of Man (in 1904), Bradford and Bristol. By 1908 the number of Marks & Spencer outlets had risen to sixty, two-thirds of them shops, the rest established penny bazaars in covered markets. But by then both Tom Spencer and Michael Marks were dead.

In 1907 Tom Spencer died, largely from drink it was believed, aged 53 – slain by a life of ease. A few months afterwards Michael Marks collapsed in the street and never recovered. A frail constitution, overwork and cheap cigars put him in the grave at 47.

Marks & Spencer later became famous for value, quality, its unique relationship with suppliers and the paternalistic way it treated its staff. The paternalism started with Michael Marks, who as well as being a shrewd businessman was both sensitive and kind. When one of his female sales assistants contracted pneumonia and died after a particularly cold spell in Birkenhead open market he was devastated, resolving never to operate in open markets again. In the covered markets he built wooden floors so the girls' feet would not get cold, he shared food with them and gave them Christmas presents. He was soon providing gas rings to make tea and to warm up food, although at the turn of the century staff were expected to bring their own lunch with them. They were also expected to work a 63-hour week with only one week's holiday a year for assistants, two weeks for manageresses.

When Michael built the first head office in Derby Street, Manchester, which initially employed a dozen people, he put in a dining room and a place where staff could cook their food.

He was quick to share his newly made wealth and became a regular bene-factor in the Jewish working men's club which he visited every week.

By 1907 the company had become well known, as had a growing food chain called Sainsbury. Shortly before his death Michael Marks bought a site from the founder, John Sainsbury, for a penny bazaar right next to the Sainsbury store. He invited John Sainsbury to the opening and proudly introduced Simon, who had just started working in the company. 'I like your son, Mr Marks,' declared Sainsbury, adding prophetically, 'He will go far.'

That Christmas Eve, Michael took Simon and Tom Spencer junior to lunch at Manchester's Victoria Hotel. It was following that, while on his way to visit the Oldham Street branch, that he collapsed in the street and died a few days later.

His funeral at Manchester's Jewish cemetery drew one of the largest crowds ever seen there. The obituaries paid tribute to his generosity and kindness. 'Pioneer of Penny Bazaars – Death of a Generous Manchester Jew', was the headline above one article, which briefly outlined the growth of the company from one stall but devoted more space to his philanthropic works. The most touching part of the article read: 'As an instance of his open-handedness and at the same time of his patriotism, it may be mentioned that during the Boer War when the "Chronicle" fund for the relief of sol-diers' families was running in our columns, Mr Marks contributed every week the sum of ten shillings under the modest description, "From a Jew".'

Once again the story could have ended there. Michael Marks had not ex-pected to die so young, despite his persistent cough. Simon at 19 had offi-cially joined the company just two months before, although he had been given a fine education and sent off round Europe to experience life outside the UK. In addition, Tom Spencer's executor William Chapman now controlled half the shares and was, after Michael's death, the only director, Simon being under 21.

Shortly after his father's death Simon wrote: 'It has been a terrible time to go through. The responsibility which so suddenly descended on me has aged me by ten years. At least that is how I feel. At home ... everything which used to be so jolly is now dispiriting. We wait for the absentee but he does not come. We speak of him so often but he cannot hear. It is only now that we are beginning to understand what death means, what a terrible chasm separates us.'

Until the moment when at 19 he stood by his father's graveside and realised in the words of the Talmud that he would have 'to be a man where there is no man', Simon had led a comfortable, secure life, rich in experience as the beloved only son in the heart of an increasingly affluent Jewish family. His four sisters, Rebecca, Miriam, Matilda and Elaine, adored him although he clashed ferociously with Becky, the eldest and most independent-minded of the three.

Simon was six when the family moved to Manchester – to the flat above the Cheetham Hill Road shop – and for the rest of his life he regarded the city as his home town: 'It is here that I spent the formative years of my life, where I married and where I helped to lay the foundations of a new Marks & Spencer.' Until he was 13, Simon went to the Manchester Jews School, a few minutes' walk from his home. Despite the name, the education was non-religious and its aim was to convert east European immigrants' children into English gentlemen and ladies. The spirit of the times was to assimilate. Most of those immigrants were sick of pogroms and persecution and grateful for the chance to prove they could make a positive contribution in their new country. Several elite Jewish families, headed by the Rothschilds, had already made their mark in the professions and commerce. These families were concerned that the influx of Russian Polish Jews should not stir up anti-Semitism and were at pains to push them towards an English way of life.

Although Simon was expected to learn Hebrew on Sunday mornings, his efforts at school were devoted to the English language, culture, games and songs. The school strongly discouraged the speaking of Yiddish – the language of the *stetl*.

By the time the family moved to the more affluent Bury New Road, Simon was able at the age of seven to write a Christmas greeting to friends. He was always slight, and grew to only 5ft 6in, but his forceful aggressive personality showed itself early. He later wrote of his schooldays: 'I always seemed to be in trouble, fighting more or less victoriously with other boys, but whether victorious or not, I always got a further scolding when I returned home, a little dirty with hair dishevelled and my clothes torn with the adventures of the day.'

At school he was good at languages and he adored cricket. At the age of 16, when answering a questionnaire he wrote that his favourite amusements were cricket and football and his idea of misery was 'To be in bed while one's cricket team is playing a match'. His idea of happiness was 'speaking to a nice, nice girl', his favourite book *The Count of Monte Cristo*, by Alexander Dumas. His favourite historical character, he wrote, was King Alfred, while his ambition was 'to have a handle to my name'. In men, he most admired the qualities of tenacity and straightforwardness and his favourite adage was 'If at first you don't succeed, try, try, try again.'

Several business dynasties have been established by a father and then taken to national success by a son – Sainsbury, Dixons and Heron Corporation are all examples. Michael and Hannah brought Simon up in the belief that he would one day take over the helm of Marks & Spencer – and they were particularly fortunate on three counts. First, Simon had both the brain and temperament for the job. Secondly he wanted to do it – there is never a suggestion that he thought of any other career. And thirdly, he found a life-long business partner, friend and supporter in Israel Sieff.

There is a saying in the company that Marks & Spencer people work together, eat together and sleep together. They certainly marry each other. Of the sixteen executive directors on the board in 1998, six were married to women who had worked or still worked in the business and two, Peter Salsbury and Chris Littmoden, had second wives from M&S. The chairman Sir Richard Greenbury had, after a second marriage that ended in divorce, remarried his first wife, Siân. Both women were former M&S employees. It went right through the business down to the store staff, who frequently married each other.

The roots of this phenomenon go right back to Simon and Israel. It happened that a teenage Israel Sieff was walking along the road one Saturday morning when he spotted three girls ahead of him, dressed in fur-trimmed heavy wool coats – Simon's three sisters. He was particularly intrigued by the shapely legs of the tallest, Becky. 'It was the first time I had noticed the shape of a girl's legs. I wanted to see if she had the kind of face I felt instinctively … should go with the legs.' He managed to overtake them and was gratified when he looked back to find that her face was 'extremely pretty'. A week later they met at a children's party and she arranged for Israel to be invited home. There Simon asked him if he wanted to play cricket, and so the two boys went out to the field behind the house to join the two teams Simon had assembled. Israel recalled Simon as 'a dark, eager, vital forceful boy, altogether quicker in his speech, gestures and movements than myself. We were as animals very different which is why, perhaps, we hit it off.'

Israel was pivotal to the growth of Marks & Spencer. Without him Simon's harshness in the company would have been intolerable. 'Simon was a monster,' recalled a former director who worked closely with him as a young man. 'He ran the company as a total autocrat and was proud of it. "Give me no pro-consuls," he would say. Disagreeing with him could end your career. One chief accountant mildly pointed out what he saw as some flaws in Simon's thinking on a minor issue and was promptly fired.'

Even at 13 his leadership qualities were plain to see as he captained the cricket team he had assembled.

'I remember the first game well,' wrote Israel in his memoirs.

It was like so many we played on the field behind his father's house. He (Simon) was not dictatorial and he did not abuse his power. But he did not conceal the fact that he was in control of the game and the players. Our friendship began that Saturday afternoon. It lasted sixty-two years, up to his death in 1964. All through it he remained the one who possessed the bat, ball and wickets and I was happy and fulfilled under his captaincy.

The friendship became a business partnership and the families became thoroughly intertwined when Israel married the long-legged Becky and later Simon married Israel's sister, Miriam. One of Simon's other sisters, Miriam, married Harry Sacher, a barrister who eventually became an M&S director.

Soon after they met the two boys started at Manchester Grammar School, the best school for miles around. Boys travelled from as far as 30 miles away, but for Simon and Israel it was a short tram ride. There they consolidated the partnership and friendship that was to last six decades. 'They married each other's sisters because they couldn't marry each other,' is the conclusion of one director. Simon, quick, arrogant, confident with a volcanic temper, Israel, an altogether more gentle philosophical character, they shared three passions: Marks & Spencer, the formation of a Jewish state and, of course, cricket.

Simon did better in exams than Israel but at 17, while Israel went to read economics at Manchester University, Simon was dispatched to the Continent. He first spent a year in Nuremberg perfecting his German and then went to Paris, which he loved but where he was lonely.

He finally returned home from this mind-broadening exercise in November 1907, just a few weeks before his father's death, to work as Michael's assistant.

For two weeks after Michael Marks died William Chapman, Tom Spencer's executor, was the only director of Marks & Spencer. At 19, Simon was still under age and found himself in a suddenly precarious position, although the family still owned nearly half the shares. He swiftly insisted that Bernhard Steel, owner of a construction company that built and converted the Marks & Spencer's stores and one of Michael's executors, be put on the board to represent the Marks family interests until Simon could become a director two years later.

In different circumstances Marks & Spencer might have become Chapman & Steel – but fortunately for Simon the two men disagreed often – and both had their own business interests to pursue. Between 1907 and 1915 William Chapman was chairman of the company while Simon learned the business, travelling widely, developing his buying skills. Simon did not get on with Chapman, who clearly wanted to gain control of the company yet made the fatal error of trying to run his handkerchief firm at the same time. Chapman and Steel clashed frequently, mainly owing to disputes over costs charged to Marks & Spencer by the building contractors. Yet despite these frequent arguments the two older men realised they were in a position to wrest control from the Marks family. In 1909 they proposed to increase the share capital to £100,000 in the sure knowledge that neither the Marks family nor the young Tom Spencer (who had become even more of a drunkard than his father) had enough money to take up their share.

Simon managed to defeat the proposal that time, but once again in 1911, the year when Simon and Tom formally became directors, Chapman and

Steel proposed to increase the share capital. But before the proposal could be implemented, relations between Steel and Chapman collapsed. Improprieties in Steel's building company were uncovered and he was forced to retire – ostensibly on grounds of ill health – in 1912.

Despite all this, Edwardian prosperity combined with Simon's buying skills meant that the company continued to power ahead. In 1912, record sales of £316,700 produced profits of £24,000.

Simon was now a junior director under Chapman's chairmanship while Tom Spencer junior fell very much under the handkerchief manufacturer's influence. Chapman blocked any attempt to install another director allied with the Marks's interests. So any major decisions went 2:1 against Simon. In response Simon, backed up by Israel, his mother and his sisters, started quietly to buy up the loose shares that had been allocated to the other signatories of the agreement when the business was incorporated and, subsequently, to senior employees. He could see all too clearly that one more attempt to increase the share capital and the Marks family would lose control of the company his father worked so hard to build. The price he found he had to pay for the shares was, in his own words 'exorbitant' – £14,000 for 1,000; but Simon managed to find £2,500, Hannah Marks put up £5,000 – half her savings – and Israel and his father Ephraim Sieff provided the rest.

Yet in the midst of this corporate turmoil the company paid out a 50 per cent dividend. It could boast 145 branches, only ten of them in market halls and fifty-six of them in London, although the war made it more difficult to fill this growing number of emporiums with exciting and varied goods.

The pace and drama of the boardroom bust-up now gathered momentum. In the autumn of 1915 Simon failed to turn up to three board meetings that had been called by Chapman. This infuriated and unnerved Chapman, who, because of the lack of a quorum, had no option but to cancel the meetings.

Then, for the meeting called for 22 November, Simon appeared, bringing with him Alexander Isaacs, a jeweller who had been an executor of Michael's will, and Israel Sieff, expressly to appoint them as directors. In the ensuing argument, Chapman declared that such appointments required a 75 per cent majority and as the Spencer trustees were against it, there was little point in putting it to the meeting. He did, however, allow a vote, presumably because he was sure of winning, which went five for the appointments and eight against.

Alexander Isaacs countered this defeat by demanding a poll of the number of shares rather than a show of hands. This time the proposal was again apparently defeated by just 44 shares. Simon then played his last card – he declared to the meeting that he held proxy votes on a further 608 shares owned by minor shareholders.

Chapman, after consulting the company solicitor (who was also his personal solicitor), refused to recognise the proxies, declared the resolution defeated and closed the meeting. Chapman retained his supremacy on the board and declared his intention to curtail all expansion – something that appalled the ambitious Simon.

So in December Simon took the matter to court. Mr Justice Peterson in the Chancery Court ruled that Simon's proxies were valid and that Israel Sieff and Alexander Isaacs had been correctly elected directors. Chapman appealed. It must have been a tense Christmas in the Marks and Sieff households, but in January 1916 the Appeal Court upheld the trial judge's decision. Simon had won back control of Marks & Spencer – even though it took more than a year before Chapman and Spencer were forced to recognise it.

At a stormy meeting in August 1916 Alexander Isaacs moved a resolution that 'Mr Simon Marks be elected Chairman of the Board of Directors of Marks and Spencer Ltd and that he now take the chair'.

Chapman stormed from the room closely followed by Tom Spencer junior, although they did not resign until nearly a year later. Tom Spencer died shortly afterwards, an alcoholic like his father but at the shockingly young age of 35 – eighteen years younger than his father had been when he died. But Chapman didn't cut himself off from what he knew was a successful business. He held his shares until the flotation in 1926 – and Marks & Spencer continued to buy handkerchiefs from Chapman's firm for many years, a remarkable sign of Simon's pragmatism, rather than magnanimity in victory, in the wake of such a bitter dispute.

For the first time Simon had a clear run at managing his family firm. There was much to be done. 'On looking back I shudder to think of the inadequacy of the board and its general management,' he told his biographer Paul Bookbinder forty years later. 'Nothing new in ideas or administration had been evolved, but more shops were added.'

From war in the boardroom Simon was forced to turn his attention to the war outside – the First World War. Israel had volunteered for a local Lancashire regiment, the Derby Fusiliers, and spent some weeks training before his father, infuriated by his son's behaviour, successfully applied for his military discharge.

Simon did not volunteer. Now married, he had also to support his mother Hannah, and two younger sisters, Matilda, who was severely epileptic and the 13-year-old Elaine. Within a year Hannah died and in May 1917, a year after conscription was extended to married men, Simon was posted to Forward Barracks in Preston, Lancashire. From there, Gunner Marks would hold M&S board meetings in the nearby Bull and Royal pub.

All their lives Simon Marks and Israel Sieff viewed themselves as British Jews. But during their late teens and early twenties they both became active Zionists. They fell under the spell of Chaim Weizmann, then president of the English Zionist movement and the man largely responsible for securing the Balfour Declaration stating that Britain supported the creation of a national home for the Jewish people in Palestine. Weizmann, desperately in need of their administrative and financial help at this time, wrote to military intelligence and secured Simon's release, just weeks after he had been called up. From then on the Marks, Sieff and Sacher families worked tirelessly to support the Zionist cause and the formation of the State of Israel. Israel Sieff became Weizmann's personal assistant while Simon put his money and intellect at his disposal. For Simon, who rarely looked up to anybody, Weizmann was the one man of whom he was in awe.

After the First World War Simon moved Miriam and his two children, Hannah and Michael, from Manchester to Hampstead in London, and the company headquarters to Chiswell Street in the City. For the first time in many years Simon was able to focus fully on the business. What he saw worried him: tawdry shops selling tawdry goods that had no theme or style. His viewpoint reflected his rising aspirations, heading a group of penny bazaars no longer appealed. The cheap assortment of crockery, haberdashery, toys and hardware gave him no pleasure and he was well aware that the pricing was all over the place – from sixpence to five shillings.

His mind was also concentrated by the growing competition. The American outlet F. W. Woolworth had come to Britain and its red and gold shop signs were appearing in seemingly every British high street. Simon had only to walk among the counters to admire and feel threatened by the wide range of goods selling for either threepence or sixpence. While Marks & Spencer had been marking time, embroiled in boardroom power struggles, Woolworth had become a household name. 'I was afraid,' Simon recalled later.

'And the question of how to react, what to do, was my concern day and night.' He realised that although on the surface Marks & Spencer was still highly successful – profits more than doubled from £29,000 to £59,000 between 1921 and 1922 – the company would have to change radically to survive. He wrote that at this stage the company had 'no direction, no leadership, no thought'.

Simon was surely being too hard on both himself and the company. But that was his nature – he was as self-critical as he was critical of others – and that is the characteristic that enabled him to reinvent the company whenever it was necessary, pushing it to new successes year after year. Simon Marks had the ability to recognise when he made mistakes and to act swiftly to put things right. Although he found criticism painful, he was able to react to it – it pushed him and the company forward. His self-critical insecurity ensured the company's survival and growth. How different from Sir Richard Greenbury in the last few years of his chairmanship in the second half of the 1990s. Any hint of criticism from fellow directors produced scathing verbal tirades while outsiders in the press and the City were treated to angry letters that became known as 'Rickograms'. Even when profits nearly halved and the competition had well and truly broken through the ramparts of fortress M&S, he insisted that the problems were temporary, that all the fundamentals were sound.

By contrast, when a store manager reported to Simon some decades earlier that two Woolworth directors had been in and had scathingly referred to some items as 'lemons' he was upset. But he was shrewd enough to see that they were right. He was also shrewd enough to change the direction of Marks & Spencer rather than enter into a head-to-head price war that he judged he could not win.

One telling anecdote describes him sitting in his office examining a wooden pencil from Woolworth. 'What can I do to improve the value of this basic pencil and increase its appeal on the counters of Marks & Spencer?' he asked himself. His answer was pessimistic as he realised that there was very little and that the same was true for other basic products such as a rolling pin or a bag of flour. He became acutely aware of his lack of practical experience. 'I had never worked in a shop, had no training in the business.' Most of all he saw that he needed new ideas. Like so many British entrepreneurs after him, he looked west for inspiration. And so, one chill February morning in 1924, he set sail from Southampton on the White Star liner *Olympic*, destined for America.

# CHAPTER TWO

# New direction

Simon's visit to the United States revolutionised his thinking. Introduced into the New York financial scene by a distant German relative in the music publishing business, he was inspired by his conversations with American businessmen. He met many retailers, although his notes reveal the name of only one – Sewell Avery of Montgomery Ward. Simon returned home bursting with new ideas and motivation. 'I did not realise how open and helpful and generous American businessmen were in showing strangers how they operated,' he wrote. 'They seemed to have no secrets from one another – so different from England, where everybody seems to have secrets from everybody else.'

The American visit more than fulfilled its aims. 'It was my first serious lesson in the chain store art,' he wrote.

> I learned the value of checking lists to control stocks and sales. I learned that new accounting machines could help to reduce the time formidably to give the necessary information in hours instead of weeks. I learned the value of counter footage and how, in the chain store operation, each foot of counter space had to pay wages, rent, overhead expenses and profit. There could be no blind spots in so far as goods are concerned. This meant a much more exhaustive study of the goods we were selling and the needs of the public. It meant that the staff who were operating had to be re-educated and retrained.

On his return he set about putting into place a three-point action plan. First, stores had to be bigger to display the goods to better effect. Second, prices were once again to be restricted – no longer to a penny, of course, but sixty times that with a ceiling of five shillings. Third, management information was to be dramatically improved by the use of 'checking lists', fortnightly records of sales and stock.

The east coast of America was, for Simon, a place where his own embryonic ideas about retailing were confirmed. Israel Sieff would later tell friends that Simon had been thinking about the new ideas for at least two years before his visit. That may have been Israel's hero worship coming out, but if he was right, what Simon experienced in America crystallised them.

The introduction of the checking-list system transformed the company. Now executives had information every two weeks as opposed to every quarter. It is a testament to its efficiency that the checking-list system he put in place remained in operation for sixty years before computers finally replaced it in the early 1980s.

As for the shops, it was clear to Simon that they needed to be larger, lighter, brighter places in which products could be displayed to their best advantage. He commissioned a report by an estate agency, Hillier, Parker, May & Rowdon, to analyse the portfolio and to point the way forward. The shopfronts, the report said, varied considerably, though 'those in new properties were of excellent design and particularly well suited for business'. Inside the old stores, the wood fixtures were described as 'somewhat rough'. But the one thing M&S had got overwhelmingly right was the location of its stores. 'Your branches occupy the most sought-after retail trading spots in their respective districts,' declared Hillier Parker. The first of the new 'big stores' was in Blackpool; it had a 60-foot frontage and that became the model for the group.

Simon believed firmly in having the right property in the right place. He would often talk about the three Ps as being crucial to success – product, people, property. He was soon employing a canny property man called Arthur Giffard who worked full time on scouting out the good potential sites in towns where Marks & Spencer wanted to be. David Norgrove, appointed commercial director in 2000, later commented: 'There were some very astute property decisions which created a virtuous circle. Those decisions were reinforced by the fact that property was in short supply because of planning controls.' Arthur Giffard was disliked by the other directors because Simon refused to let anyone else near him and, although he became a director, he never attended board meetings. He and Simon would go on property forays together to view sites and acquire them for future development. They rarely told anyone else what they had bought. Often they would buy more than one site in a town and later sell them to other retailers. In effect it was a way of controlling the provincial high street – they would sell to those retailers they felt would be good for business. Some decisions were wiser than others. At one time in the 1950s, M&S owned large amounts of farmland in the Isle of Wight.

Simon's policy of owning freehold property rather than leasing or renting meant that, even after the high price paid for Littlewoods's stores in 1997, M&S operated in the UK from a lower property-cost base – around 2 per cent of sales – than any other large British retailer.

His plan to expand the stores and to build new ones would require capital on a scale not needed before. Neither Michael Marks nor Simon had ever been afraid of a robust level of debt – and in those years interest rates were both lower and less volatile than they became in the last third of the century – but raising equity capital was a new adventure.

The mighty Prudential became Marks & Spencer's first substantial outside shareholder when the company floated on the stock market in 1926 – the year of the General Strike. Before the flotation, Sir George May, the Prudential secretary, examined the accounts and prepared a chart of the future development of the business. It was a chart that proved extraordinarily accurate. The initial capital of 1 million shares at 10 shillings each valued the company at £500,000. There were also 350,000 cumulative participating preference shares of £1.

Initially both issues proved unpopular with private investors. 'The issues were underwritten by the Prudential. But they had no attraction for the public and were complete flops, so that the Prudential had to take up practically the whole amount,' wrote Lionel Fraser of the Pru in his autobiography *All to the Good*. 'I had to look after the market on their behalf, and strangely enough, although the public issue had been so poorly received, a demand soon arose on the Stock Exchange. By feeding it gently and carefully, the whole of both blocks were sold at a satisfactory profit within a fairly brief space of time, thus fully justifying the confidence of the sponsors.'

He added: 'We were very proud of our early connection with Marks & Spencer. Even in those days, it was obvious to us that this concern had genius behind it.'

The money from the first offering seemed more than enough to be getting on with, but development – even at a time of deep recession – proceeded at such a pace that the firm went to the market to raise more funds in 1929, 1930 and 1934.

The first report and accounts of the newly floated company showed a profit of £74,938 12s 9d and was audited by Messrs Edwin Guthrie & Co. The new stores required plate glass windows and it is a sign of the relative expense of glass at the time that there is a special 'plate glass renewal fund' of £100 in those accounts.

By 1927 the company was a substantial enterprise with 135 stores employing nearly 10,000 people. But despite what appeared to outsiders to be rapid progress, Simon felt constantly held back by his fellow directors. Moreover, now he was based in London, he missed his friend Israel, who as a non-executive director appeared only for board meetings. Israel had his own family business to run in Manchester, but following a board meeting in 1926 when staying with the Marks family, he noticed that Simon seemed morose and preoccupied and so he probed and prodded as best friends do until Simon exploded in a tirade. 'I have nobody to talk to. I'm surrounded by a bunch of morons,' he said finally.

From that moment the future of M&S was assured. 'Well, that's all right. I'll join you for six months and sit in the next room so that you will have somebody to talk to,' was Israel's reply.

On the first day of the General Strike in 1926 Simon installed Israel's desk in his own office so that they sat side by side. When Israel arrived and was shown the arrangement he protested: 'I wanted to go in the next room, because if I'm in the same room I'll only bother you with questions.' Simon retorted: 'You must be in here because I want you to ask me questions. That's exactly what I want.'

The temporary six-month agreement soon became permanent and Simon and Israel were to remain joint managing directors until Simon's death in 1964, when Israel became chairman. It was a magical partnership. 'They were two men who together were worth ten,' was the verdict of Henry Lewis, one of Simon's protégés and a director from 1966 to 1984.

Of course, the company should then have been renamed Marks & Sieff, but the name was already so well established that they must have judged it folly to tamper with success. Israel appears to have been that rare thing, a hugely talented man with a modestly sized ego. Also both men had been educated to believe assimilation was the intelligent attitude and, with the spectre of anti-Semitism never far away, Simon and Israel would have reckoned that Spencer gave the name a sufficiently Anglo-Saxon air.

In the early 1930s Oswald Mosley was gaining popularity in Britain with his New Party, which later became the British Union of Fascists. He intrigued Israel Sieff who was involved with various industrialists and economists. One evening in 1932 Mosley was invited to speak at one of Israel's grand London dinner parties where everyone listened attentively to what he had to say. Suddenly he began to talk about how a political party comes to power. 'It must capitalise emotion and a political party in a hurry must have a hate plank in its platform. Today, the best hate plank is the Jews,' declared the man who later so admired Hitler.

Apparently this was the first time Mosley had openly expressed anti-Semitism and the assembled company, many of whom were Jewish, were appalled. Mosley added, 'Of course, this doesn't apply to Jews like you, Israel.' His son Marcus recalled: 'I remember Father rang the bell and said to the butler: "Sir Oswald is leaving".'

Even at that time Marks & Spencer was different from most other businesses. It had already developed a powerful corporate culture. Marcus Sieff became aware of this even as a teenager. 'I had already come to think of it as more than a business; I suppose I dimly perceived it as a way of life ... I used to hear Simon and Father talking about our business, what it stood for and what they were going to do with it. They discussed what its role in society should be and I felt there was something special about it that had nothing to do with size – and that it stood for more than making money.'

Chaim Weizmann contributed to this culture. The future first president of Israel was an erudite industrial chemist who believed passionately in the ability of technology to deliver benefits to the masses, and as a close friend of Israel and Simon he had a huge influence on their thinking in pushing them to innovate. Machine-washable wool was at this stage a distant dream but nylon, terylene and polyester were all embraced and adapted by Marks & Spencer, working closely with its suppliers. Israel recalled: 'We came to regard ourselves as a technical laboratory. We felt we should provide our suppliers with good technical information about the new materials and processes which the advance of technology was making available. We saw ourselves, in a limited way, as production engineers, industrial chemists, laboratory technicians.'

Simon's visit to America confirmed his own belief that the public wanted quality for their money, not just low prices. Price was important, but M&S had to deliver quality and value, and that became one of the key principles of the company that enabled it to perform strongly, not only in good times but also in times of recession. As one retired executive put it: 'Quality and value became the lifeblood of Marks & Spencer, and Simon was its beating heart.'

All through the depression years of the 1930s Marks & Spencer's profits kept on rising. From 1929 to 1939 sales increased tenfold from £2.4m to £23.4m, and pre-tax profits increased by around 700 per cent from £0.24m to £1.7m.

M&S also performed well in the recession of the early 1990s when, in the words of Sir Richard Greenbury, 'We murdered the competition.' From 1991 to 1994 profits before tax rose from £607m to £851m. Sadly, he and his board forgot that in retailing the dead competition either resurrects itself or is soon replaced by newcomers.

At the time of the flotation in 1926 M&S was still largely using wholesalers to supply its shops, although certain relationships with manufacturers had been established – such as the special relationship with William Chapman's handkerchief factory. But then Simon changed tack. In order to differentiate Marks & Spencer from its main rival Woolworth, he decided to launch a completely new area of merchandise – clothing. The changes in the British class system after the First World War and the growing independence of newly enfranchised women resulted in rising demand for women's clothing. Working-class girls were coming out of service, where they wore uniform all the time apart from one day off a week, and were finding employment in factories and in the growing numbers of shops. The growth of the cinema and magazine advertising meant consumers' appetites were whetted for affordable but fashionable clothes. Customers were beginning to behave more like each other and M&S had its share of middle- or even upper-middle-class customers, particularly after Queen Mary's groundbreaking visit in 1932, although some of them would claim 'to be buying for the maid'. And even if they did not buy outerwear there, women flocked to M&S for underwear. It was said that 'many a débutante wears a M&S slip beneath her gown'.

In order to deliver something affordable to the factory worker and wearable by the débutante and her male counterpart, Simon and Israel realised they had to cut out the middle man and go direct to the manufacturers.

Such a practice was rare in clothing retailing at the time. The powerful Wholesalers Association, who saw the livelihoods of their members threatened, put pressure on the manufacturers not to supply these upstarts. So there were a number of fruitless overtures and conversations, mainly with Israel – the diplomat of the duo who, in Middle Eastern affairs, as Chaim Weizmann's personal assistant had become skilled in negotiating with wary counterparts. He was also wonderfully persistent.

The first big direct delivery came from Corah, a much admired clothing manufacturer in Leicester. Three times Israel visited the company and three times he was shown the door. On the fourth visit he got to see the chairman, Robert Wessel, and explained that M&S could give him bulk orders in limited ranges which would enable him to increase his profit. The chairman told him that if he did that, all his other customers, mainly wholesalers, would stop ordering from Corah. 'But we are the future, I wish you would come with us,' Israel protested. It was to no avail, but as he was walking out along the corridor he was approached by the production director, Cecil Coleman, who had clearly been listening in. To him the logic of supplying M&S was all too clear and he struck a secret deal with Israel to supply 1,000 dozen pairs of men's socks. When Israel arrived back at St Pancras Simon was waiting for him on the platform. 'Simon,' he said, 'I think we've made a breakthrough.'

When Corah's chairman found out about the deal he fired Coleman, but a few weeks later, on discovering the company was doing more business with Marks & Spencer than with anyone else, reinstated him. Corah's relationship with Marks & Spencer lasted sixty years and made all the directors rich when the company was floated on the stock market. (Unfortunately the strength of sterling in the late 1980s almost put Corah out of business and it was taken over by Charterhall, an Australian investment company, and merged with another M&S supplier, Textured Jersey, which had also hit hard times. When Charterhall went into liquidation they were both sold to Coats Viyella.)

Corah was also the inspiration for Simon to sanctify his father's name and to create one of the most famous household names in the world. Corah's goods sold under the brand name St Margaret, which gave Simon and Israel the inspiration for creating something similar, using the name of the founder – and so St Michael came into being. Simon, with Corah's permission, decided to adapt his father's name into a trademark, which he saw as giving a seal of authority to his goods. Thus in November 1928 St Michael was registered under the Trademarks Act. For sixty years it was a mark of quality and reliability. It survived unchanged until 1999 when M&S recognised that, compared with modern brands, it had become a trifle old-fashioned. The name Marks & Spencer became more prominent on garment labels and St Michael was either dropped altogether or appeared in much smaller lettering.

Once Corah had thrown its lot in with M&S, other manufacturers had the courage to defy the wholesalers and sign up as direct suppliers. There were clear cost advantages, fewer sales staff being needed if most of the business is with one customer. At the same time manufacturers had to allow M&S staff into every aspect of their business – an intrusion that some saw as a disadvantage. 'For their part, they were to study new methods, new machines and the rationalisation of their buying of raw materials at the most appropriate times,' wrote Simon. 'For our part, we assured them of a ready market which was expanding year by year.' As a result of these partnerships, M&S was able to sell dresses, knitwear and socks at a price that could not be beaten by anyone who bought supplies from a wholesaler. At the time it was a virtuous circle – the supplier benefited, M&S benefited and, most important of all, the customer benefited.

In a 1932 house magazine article the authors stressed the emphasis on value: 'M&S amazing values are the result of our trading direct with manufacturers for cash. All benefits of price reductions and its relationship to its suppliers are passed on to our customers.' But there was also a reference to quality. 'M&S do not buy seconds or sub-standard articles. Satisfaction is guaranteed either by a refund of money or exchange of articles.' Simon believed passionately that M&S should never sell shoddy goods – 'even if they sold well'. It was fatal for a store manager or assistant to defend goods on the basis that they sold well. He would say: 'I'll tell you if it sells, sonny.'

Simon and Israel did not want M&S to sell cheap and cheerful stuff that fell apart. In Simon's 'notes on the business', first printed in 1954, he wrote: 'We are earning a reputation for good value and good taste. We must continue to deserve that reputation by avoiding garish and tawdry merchandise … An inexpensive article need not be shoddy.'

Anything he saw in the stores that did not reflect this philosophy would infuriate him. Instinctively he knew that the reputation of the business hinged on quality. Nobody inside the company at that time, or indeed until very recently, ever talked about M&S or even St Michael as a brand – they talked about 'the business'. But in effect it was the same thing – Simon and Israel were building the most powerful clothing brand in British retailing history – a brand that became trusted by the public to deliver on value and quality. It was like a reliable friend – which perhaps explains how angry the customers became when that friend let them down in the late 1990s.

Clothing now took pride of place yet there were still many items in a 1930s Marks & Spencer shop that were later to disappear from the shelves such as fancy goods, toys, china, enamel and aluminiumware, stationery and watches, although some returned to the stores in the last decade of the millennium. In the 1930s M&S was particularly proud of its 'unbreakable watches at 2s 11d and 3s 11d'. In 2000 the stores were selling watches priced between £19.99 and £29.99.

In 1931 a new food department opened selling fruit, vegetables and canned goods and in 1933, when the government was promoting fruit to the public, a separate fruit department was set up dealing in Jaffa oranges and grapefruit from Palestine. Four years later a fruit distribution centre was established in Covent Garden.

The other area where the M&S approach was ahead of its time was in its attitude to staff. Simon and Israel – liberal Jews to their fingertips – developed Michael Marks's nascent paternalism. A formal welfare policy as such did not emerge until 1934, but by then the company was providing free medical examinations and canteens where all the staff were expected to eat. Once, in the early days, Simon and Israel had made a purchase while visiting one of the old penny bazaars. As the assistant started to wrap it up, Simon said, 'Don't you start on that or you will be late for your lunch.' 'Oh, that's all right, I won't be having any lunch,' she replied. 'I can't afford it.' When pressed, it turned out that her whole family was unemployed and dependent on her wages for survival. Simon and Israel talked late into the night after this incident and concluded, 'There was only one thing that could cope with this, and that was to provide a hot meal at a cost so low that an employee would have to recognise it as uneconomical not to pay for it and eat it.' It soon became an iron rule that staff ate lunch in the company facilities. Behind the scenes, most stores established a 'Café Marks' – an old-fashioned name and format that survived, in some stores, into the present century.

The company also took an interest in its staff as individuals – not least because Simon and Israel recognised them as the best source of information on customers. Stores were told that birthdays should be noted. Anyone who excelled in sport should be congratulated and have their names displayed on the notice board. Occasional staff dances became a feature. But by modern standards, staff still worked long, hard hours for low wages in tough conditions. One evening at a dinner party Simon found himself next to a woman who suddenly turned on him and harangued him for his treatment of staff. 'It's firms like Marks & Spencer that give the Jews a bad name,' she declared. Her name was Flora Solomon and Simon was so impressed that he recruited her to head up a new welfare department in 1934. According to Asa Briggs, 'It represented a genuine breakthrough fostering a sense of belonging among all M&S staff at work and at play. Many social activities of the 1930s are recalled by long-serving members of staff and by pensioners including amateur dramatic societies, concerts, cricket matches and swimming galas as well as memorable holiday outings and trips abroad.' The welfare department arranged all these and ensured a common staffing policy in all M&S stores. By the time Marcus Sieff became chairman in 1972 Marks & Spencer had the highest reputation as an employer. In the Baker Street head office staff received free cancer screening, flu jabs, subsidised dentistry and chiropody. A generous non-contributory pension scheme was also put in place.

Such policies were a mixture of philanthropy and pragmatism, a reflection of Simon's view that his business was an extended family. Indeed, wherever possible Simon employed family, even distant cousins. He believed the business received more productive work and loyalty from a happy workforce. Not that he was ever soft.

The price for such nurturing was total commitment and loyalty to the company and rigid adherence to its rules, of which there were many. No one was allowed to eat at their desk, supervisors monitored working hours and everyone was expected to know their place in the hierarchy and not to challenge it. Anyone on the management ladder would be expected to uproot his family and move to whichever part of the country was deemed to need him. It was a bit like life in the army. Managers were the officers, store staff the footsoldiers. Provided the generals gave the right orders – which for so long they did – success was assured.

During the 1930s expansion continued at breakneck pace. Some 129 new stores were built or rebuilt between 1931 and 1935. Another 33 were built by the outbreak of the Second World War and by that time more than half the total of 234 stores had been built from new or rebuilt. 'An M&S store of today,' Simon told his shareholders in 1939, 'is in size, equipment and appearance a very different institution from what it was even two or three years ago.' The newest stores had plate glass windows, modern lighting, and the distinctive green and gold fascia most of us grew up with – in contrast to Woolworth's red and gold – had appeared. The word bazaar had disappeared from all but the oldest shops. Turnover and profits were both healthy and growing.

Simon often took decisions that fellow directors and advisors thought risky. He lived and breathed his business and had total confidence in his ability to make the right decision. Self doubt didn't come into it and he drove the business harder and expanded faster than others deemed prudent.

One decision, made against almost unanimous advice, was to buy the site on the corner of Oxford Street and Orchard Street in London near Marble Arch, a site that became the company's first big West End store. Sir George May of the Prudential urged caution before embarking on such a large and expensive project and most M&S directors felt it was too early to tie up so much capital in such a big store.

But Simon was convinced. 'Even if it never makes a profit, it will be a good advertisement for the business,' he said. The press came to the opening. One reporter wrote that he was 'quite lost in amazement at what I saw. It was the price and value of the goods which made me wonder. Nothing was over five shillings and yet similar goods in many shops would cost at least two or three shillings more.'

'The Arch', as it became known, was soon one of the most profitable stores and, as Simon's gamble paid off, it became the store where new lines were tried out and experiments made. Shrewd shoppers in London still go to the Marble Arch store to see the latest offerings and to take their pick from a vast array of goods. As the nearest outlet to the Baker Street head office it became Simon's personal store.

Although he had instigated the checking-list system which gave a written fortnightly snapshot of the sales and stocks, Simon (and Israel) believed there was no substitute for personal investigation – or 'probing', as it was known. In 1958 Israel wrote down his definition of probing, which included the following:

> Probing is the method whereby the interested and enquiring mind of the executive and his colleagues penetrates beneath the surface of things and discovers the real facts. It throws a bright light on the 'cloggers' which lurk on the counters and shows up the fast sellers.

Probing is an effort to bring the minds of the executive and his staff closer to the operational level of the stores which are the arteries of the business.

Sole dependence on statistics or electronic devices can only result in remoteness of control and lack of knowledge of what is really happening in the stores. Statistics, anyhow, are mainly post-mortem and can deal only in a mechanical fashion with what has happened. They ignore all feeling for merchandise, which is essential for upgrading. The robot-mind merely records. It has no perception, no understanding, and it cannot take initiative – vital elements in the art of probing.

So vital was the principle of probing that it became part of the company motto on the coat of arms that adorned the cover of the annual report up until 1983. Beneath a lion and an owl were the words 'Strive, probe, apply'.

Simon, who invariably wore a trilby and carried a briefcase, would visit the Marble Arch store once a day, questioning the staff over what was selling, what was not. So hands-on was his style that even the layout of the goods had to be cleared with him. Being store manager there was both heady and stressful. 'Simon could be a forbidding man; his manner was extremely blunt and direct,' recalled Greenbury, who was a departmental manager at Marble Arch in the 1950s. 'It was obvious to me that he was not only the chairman of the business but also its owner and proprietor. Probably the most frightening thing about him was that he was always right.'

Through the 1930s a more formal corporate structure began to develop. There were now the stores, the suppliers and the head office, then still in Chiswell Street. A year after the formation of the welfare department in 1943, a small textile laboratory was set up and a merchandise development department was created along with a design department. The merchandise department's brief was to improve the quality and appearance of goods and was headed by Dr Eric Kann, a refugee from Nazi Germany where he had been head of the chain-store firm of Samuel Schocken. He brought considerable expertise.

The growth of the Nazi regime affected the company in another significant way. Although Marks & Spencer sourced most of its goods within Britain because at that time it was more convenient, it had always been a significant importer from continental Europe. Simon had spent a very enjoyable year in Nuremberg in his late teens and had made valuable business contacts there. But from the time Adolf Hitler came to power, Jews whose families had lived in Germany for generations began to be hounded and their businesses boycotted.

Simon and Israel, along with most of British Jewry, were horrified and they immediately barred German-made goods from the stores. One order of 25,000 dozen artificial silk stockings, only available from Germany, was cancelled and all the wall clocks in the staff canteens were disposed of when it was realised they were of German origin. The Second World War when it came also made importing increasingly difficult and these two factors sowed the seeds of the buy-British policy of which Marks & Spencer later became so proud – and which was probably partly to blame for its eventual downfall.

By 1934, two years after Queen Mary's visit, Marks & Spencer was firmly established as a leading retailer of clothing and food. It was no longer a direct competitor with Woolworth and its green and gold fascia was increasingly to be found next to the red and gold on every significant high street in the land. Simon Marks and Israel Sieff had become influential figures, as businessmen and as active supporters of Zionism. When German Jews began flooding into the United Kingdom, to a certain resistance from the government of the day, Simon rallied his Jewish associates to form the Central British Fund for German Jewry. The aim was to help people escape from Germany to Britain and ensure that the refugees would be looked after by the Jewish community and not become a drain on the British taxpayer. A year later he toured America in an effort to raise funds. 'May the future Jewish historian,' he declared in one speech, 'be able to write of our generation that we did not yield supinely to the resurgence of barbarism but dealt with every problem as it arose with courage and wisdom.' Simon personally donated more than £1m to the Central British Fund, no mean sum in the 1930s and equivalent to approximately £42m in 2001.

Simon and Israel became prominent in British society. The Marks family lived in Cleeve Lodge, a beautiful turreted house near Hyde Park Gate. From there, Simon's daughter Hannah came out as a débutante. In November 1934 Simon was a guest at the royal wedding of Prince George, Duke of Kent to Princess Marina of Greece.

Despite the depression profits hit £1m for the first time in 1935. Simon ruled his business with a firm hand. By modern standards he was a despot. Command came from the top and nobody was expected to question his authority. Thus Simon, who chaired the company for forty years from 1924 to

1964, set the culture of a company that became slavishly responsive to the man at the top. Thinking for yourself, taking initiative, unless it was to point out faulty products, were not encouraged. Head office decided what goods would be sent where, how they would be displayed and what price they would be. Store managers were expected to follow instructions to the letter. Total obedience combined with a zeal for quality products were what counted and so those who rose towards the top naturally displayed these qualities.

'There was a depth and quality of management rare in companies at the time,' recalled Henry Lewis, Simon's protégé who rose to the rank of joint managing director. 'But it bred something of a civil service mentality. I used to say that to do well at Marks & Spencer you had to have first, a little above average intelligence, second, a lot of common sense, and third, a slight Manchester accent.'

In the early years such structured attitudes went with the times. Britain was still a society divided by class and the working classes, even though they might be beginning to wear clothes of the same style as wealthier people, were expected to know their place and stay there.

Fortunately for M&S, and all its employees, Simon Marks was a genius. His commands were generally the right ones. He was passionate about every aspect of the business and he had a legendary eye for detail. The company was his baby, his mother, his lover all rolled into one. 'There is nothing relating to Marks & Spencer that does not interest me,' he would say. When the head office moved to 82 Baker Street, Simon researched the latest trends in head office decor by secretly visiting other firms' headquarters with the company architect. It was Simon who oversaw the design of the office lift, Simon who chose the ornamental lamps.

Having spent his early days as the principal buyer he took a keen, some would say obsessive, interest in product. He made a point of inspecting every new line, examining the stitching and the lining. He would pass judgement on garments he considered inferior or unsuitable with 'It's not our business' or he would berate the selector with 'Why are you trying to ruin my business?' He took it all intensely personally. A pulled thread on a jumper was like a knife in his soul.

And because of this passion, this obsession with quality to the smallest detail, the business prospered during a time of mass unemployment and when retailing in general was struggling. 'Why did we continue ... to grow when all around us our competitors found themselves in difficulties?' asked Israel Sieff in his memoirs. 'Because we answered the people's prayer. Their prayer for goods at prices which even in their days of impoverishment they could just about afford to buy.'

It is hardly surprising that Simon's son Michael rebelled against this all-consuming passion. Every family mealtime included a discussion about some aspect of Marks & Spencer and this particular small boy found it immensely tedious. Either children became swept up in the business, as Simon had been, or like Michael they turned away. Uninterested in commerce, he resented being born into such success and wealth. 'When I was a child, I caught my death of gold,' was one of his favourite quirky sayings. He liked neither his father nor his mother and wrote children's stories featuring a wicked witch based, it was said, on his mother Miriam. He married five times – first to a member of the Rothschild family, then to Japanese, Chinese and Greek women. The last marriage caused a scandal when he converted to the Greek Orthodox church.

He was dragooned into working for Marks & Spencer for a few years, but he always avoided his father if he could, preferring to eat in the staff canteen with the clerical staff rather than with the executives. To Simon, he was a source of anger and grief. At one famous family gathering at home, Simon asked Michael's opinion of an M&S cake. 'I'm sorry, I just can't get interested in Devon splits,' he replied witheringly. Michael produced one son, Simon, the current Lord Marks, and a daughter.

Always a shabby figure with an unkempt mop of black hair, Michael eschewed all signs of wealth, opting for a somewhat bohemian life after he left the company. Hannah, his sister, was much more of a businesswoman with an aptitude for figures. But just as Simon had kept his own sister Rebecca out of the business despite her obvious abilities, so it was with Hannah. In that sense, Simon was a creature of his time, a male chauvinist, at least where the women in his family were concerned.

The Second World War with its rationing, national service and restricted overseas travel put huge constraints on the business. The annihilation of Jewry in Germany, Poland and Czechoslovakia deeply affected Israel and Simon and their families. Both men's fathers had arrived in Britain with nothing, had built businesses and had joyously received their naturalisation papers. Israel's father Ephraim actually kissed his papers when they arrived. They were both proud to be British. So the British government's obstructive attitude towards Jewish refugees fleeing certain death in the concentration camps tore them apart. The Balfour Declaration endorsing Britain's commitment to a Jewish homeland was virtually overturned – and Jewish immigration into Palestine was severely restricted. Ships full of desperately ill refugees were refused entry and many of the passengers died.

Yet Simon and Israel held on to their patriotism. 'We would be unjust if we were to confuse those responsible for this outrage with the great British people whose ideals are still justice, mercy and charity,' Simon declared in a speech to a group of American Zionists.

At the beginning of the war Marks & Spencer employed 17,000 people and could boast 234 stores with 44 miles of counters selling 300 million individual items a year. This was another empire that needed protecting and by the outbreak of war almost 5,000 staff members, more than 25 per cent of the total, had been trained in first aid, fire watching and decontaminating duties. Once again what the top men decreed, the middle and junior management implemented with rigorous efficiency.

Simon Marks became a founder and major sponsor to a new cadet force for the RAF, funded partly by private money. At an early lunch at Londonderry House to discuss the project the guests were told that a lump sum of £25,000 was needed to set up central administration and so far they only had £7,000. Simon simply wrote out a cheque for the balance and told the Air Commodore to request more if needed. He remained involved with the Air Defence Cadet Corps throughout the war.

One of the strangest and least-known chapters of M&S history was its role as an exporter to the United States during the Second World War. In May 1940 Israel Sieff, who was taking a selection of garment fabrics to show to American retailers, narrowly escaped a U-boat torpedo attack on the way to America to investigate how M&S could help generate US dollars for the war effort. During the course of the war the Marks & Spencer Export Corporation generated more than £10m for the Treasury, but in Britain trading during the war was a shadow of that in peacetime years. Half the staff were away serving in the armed forces and what customers there were found a vastly reduced variety of goods. On top of that M&S found parts of its property requisitioned for the war effort. The two upper floors of the head office housed the clandestine Special Operations Executive – a crack force of spies whose job was 'to set Europe ablaze'. It may have been inconvenient for the business but Simon and Israel, as sons of Russian immigrants, saw it as an honour for the British government to use their headquarters for such a vital task.

M&S continued to look after many of its staff members even when they were in the forces. A company service sheet was sent to them wherever they were posted and their military pay made up to their M&S level.

By the end of the war more than a hundred M&S stores had been damaged by bombing and sixteen destroyed. Rebuilding could not start until 1951 because of government edicts and took until 1957 to complete. Characteristically Simon and Israel saw this as an opportunity to reinvent the business once again. Simon decided on 'a new look and a new character more in keeping with the specialized goods we are selling'. He also decided to try to make the style of each store blend in with the character of the high street where it was located.

Part of the genius of Simon Marks was that he was always ready to kiss goodbye to the past and start again. He understood, as all great retailers have done, that change is the nature of retailing. Those who do not adapt to the changing needs and tastes of the public do not survive. And neither do those who let costs spiral without check. Ten years after the war ended he took the knife to an organisation that had become burdened with bureaucracy and swamped in paper.

The most dangerous aspect was that overheads were growing faster than sales. Overheads as a percentage of turnover had risen from 8.5 per cent to 10.5 per cent in the ten years from 1945. Hence in 1956, after long debate with Israel, Simon initiated 'Operation Simplification'. Despite this innocuous title this process swept away outdated systems in a far reaching and ruthless restructuring of the business. M&S had become heavily overstaffed with many people engaged upon tasks that were no longer necessary.

The company records show that in 1956 M&S employed 26,700 people; just a year later that figure had dropped to 21,500. The axe fell more slowly at head office, but it still fell. In 1956 there were 2,600 people working in and around Baker Street; by 1959 the number was down to 1,900. Some of them had retired, the rest had been fired.

There were ceremonial bonfires of the superfluous paperwork and an exhibition was held showing examples of unnecessary documents. Simon Marks's biographer Paul Bookbinder estimated that 18 million forms were scrapped, saving 80 tonnes of paper a year. Around £4m of overheads were saved over two years. Information kept on the off chance that it might be required years later was destroyed.

The cumbersome invoicing system was drastically revised. Until then, a supplier would invoice every store for every item. Each store then checked that it had been received, endorsed the invoice and sent it to head office for payment. With 240 stores this meant the supplier had to send 240 invoices per item, 240 store staff had to endorse them and send them to head office. After Operation Simplification the supplier sent one invoice to head office to cover deliveries of a line to all stores. Sales girls no longer had to fill in forms to get goods from the stockroom. The practice of long weekly reports to head office from the store managers was abandoned.

Israel was so thrilled with the result that, shortly after being made a life baron in 1966, he regaled the House of Lords with the benefits of getting rid of paperwork: 'Our salesgirls, the people in the office, all the employees suddenly began to blossom out. They felt that we trusted them, because the systems we adopted gave them the freedom to do what they wanted in so far as goods were concerned. Everywhere I went I found evidence that a hidden treasure of ability had been unlocked.'

A new era had dawned.

# CHAPTER THREE

# *After Simon*

S imon Marks died as he would have liked – at work. On 8 December 1964, the day before the staff Christmas lunch, he visited the ladies' tailoring department with his favourite nephew, Michael Sieff, brother of Marcus. The garments did not please him and, in characteristic style, he began hurling them on the floor, declaring as he had so many times over the previous four decades, 'You are trying to ruin my business.' He stormed out and minutes later collapsed with a massive heart attack. He died almost instantly.

Simon was 76, had been suffering from heart problems for some months and clearly should have stopped working after the first attack. But like his father before him he preferred to work, to build, to perfect his empire to the very last. He had doubtless hung on too long, as great entrepreneurs do.

A much tougher and more abrasive character than his father, Simon dominated the business for forty-eight years, transforming a chain of penny bazaars into a national institution. In St Michael he had created one of the most famous trademarks in the world. He had led a retail revolution in Britain, constantly overturning old ways of doing things and reinventing the business. 'I am the greatest rebel of you all,' he used to boast.

People outside the business found him a less awesome character. Michael Sorkin, the managing director of the investment bank SG Hambros, recalled meeting him during the fourteenth-birthday celebration of Simon's son Michael. 'I remember him as a very warm, down to earth person,' said Sorkin. 'After a birthday tea at their flat in Grosvenor Square we set off to the Palladium for a show. Lady Marks took the girls in the Rolls, but Lord Marks said, "Come on boys, we'll walk".' And so Simon Marks led a small troupe of teenage boys through the West End to the London Palladium.

He was knighted for his efforts during the Second World War and received a hereditary peerage in 1961, taking the title Lord Marks of

Broughton, the district of Manchester where he grew up. He had also found time to advise Chaim Weizmann, visiting Israel regularly, and by the time of his death his charitable trust had given away more than £600,000 to various good causes, by no means all of them Jewish. He also gave large sums personally. All told, his charitable giving up to his death in 1964 is estimated to have totalled more than £2m.

The greatest tribute to Simon was that Marks & Spencer continued to grow so successfully for so many years after his death. He left behind a well-oiled, structurally brilliant if hierarchical machine, whose people were so imbued with his standards of value, quality and service that it continued to function pretty well, maintaining almost all of its agility and sensitivity to change, first under Israel, and then under four subsequent chairmen, until the mid 1990s.

Henry Lewis, who joined the company in 1950, and became a director in 1965 and joint managing director with Derek Rayner in 1973, was by the turn of the century one of only three executives still living who had lunched regularly with Simon Marks. A former RAF navigator from Stockport, Lewis had joined M&S after taking an economics degree at Manchester University and a one-year course in personnel management at the London School of Economics.

The directors would meet at 12.30 in an opulent dining room where the walls were hung with Impressionist paintings. 'We used to gather there, eight to ten of us, every day for drinks,' recalled Lewis. 'Then the butler would come in and say, "The chairman is coming up for lunch," and we would all stand up as he came in. It seems incredible now, but this happened every day. Once we sat down nobody ever spoke across the table, the conversation always came from Simon to the rest of us and back. It was really a continuing board meeting.'

According to Lewis, three topics dominated those lunches: the development of new products and the latest technology, trading in the stores and the performance and welfare of the staff. But three topics that Lewis noted took up a great deal of management time in other companies were rarely mentioned at M&S. One was finance – because the money came in one week from the stores and the suppliers were paid the next. The second was marketing – 'good goods will sell arse upwards' remained Simon's philosophy to the end, so he had no interest in sales campaigns, advertising or promotions. The third was service – not service by the sales assistants to the customers – which Simon did believe was important – but service in the sense of providing what he viewed as non-essentials. There were no fitting rooms, no toilets, no extra-large clothes, no baby clothes and no credit facilities. Marks believed in the simple maxim that if you delivered the right goods to the right place at the right time they would sell. Only thirty years after his death, in the mid 1990s, did that philosophy begin to appear flawed.

Many in the company were relieved that Simon Marks had gone. As he grew older, what had been strong leadership became tyrannical; people under him had felt constrained, if not constantly terrified. So domineering had he become that when Israel addressed the staff after Simon's death, he felt the need to explain that such behaviour always sprang from a love of the business and a desire to see it perform to its best.

Yet Simon's death left a huge vacuum in the company and a belief among many directors who had worshipped as well as feared him that, if they had any problem, all they had to do, as an officer once said of Wellington, 'was to wonder what the old Duke would have done'.

This practice worked well when it came to day-to-day operations. The insistence on high standards and quality control, continuing technological advance, staff training and care all continued. But the company lost his touch of genius, his instinct, his intuition.

As Israel wrote five years after Simon's death: 'He rode the market like a jockey rides a great race – sensing what is happening before anybody else does, and boldly and swiftly acting on his judgement.'

Few are blessed with that special touch and, because of the huge success of Marks & Spencer under his chairmanship, nobody would attempt to alter the ways things were done for a very long time. On his foundation, the next five chairmen drove the company to ever greater glory. Profits leapt ahead – although the figures were distorted by the high inflation of the 1970s and early 1980s. The year Simon Marks died the company made £25m in profits on sales of £201.5m. By 1973, when Marcus Sieff became chairman, profits were up to £70m on sales of £496m. In 1984, when Marcus moved up to be president and Derek Rayner became chairman – the first non-family member to do so – profits had almost quadrupled to £265m. From 1991, when Sir Richard Greenbury took over as chairman from Rayner, to 1998 profits almost doubled from £615.5m on sales of £5.8bn, to a peak of £1.2bn on turnover of £8.24bn. Buoyed by increasing consumer demand and, for so long, a lack of effective competition, the company received accolade after accolade. 'The cupboards are stuffed with management awards,' remarked one director. As chairmen, Marcus Sieff, Derek Rayner and Rick Greenbury made their own contribution – all helping the company to grow in their different ways. But they had the advantage of building on excellence.

Some things had to change. Simon believed in employing the family. Although his own son Michael worked reluctantly in the business for only a few years, shunning it thereafter, there were plenty of other family members employed in Marks & Spencer. A photograph of the board of directors in 1960 shows fourteen men, nine of whom belonged to one or other branch of the family. There were by now five separate strands. Simon's daughter Hannah had married Dr Alec Lerner, who joined the board, and produced Joel, who became one of his grandfather's favourites, although despite working briefly in the company he never became a director. Simon's sister Miriam married Harry Sacher, who rose to be a director, and their two sons Michael and Gabriel later worked in the business and eventually joined the board, as did Michael Sacher's son, John. Elaine Marks – Simon's youngest sister – married Norman Laski, whose daughter Ann married David Susman, who also came into the business. And then there were the Sieffs. Israel Sieff and Rebecca Marks produced Michael and Marcus. Both became directors and Marcus rose to be chairman. Marcus's first marriage to Rosalie Fromson gave him his only son, David, who was an M&S director for many years and became the last family member to leave the board when he retired in July 2001. Marcus also produced two daughters, Daniela and Amanda, in subsequent marriages, but only Amanda worked in the family firm, and then only briefly.

A 1960 photograph shows three Sieffs: Israel, his younger brother Teddy and Marcus; with them are Harry Sacher and his son Michael, Alec Lerner, Norman Laski and Simon Marks.

Simon not only believed in employing family in the business, he held out against having non-family directors, even when he admired them. He discovered Henry Lewis in 1958, temporarily running lingerie following the sudden death of the executive in charge, Cecil Speelman, who collapsed with a heart attack at a New Year's Eve party. 'Israel had asked if I could cope for a day or two, which became a week, which became a month,' said Lewis. One day Simon appeared in the department and soon it was clear that Lewis had become a protégé – not always an easy role. One particular morning Simon berated Lewis for a frayed nightdress ribbon he had discovered.

'When he left I was like a rag,' said Lewis. The next day he asked Lewis if he had been upset. Lewis said he had not. 'In that case, you didn't understand what I was talking about,' declared Simon. Within a couple of years Lewis received regular invitations to lunch with the board and was, in most ways, treated like one of them. Yet Simon never made Lewis a director. It was only after his death that Israel, having recognised the unfairness of the situation, appointed him to the board.

Today such family dominance in a publicly quoted company would be unthinkable. Even in 1960 it was unusual, although Sainsbury and Tesco were also family-run affairs. But while shares had been sold to the public ever since 1926, Simon still controlled the 'A' voting shares and he resolutely refused to enfranchise the ordinary shareholders. 'It may be the right thing to happen, but it will never happen in my lifetime,' he would say. So until his death he remained the proprietor and, perhaps because he had fought so hard and long to win that control back, he never for a second allowed anyone to doubt it.

There may have been relief among some store managers that they would no longer be terrorised by Simon's 'royal visits'. So fearsome was his reputation that one petrified shop assistant could not even say his own name when Simon enquired it. But other more robust characters adored him and mourned the regular appearances of the short, dark figure carrying a briefcase and wearing the omnipresent trilby.

Israel took over the chairmanship for three years before handing over to his younger brother Edward, or Teddy as he was known. Israel opened up the company to new ideas while Teddy brought a unique feel for fabric and design to the task. As chairman he was famous for dismissing any criticism or suggestion with the phrase: 'Nonsense, laddie' and moving on. Teddy was chairman for five years until 1972, but is perhaps most famous for surviving an assassination attempt by the terrorist Carlos the Jackal in December 1973. Carlos, who shot Teddy through the nose, was believed to have been working for one of the Middle Eastern countries hostile to Israel and from that time on Marks & Spencer's chairmen were always viewed as terrorist targets by the security services.

It was a time when some of the constraints were being loosened and more junior staff were allowed to take some decisions. Israel's chief legacy was his attention to and care of the staff – 'fostering good human relations'. His empathy for people was one reason he and Simon made such good partners. After a tirade from Simon, many a shaken store manager would be comforted by Israel's arm round his shoulder and a little chat away from his colleagues. Left alone, Israel conducted a more benign administration and five years later realised, as many initially bereft spouses do, that despite his grief he had gained a new freedom. 'While he [Simon] was alive he dominated me,' he wrote in his memoirs. 'I always deferred to him; it never occurred to me to do anything else. I grew up in the assumption of his superiority, as a brain, a business leader and as a human being. Since he died I have in one sense felt a freer person; my decisions and judgements are not related to those of anybody else as they were to Simon's.'

It had been an astonishing partnership between these 'two men who together, were worth ten'. Their friendship was as solid at the end as at the beginning. They were perfect foils for each other. Where Simon ruffled, Israel smoothed. Simon's nasty medicine was followed by Israel's spoonful of sugar. Where Simon saw everything – even music – in terms of 'the business', Israel possessed a much broader intellect. He was interested in foreign affairs and spent a lot more time and energy on Zionism than Simon did. He studied economics at Manchester University and was a founder member of a 'think-tank' called Political and Economic Planning or PEP for short. Independent of party politics, its role was to garner and analyse economic and industrial information and make it available to policy makers in Whitehall. Israel also wrote eloquently and communicated his ideas through articles in the press and talks on the radio. He had been the velvet glove round Simon's iron fist.

Freed from Simon's dominance, Israel enfranchised all the non-voting shares in 1966. From then on the shareholdings became increasingly diluted and fragmented as family members sold shares and split them up among their children. The sense of ownership was lost. Although members of the founding families, they became hired hands like everyone else. As the 1960s progressed the management recognised that the company needed a more meritocratic approach to meet more modern times.

But questing for the highest standards remained endemic to the culture and so did the search for something new. 'Whenever you met a director in the corridor, they would always ask, "what's new",' said Paul Smith, who joined M&S as a management trainee in the 1960s. And the affection for Manchester as the original home of the company remained – as ambitious young executives were well aware. 'We always used to thicken up our Manchester accents when making presentations to directors,' admitted Smith.

By the time Israel's son Marcus, later Lord Sieff, became chairman and chief executive in 1972, more non-family members had made it into the boardroom. Sir Richard Greenbury became a director under Teddy Sieff in 1971 and Derek Rayner and Henry Lewis became joint managing directors in 1973. As the battalion of non-family executives who started as trainees after the war rose to senior positions, a noticeable antagonism grew towards the family. By the 1990s being a Sieff or a Sacher had become a disadvantage – or so felt the young Sieffs and Sachers coming into the business.

One thing that did not change was the supremacy of the chairman. Simon created a culture where the top man was all-powerful and this was to continue right into the 1990s. The chairmanship of Marks & Spencer held within its powers almost divine governance and was handed on like some kind of papal see. Once the new chairman was named, everyone metaphorically bowed their heads in obeisance. Questioning the chairman, vigorous debating of issues and policy were frowned on. Flagrant disagreement was seen as a resigning matter.

There was always the example of the unfortunate Mr J. H. Nellist, chief accountant in 1945, who dared to disagree with the chairman. Simon had been telling him about a new plan for the business when Nellist reputedly said: ' I am concerned that might damage the business.' 'Well,' said Simon, 'if it does, you won't be around to see it.' Nellist was then dismissed. In the light of such a draconian tradition, few openly disagreed with the chairman.

In 1958 the company moved from 82 Baker Street to the huge purpose-built headquarters stretching from 37 to 67 Baker Street. Initially there were three seven-storey blocks running between Baker Street and Gloucester Place linked by a central narrow block – an endless internal walkway. A fourth tower was acquired later and even in 2001 the towers were labelled A Block, B block, C Block and D block with signs hanging from the ceiling to reorientate those who were lost. On each individual office door was the name and title of the occupant – some larger offices had the name of the department. Typically Baker Street housed 3,000 people, although when temporary staff were thrown in that number could rise to nearer 4,000.

From the main visitors' entrance hall at number 67 a fine curving staircase led to the first floor, where the chairman and some of the senior directors had their offices. The chairman's office until the late 1990s was approached along the 'royal corridor' which, by Marcus Sieff's time, was carpeted in a deep blue, deep pile formal carpet. A uniformed commissionaire at a small table

49

was stationed at one end to prevent anyone without an appointment from entering. This arrangement was dropped only in 1999 when Peter Salsbury, who took over as chief executive from Greenbury, attempted to sweep away the old-fashioned elitist ways. Not that this policy prevented him from moving into Greenbury's old office and having it redecorated at considerable expense.

Other full-time directors and senior executives had offices on the second floor, while the rest of the operation was on the third to sixth floors. Compared with the staff dining quarters, the directors' dining rooms on the seventh floor were like another world. Tastefully decorated, the airy rooms were hung with original paintings, the antique furniture kept in gleaming condition by a small army of staff. First-time visitors would be struck by the atmosphere of hushed elegance and were surprised to find a retinue of white-gloved waiters. According to Sir David Sieff, the gloves were a legacy of Simon's obsession with hygiene, rather than mere formality. There the directors and their guests dined in considerable style under the watchful eye of the extraordinary George, the head butler and a man of high camp wit and style. Despite his manner, he was married with one son and also had a shrewd head for business, running a catering company for high-class parties and weddings on the side. He was, though, the sort of eccentric that only family businesses can accommodate.

Apart from the main directors' dining room there were a number of private rooms for entertaining suppliers and guests. The catering for this was done separately from the main staff restaurants by the 'directors' servery', as was the tea and coffee service provided on silver trays with fine bone china rimmed with gold, leading to the aphorism, 'gold-topped directors'. But the food, where possible, was always Marks & Spencer's own. 'If the food – or the clothes for that matter – was not good enough for the directors, then it was not good enough for the customers,' said Sieff.

After Simon's death the hierarchical structure became more entrenched, with directors and more junior executives increasingly conscious of rank. As the family's grip weakened, those coming up jockeyed for position, keen to show they were as good if not better than those called Sieff, Sacher or Lerner. Seniority was designated by how many of the big square windows your office sported, how large your desk was, the depth of pile of the carpet, the fabric of the curtains, how many easy chairs you had, how big was your secretary's office, what kind of car you had and so on.

'Simon would not have allowed it,' said David Sieff. 'He would have seen it as taking energy from the business.' But for the directors who emerged in the last thirty years of the century it was endemic. 'Marks & Spencer has always been the sort of place where if A has something, then B has to have one too,' one former director said.

Simon started his career travelling around Europe to buy the best and cheapest merchandise. From then on, his interest always focused on the buying operations. So the central power of the organisation resided with the buyers, often formidable women who had fought their way up to senior positions. 'They were Queens of their domain, frightening people,' recalled Peter Wolff, a onetime M&S executive and later a supplier through his company, SR Gent.

The buying teams were organised as triumvirates. There was a selector, whose job was to sense the coming fashions, to choose the styles, the colours, the type of fabric. To do so she would travel the world to fashion shows, always looking ahead to the next trends. Working with her – some would say against her – would be a merchandiser, whose job was to make the figures stack up. It was a delicate balance of power. The selectors were the creative animals and like creative animals everywhere tended to be ego-centric and temperamental. They were almost always women. If a garment was too expensively made to make a decent margin, the merchandiser would veto it or encourage the selector to make some compromises. Perhaps a cheaper fabric could be used, a pocket dispensed with, expensive trim on the collar replaced. The merchandisers were almost always men and, because of the nature of the job, more practical in their approach. The third member of this triumvirate would be the clothing technologist, who would often help the other two achieve a compromise on the fabric or design.

Such a structure may have appeared cumbersome to the outside world, but for decades it delivered 'the right goods at the right time at the right price to the stores'. It was the system that gave M&S a 10 per cent market share in clothing in the UK by 1966 and 15 per cent by 1996. Twice a year the senior executives in each department – ladies' casual wear, say, or men's knitwear – would present their ranges to the chairman and he would have the power to change or veto any garment. That was the way it worked under Simon Marks and that was the way it still worked under Sir Richard Green-bury until he left in 1999.

The Baker Street headquarters was the nerve centre of Marks & Spencer.

There, up to 4,000 people worked together, ate together, and many slept together – some because they were married or dating – others because they were engaged in illicit affairs. The frequent trips to visit suppliers, to training events and management conferences gave ample opportunity for liaisons to be formed. And there was an air of droit de seigneur about the place. It was a strong-minded young selector who ignored the flirtatious attentions of her superior male colleagues. 'We had a phrase for it,' recalled one former female employee. 'We called it corridor creeping.'

The enclosed world of the Baker Street office would have made a successful soap opera. It was a hotbed of feuding, power play and above all gossip. It was also where the training of graduate trainees and managers was based. From the 1970s to the 1980s M&S paid more than most other companies to secure the cream of the graduates. And once they had them, they drilled them without mercy. 'M&S was driven by divine discontent,' remembered one former selector who joined in the 1980s, but moved on to work for a supplier. 'They drilled quality and standards into you at every opportunity, they trained you to want to improve products, it was extremely intense – they got into your blood completely.' They also instilled confidence verging on the arrogant 'After a year I was sent off to a supplier to tell the management what was wrong with their factory. It was heady stuff,' she said.

Expense was no object. One recruit into the food side remembered being urged to eat at the best restaurants – 'to educate our palates'. Trainees stayed at top hotels and travelled first class on trains and planes. The company offered them interest-free loans to enable them to buy their first homes and they had access to all the medical facilities and free run of the gym and the various sporting clubs. At Christmas there were lavish parties at the Café Royal.

But although it was enjoyable, there was a price to pay. 'If you were not shaping up quite as they wanted they would slap you down hard and rebuild you in their own image,' one former merchandiser said. 'And you had to be on call seven days a week, twenty-four hours a day, ready to go anywhere. They took over your life.'

Stuart Rose, who began improving the fortunes of the rival Arcadia group (formerly Burton) in 2000, worked for M&S in the 1980s but rebelled against the culture. 'They were very good at lifting you up and dumping you back down again. They constantly wanted to turn you into the same kind of gingerbread man as everyone else. I was slightly different,' he said.

Above all, Baker Street was the place where all the decisions were made –

who the suppliers would be, the styles, the colour, the fabric or, in the case of food, the type of tomatoes, the choice of recipe dishes that would be sold. In addition, Baker Street decided the quantities of each line and which store would get what.

Life in the stores was always defensive, according to Bill Green, who ran the Folkestone store for twenty years until the late 1970s. 'We had hardly any control,' he said as he recalled his frustration with head office. 'Half the time when a line was doing well, you could never get enough of it. Sometimes we were screaming for stock and we just couldn't get it. Yet if anything went wrong a deputation from Baker Street would come and "investigate and discipline". You felt you always had to defend your corner, they were never supportive.' A store manager's job was to make sure the store worked, that the place was spotlessly clean, that the displays were in order and to head-office specifications, that the staff were well trained and motivated. But to decide what that store needed in stock – never.

When Teddy Sieff handed over the chairmanship to his nephew Marcus in 1972, it heralded a change of emphasis. Marcus, later Sir Marcus and then Lord Sieff, had grown up as Israel's son with all the advantages that money and position could buy. Although the family fortunes waxed and waned, he had a comfortable childhood and, unlike Simon's son Michael, who loathed the business, he soaked up its culture and its values. Occasionally he would breakfast with his uncle Simon at the Midland Hotel in Manchester, which had a high reputation for its cuisine. In his memoirs *Don't Ask the Price* he describes how Simon sent a plate of kippers back three times before he was satisfied. When a plump, juicy kipper finally arrived Marcus recalled his uncle's face relaxing into a smile. 'Ah now, that is quality,' Simon said.

Marcus joined the business straight from the army and soon learned that it was all right to speak up if it was in the interests of improving the product. A few weeks into the job he complained about the standard of the tomatoes in the food department and claimed M&S should not be selling them. His superior disagreed and marched him up to see Simon, complaining that he was 'making a nuisance of himself'. But Simon, after investigating, agreed with his nephew and for a few years there were no tomatoes for sale at M&S in the winter months. Years later, Marcus discovered that if he air-freighted tomatoes from the Canary Islands into Britain already ripe, the result was juicy and full of flavour. They cost 50 per cent more, but the discerning shopper would pay and they sold faster than the sea-freight tomatoes.

Marcus enjoyed the high life and liked to hob-nob with Hollywood stars such as Rosalind Russell and Cary Grant. He also liked the power of high office and the access it brought to top politicians at home in the UK and in Israel. One of the speakers at his memorial service recalled how for most of his adult life he was able to telephone the prime minister of both countries and be put through without a question.

He was also an irrepressible ladies' man. He married four times and pulled off the difficult trick of staying on good terms with all his wives. And he had countless mistresses – although unlike many M&S directors he was shrewd enough to keep his personal life outside the business. It was said that his decision to expand M&S into Canada – his one outstanding mistake – was swayed by his fondness for a girlfriend there.

Nevertheless, he was a true leader who commanded respect and affection. He had a vision for the company's growth and saw the need to modernise the management. Unlike Simon, who wanted to dominate all, Marcus saw that the company had grown to such a size that one man could no longer run everything. 'The development of able leaders and executives with delegated responsibility was essential,' he wrote in his memoirs. He brought in non-executive directors for the first time – the Marquis of Milford Haven and the first industry heavyweight, Albert Frost, the former treasurer of Imperial Chemical Industries and Sir Leopold Amery. Clinton Silver, who Marcus made a director, remembered him as a charismatic figure who could also use his temper to effect. 'I loved Marcus and he was the first to empower people within the business,' he said, before adding, 'But he could be so oppressive – he liked his own way.'

The underlying principles of the business, though, remained the same. There have been three Harvard case studies on M&S, one undertaken in 1975, three years after Marcus took over. The principles he supplied to the researchers then were exactly the same as they had been under Simon.

1. To offer our customers a selective range of high-quality, well-designed and attractive merchandise at reasonable prices.
2. To encourage our suppliers to use the most modern and efficient techniques of production and quality control dictated by the latest discoveries in science and technology.
3. With the cooperation of our suppliers, to enforce the highest standard of quality control.

4. To plan the expansion of our stores for the better display of a widening range of goods and for the convenience of our customers.
5. To foster good human relations with customers, suppliers and staff.

When he became chairman, Marcus mapped out a four-pronged plan: first, to develop production in the UK and so increase employment at home; second, to improve human relations within M&S and with suppliers; third, to become more involved with the communities with which M&S traded; and fourth – in hindsight a mistake – to expand overseas.

His main hobby-horses were the first two. Arriving in the company in 1951, just a few years after the end of the war, he was understandably patriotic and became passionate about sourcing as many M&S products as possible at home. To this end manufacturing techniques were taken from other countries and transplanted into Britain. One example was the production of men's suits.

In 1971 M&S decided to start selling men's suits but discovered that UK production of off-the-peg suits had almost died out. In the first year, 90 per cent of the suits sold by M&S came from Scandinavia, Italy and Israel. That same year Marcus 'bumped' into Sandy Dewhirst, grandson of the Isaac Dewhirst who had lent Michael Marks his crucial first five pounds. Dewhirst told him the company had a lot of spare cash and Marcus persuaded him to go into the production of men's suits for M&S. Dewhirst imported a technologist from Sweden and used an Italian designer employed by M&S to set up a plant in Sunderland in 1973. Two more plants followed and by 1985 they were employing more than 1,000 people.

His commitment to British suppliers is highlighted in his memoirs again and again. It became almost like a religion; all the senior management were imbued with a buy-British ethos and the belief that as well as serving their country, they gained quality and flexibility unavailable overseas. It worked so well for so long that when competitors began to source cheaper high-quality products from overseas in the 1990s M&S was slow to recognise the challenge. The company's loyalty encouraged inefficiencies in the UK manufacturers and protected them from international competition. As one commentator put it: 'M&S provided a vast system of outdoor relief for the British textile industry that enabled some companies to survive for longer than they perhaps should have.'

While Sieff was in charge the old ways of doing business round the dining-room table on a Sunday lunchtime continued. It may have been cosy, it may have been partisan, but as a means of delivering what 'she' the customer wanted, it was very effective. By helping small manufacturers expand and taking the lion's share of production it also ensured total loyalty and what some saw as an unhealthy dependence on M&S as a customer. In Simon's day, M&S was not above putting the squeeze on suppliers when things got tough. M&S was not alone among retailers in doing so, but in clothing at least it was bigger than all the others. During the recession of the mid 1970s British textile companies went though an extremely difficult time with M&S under Sieff 'asking' them to reduce their profit margins. 'There would come that time when they would arrive and tell us it was time for the suppliers to "make a contribution",' said a former director of William Baird, a clothing supplier.

Marcus, who had been in charge of the food side in his early career and was something of a bon viveur, took far more interest in the food department than the previous chairmen and led the company into the lucrative chilled-food market. Simon had grumbled at his early efforts: 'Are you trying to turn me into a grocer?' he had asked sternly when Marcus had put loose vegetables into the food departments. But he persevered, and when he became chairman he pushed at the frontiers of innovation. Although much M&S fruit and vegetables came from overseas, Marcus was instrumental in persuading British farmers to grow new lines. One example was the Californian 'crispheart' lettuce. He sent technologists to California to study growing techniques and spent two years experimenting in the UK before a way was found to grow crispheart lettuces at home.

Simon's legacy to the food side was his fanaticism about hygiene standards – he realised that one case of food poisoning could do immeasurable damage to the company's reputation. Several versions are told of the tale of the store manager who interviewed a young female recruit with her mother – as was normal in the 1950s. Initially the mother was thrilled that her daughter was joining M&S. Several weeks or months later she returned distraught, complaining that her daughter had become unduly critical of the hygiene in the home, in other words, critical of her mother. 'She even wants me to wash my hands before making pastry,' she said according to one version. Another tells how the daughter insisted on cleaning the walls of the fridge, something that particular mother judged excessive.

Equally important as in-store hygiene was the hygiene of the suppliers,

56

which were cajoled or bullied into improving their standards. This included manufacturers of pies, cakes, biscuits and so on but also extended to farms that supplied dairy produce and meat. If they refused or failed to improve, they were reluctantly dropped. While Marcus was running the food side, his deputy was the extraordinary Nathan 'Dr No' Goldenberg, a food technologist who laid down what some considered almost impossibly high standards. One director described him as 'mentally incapable of any form of compromise in the fields he considered important'. An example of his diligence emerged when M&S started doing business with a well-known biscuit supplier. Despite the firm's good reputation, Goldenberg was suspicious about the standards of hygiene and stayed late one night in the offices until the factory had closed. He persuaded one of the company's young executives to take him back into the factory and when they turned on the lights they saw the floor alive with red ants scurrying back under the ovens. M&S immediately stopped using the company until it submitted to a rigorous overhaul of standards.

But what others regarded as fanaticism paid off. Between 1960 and 1970 M&S food sales rose from £24m to £97m. The company does not reveal specifically its profits from food – but assuming a conservative 6 per cent return on sales, turnover of £97m would produce profits of £5.8m. By 1970 M&S had set up a national system of food depots and chilled or frozen transport, which ensured produce could reach stores in prime condition within thirty-six hours.

Marcus's jetsetting lifestyle enabled him to sample different kinds of food around the world, giving him ideas that he would bring back home. In his memoirs he recounted his conversion to frozen foods, having been totally set against them, while staying with the film star Rosalind Russell in Beverly Hills. 'One afternoon I was given a piece of cake which I found delicious. I said to Ros, "Your cook is remarkable, but I didn't know she was that good." She replied: "Don't be silly Marcus, this is a frozen cake bought in a supermarket".' The following day he went to several supermarkets and bought a number of brands of frozen cakes, which he and Russell sampled. Way ahead of the rest was a cake made by The Kitchens of Sara Lee, of Chicago. Marcus soon arranged to meet Charlie Lubin, the head of Sara Lee. They formed an instant rapport and Lubin took him on a tour of the bakery.

But the two men were soon at loggerheads. Lubin refused to supply Sara

Lee cakes under the Marks & Spencer name and M&S refused to sell them under the Sara Lee brand. It took several years before agreement that the cakes would sell under the M&S name could be reached, at which point Sara Lee took over an old bakery in Yorkshire, rebuilt it and supplied the company from then on. Yet the incident marked the start of M&S frozen foods.

His frequent visits to the USA gave Marcus expansionary ideas. Under Simon, the growth of the company had always been through the building of new stores and the expansion of older ones. He never made an acquisition of another company and neither did Israel or Teddy. But the next three chairmen of Marks and Spencer – Marcus, Derek Rayner and Rick Greenbury – in their quest to speed up the company's growth all made expensive and ultimately disastrous acquisitions at the apogees of their careers. Marcus was the first, paying way too much for a controlling interest in People's Department Stores of Canada in 1974. Then, in 1989, Rayner bought the Brooks Brothers menswear chain for roughly double what it was worth. Finally, in 1997, just when it seemed Marks & Spencer was at the peak of its success making more than £1bn a year, Greenbury bought nineteen stores from the Littlewoods group. None of these acquisitions ever fulfilled its promise.

When Marcus took over as chairman in 1972, Britain was in the grip of a Labour administration hostile to big business. Because of this, and his feeling that further growth in the UK would be difficult, he looked around for acquisitions on the other side of the Atlantic. He put his toe in the water carefully, starting a joint venture with People's Department Stores in Canada. In 1974 M&S bought 55 per cent of People's, which also owned a chain called D'Allairds and a 51 per cent stake in Walkers Stores. It was a mistake from the start. Despite continued investment and efforts to improve trading, the Canadian operations at best made a modest profit and at worst lost money and continued to limp along until they were finally sold in 1999.

In 1982 Marcus presided over the nearest thing Marks & Spencer has ever had to a scandal. At the annual meeting in July, Ralph Quartano, head of the Post Office pension fund, openly criticised M&S for a scheme that had allowed eight directors including the chairman to rent their houses cheaply from the company and then buy them back at cost, netting large personal profits. The arrangement had started in 1973 but was only disclosed for the first time in the 1982 accounts because of a new stipulation in the 1981 Companies Act. Quartano declared that the scheme should have been disclosed from the beginning and pointed out that M&S was breaking Stock Exchange rules by not securing shareholder approval for the deals. 'It is important for St Michael to be on the side of the angels,' he told the meeting. Such was the ensuing furore in the press that a special shareholders' meeting was held on 3 November to thrash out the issue.

From their cocooned standpoint, M&S directors could not understand what all the fuss was about. For many years the company had lent money at advantageous rates to executives and management staff to help them buy their houses. But the law prevented M&S from doing the same for directors. The directors felt this was unfair – despite their superior salaries – and so in 1973 they devised the scheme, which had seemed to them a perfectly reasonable way round the problem.

The scheme was quite legal and nobody would have been much concerned if house prices had remained stable, but they had shot up in the intervening years, providing the directors with huge profits, which provoked accusations of greed. The story proved to be a taster for the 'fat cattery' furore of the 1990s and the press whipped up a frenzy of shareholder indignation. The November meeting was a stormy affair with 800 shareholders turning up and Marcus admitting that the transactions 'should have been referred to the Stock Exchange and were not – an omission I regret'. He added that no further housing transactions were envisaged.

It says a lot for his charm and humour that Marcus was able to diffuse the anger to such an extent that, at the end of the meeting, the majority of those present voted in favour of the arrangement. Even so, M&S realised its blunder and quickly wound up any remaining housing transactions. But the episode was a glaring example of how inward-looking companies, particularly successful inward-looking companies, can be dismissive of the outside world. M&S executives regarded themselves as above reproach, and were shocked and hurt when the reproach came. It was, they were to discover, a mere dress rehearsal for what was to come in 1998.

Two years later, in 1984, Marcus stepped up to become president, which he turned into an aggressively ambassadorial role, travelling the world lecturing on the M&S ethos. He retained an office in Baker Street but stepped back from the day-to-day business. The man who took over from him, the first chairman to come from outside the family, was his own discovery – a brilliant, irritable, chain-smoking homosexual called Derek Rayner.

# CHAPTER FOUR

# Goodbye to the family

Derek George Rayner had waited a long time to be chairman of Marks & Spencer. Marcus Sieff would sometimes say he had not only discovered and developed his successor, he had also discovered his successor's successor in Rick Greenbury – a measure of the way things were done in those days. Yet Sieff was reluctant to release the reins of power, leaving it until he was 70 before becoming president, an exclusively ambassadorial role.

By then Rayner, already knighted, was 58, impatient for power and privately disparaging of his benefactor for hanging on for so long. He had been a main board director for seventeen years and joint managing director for eleven years when he took on the mantle of the chairmanship in July 1984. A tall, bulky man with thinning grey hair and blue eyes, he had long artistic hands that in waking hours almost always held a cigarette – he would frequently light the new one from the glowing stub of the old. When, towards the end of his chairmanship, he was forced to give up his seventy-a-day habit after being rushed to hospital from an overnight Hong Kong flight, his already irascible temper became even more ferocious. Always difficult, edgy and petulant, he could reduce middle managers to quivering wrecks with a volley of four-letter words.

'He was a very forceful man,' recalled Greenbury. 'If you think I was autocratic, Derek was a real autocrat.' Hugh Walker, who became a divisional director of foods, spent four years as Rayner's personal assistant and remembered him as a shrewd visionary with little time for those he considered his inferiors. 'Derek had huge impatience, partly because he was four steps ahead of other people,' said Walker. 'He led from about a mile in front and could be impossible to argue with. At operational meetings he would regularly say: "If you don't do it I'm going to resign."'

But Rayner could also be charming when relaxed. He loved good food,

J&B whisky, which his minions had to procure wherever he was in the world, and classical music, particularly Bach. He lavished affection on his two Yorkshire terriers and he adored gardening. At Gorsewick, his Sussex country house, where he would entertain old friends such as Leon Brittan, Geoffrey and Elspeth Howe and Lois Sieff, Teddy Sieff's widow, he transformed the garden into a work of art. He had an encyclopaedic knowledge of plants and once spent an afternoon showing a director from Kew Gardens round, growing increasingly irritated as each time he announced the Latin name of a plant, the man from Kew would trump him with the Latin for the sub-species.

He also enjoyed giving advice. One M&S supplier invited Rayner to his house for tea on a summer afternoon for a quasi-business meeting. 'Suddenly Derek said: "I would do something about those roses if I were you," and for the rest of the two-hour meeting we discussed my roses,' he said.

But most importantly for Marks & Spencer, Rayner possessed a fine intellect – he was 'a very bright man, highly articulate and mentally structured', according to a former colleague.

Although Rayner was Sieff's choice, he was about as different from his predecessor as it was possible to be. If Sieff was a charismatic leader who charmed customers, suppliers and staff, Rayner was publicly cold and shy. On a visit to a textile factory Sieff would kiss the girls working the machines and ask to have his photograph taken with them; Rayner would walk straight past without a word. Sieff was a notorious womaniser who loved a good party; Rayner found M&S's young glamorous female selectors daunting – although he enjoyed the company of strong women such as Margaret Thatcher and Princess Margaret. He preferred the intimacy of the dinner party to larger gatherings. If Sieff believed in the tradition that the product was everything, Rayner had modern ideas about marketing and professional management. 'I have to create the future, not preside over the past,' was one of his favourite sayings. Marcus Sieff's idea of a good holiday was a trip to the French Riviera or Barbados in winter; Rayner preferred the exotic delights of Thailand, which he visited so regularly on business that he eventually bought two apartments in a peaceful fishing village near Pattaya, 50 miles from Bangkok. And while Sieff was Jewish, Rayner was of pure Anglo-Saxon stock and had considered taking holy orders while reading theology at Cambridge – although once he became chairman he put great efforts into supporting the state of Israel.

Yet despite their differences in style, Rayner felt he was as imbued with the values of the founding family as it was possible to be without having Marks or Sieff blood in his veins. Greenbury agreed, claiming that he and Rayner made little real break with the family ethos. 'Derek and I had been brought up by the family. They took us under their wing and developed us. And although we were not family, we were the nearest thing,' he said passionately. 'We both believed in the principles by which Simon had grown the business and Marcus and Teddy ran it – we believed that those principles were fundamental to its success. Therefore although Derek and I modernised them – the attitude to people, to suppliers, to customers – we stuck to them so there was real continuity.'

The family itself believed that blood was thicker than water and perceived things slightly differently. 'We felt things did begin to change under Derek,' said one of the Sieffs. 'He kept the values but managers became more competitive and status conscious with each other, and it became almost a disadvantage to be a family member.'

Stuart Rose, who became chief executive of Arcadia in 2000, was a junior executive under Sieff and Rayner. 'Under Marcus it was a benign dictatorship. He would shout at you but then he'd put his arm round you and say: "I'm only trying to teach you boy,"' he said. 'Derek started to squeeze the business for profit and the organisation became more political. You always had to mind your back.' Suppliers also noticed the difference. Rayner was less clubbable – the days of chewing the fat in each other's homes were gone. 'It was no longer possible to sit round the dinner table and discuss things privately,' said one.

One thing Sieff and Rayner shared was a passion for overseas expansion. Between them they squandered nearly £1.3bn on acquisitions in North America and attempts to make those acquisitions pay. European expansion was less expensive but almost as unrewarding. Although the Continental stores prospered at various times, the returns were always a fraction of those in the UK.

Even though his predecessor's investment in Canada had been a dismal failure, Rayner saw a future for M&S beyond the British Isles and Europe. In December 1990, in one of the Harvard Business School case studies, he was quoted as saying: 'The world is what it's about, not little Europe. We've got to be entrepreneurs and take some risks. This retailing field is becoming crowded.'

By the time Rayner took the chair he had already made a name for himself outside the company advising government – and to outsiders who met him, he appeared more like a senior civil servant than a retailer. For a man who had flirted with the priesthood, the cloister and the corridors of Whitehall had much in common – both serving a greater power. His first secondment from M&S was to Ted Heath after he won the 1970 general election. Rayner's role was to examine and make recommendations about the way defence equipment was bought. Later, in 1979 Margaret Thatcher invited him to set up a group to 'improve efficiency and eliminate waste' in government.

According to Marcus Sieff, who told the story in his memoirs, the defence job had come out of a grand dinner party in 1970 at Heath's flat in Albany for a dozen or so big-company chairmen including Val Duncan of RTZ and George Cole of Unilever. After the dinner, during which, as Sieff characteristically recalled, Cheval Blanc 1945 was served, Heath declared that if he became prime minister he wanted to work more closely with industry. But there was a price – and it was that industry would have to give up some of its most valued executives to work with government. According to Sieff, he returned to M&S and, after various discussions, volunteered Rayner. But Rayner, who since his Cambridge days had mingled in political circles, always dismissed the story with some irritation, claiming that he and Heath already knew each other and the Tory leader had himself requested Rayner for the job. Certainly Rayner and Heath had much in common with their finely educated minds, their bachelor status and love of classical music.

Rayner's first task was to look at defence procurement. The big issue in those days of state-owned airlines was the conflict between purchases of civil aircraft and military aircraft, purchases that at the time were both handled by the Ministry of Aviation and Supply. One senior civil servant recalled that Rayner sized up the problem almost immediately. His report recommended the establishment of a more broadly based defence procurement executive, which would oversee the purchase of military aircraft as well as tanks, armaments and so on. 'Derek was very impressive to watch. He got to the heart of the issue and I thought he did Whitehall a considerable service,' he said. When Rayner put forward his recommendations after a year, they were so warmly received that Heath invited him to stay and put them into practice as chief executive of the Procurement Executive, Defence. He got the department up and running in record time and the proof of its success is that a version of it still exists today.

In 1973 Rayner returned to M&S, where he was made joint managing director along with Henry Lewis. But in 1979 Rayner was back in government, this time with Margaret Thatcher, for whom he created the 'Rayner scrutinies' to probe Whitehall waste. The idea was to send a young, ambitious civil servant into each government department with the task of 'scrutinising' it and devising a plan of action within a few weeks. It was a way of throwing a searchlight on to a particular problem. Altogether 135 government departments were scrutinised in this way and had to endure an assault on waste. The government declared the scrutinies a great success, claiming they had saved £275m a year and eliminated 10,000 jobs, and M&S colleagues felt Rayner enjoyed every moment of his time in Whitehall, particularly relishing his relationship with Thatcher, with whom he had a special rapport. 'He played her like a Stradivarius,' said one Downing Street aide, 'and he would use her influence whenever he felt the need.' Indeed, he subsequently maintained he could never have done the job without her support.

Even so, Rayner felt he was held back when it came to implementing the recommendations of his scrutineers. In some ways he found his three years with Thatcher as frustrating as they were fascinating and was later surprisingly frank about his disappointment in making so little impact on the overall Whitehall culture. In the political world he found a body of people resistant to radical change. 'It has been worthwhile, but I would not claim the change has been significant,' he told Sir Geoffrey Owen, then editor of the *Financial Times*, in 1991.

His work for Heath and Thatcher had the disadvantage of making him a target for the IRA, which viewed high-ranking businessmen who helped the British government as worthy of attention. But as Marks & Spencer chairmen had lived with the terrorist threat from Arab extremists ever since the assassination attempt on Edward Sieff, Rayner was already well practised in security precautions.

Knighted by Heath and made a peer by Thatcher, Rayner was born and brought up with his sister Audrey in Norwich. He spent two years at the end of the Second World War in the RAF and dreamed of active combat but by that time there was a shortage of aircraft and his flying ambitions were never realised. He was sent instead to the Middle East, where he served as an adjutant. Returning to post-war Britain he read theology at Selwyn College, Cambridge, where he shared rooms with Alistair Sampson, who went on to become the pre-eminent dealer in antique oak furniture, and a young

Geoffrey Howe, future stalwart of the Thatcher government and later a Lord. At Cambridge he wrestled with the idea of joining the priesthood, yet ironically, it was his study of theology that, he later wrote, 'somehow stopped me believing', although he continued to be a regular churchgoer. Such were his misgivings he failed to finish his degree and, unsure of what to do, he started managing what Sieff in his memoirs described as a 'fancy goods shop' in Norwich. When the shop ran out of capital in 1953 he joined the Oxford branch of M&S. He was by then 27 – a late starter compared with most of those who became M&S directors, including Greenbury, who joined at 17, straight from school.

While he was working away in the food department of the Oxford store Rayner's luck changed. Marcus Sieff, then head of the food operation, came by on a store visit and discovered him. Tall and highly educated, he must have appeared instantly different from the average shelf stacker and the chairman was immediately impressed by the speed with which he had acquired knowledge about the food business. Indeed, Sieff was so impressed he tried to persuade the personnel director Norman Laski to break his iron rule of not allowing anyone into head office in Baker Street before they had served two years in stores. After one conversation with Laski, Sieff thought he had won the argument – but then a few weeks later, on another chance store visit, he found Rayner in the Watford branch, to which he had been transferred. Sieff lost his infamous temper. In his own words: 'I played merry hell and said that unless Derek Rayner was in head office by the following Monday, I would take up the matter with the chairman.' The chairman was his uncle Simon and Laski deduced that Sieff's relationship with him was stronger than his own. In October 1954 Rayner was transferred.

From then on Rayner became Marcus Sieff's right-hand man, helping him to build up the food side and becoming manager of canned goods in 1963. One store manager who met him then remembers a charming young man: 'He was a very pleasant fellow in those days, very easy to talk to and he certainly gave the impression of listening.' Rayner also worked abroad, promoting export business for M&S. Thanks to his obvious talent and Sieff's patronage he zipped up the ranks and was promoted to the board in 1967 at 41, fourteen years after signing on at Oxford.

Soon after Marcus Sieff took the chair from his uncle Teddy in 1972, it became clear to everyone, including Henry Lewis, who had felt secure under Simon Marks's patronage, and Michael Sacher, the main family contender for the succession, that Rayner was likely to be his heir and anyone else who wanted the top job would face an uphill struggle. Not only did they get on well at work, but Rayner would spend almost every other weekend with Sieff and his wife in their country house.

Henry Lewis had clashed frequently with Sieff. Although Sieff had developed the food group in the teeth of opposition from his uncle Simon, his enthusiasm focused on fresh exotic produce rather than the development of new dishes. Lewis recalled one occasion when he and Angus Monro, who later ran the Matalan discount chain, were testing a new product – a washed and bagged salad that was quite revolutionary at the time. 'Marcus came in and was scathing about the product, said it would never catch on, that it was rubbish,' Lewis recounted. 'And today, bagged salad is on sale everywhere.'

Having seen the writing on the wall, Lewis, then still in his early fifties, decided to make plans to leave the company and start a new career, although he was delayed by a heart bypass operation and stayed on until 1985. But if Lewis dropped out of the race Rayner still had to contend with Michael Sacher, the son of Simon's sister Miriam and her husband Harry Sacher. Even in a company as hierarchical as M&S the power of deciding the next chairman was not entirely in the incumbent's gift.

Sacher, who was deputy chairman to Sieff and who was the only director in the mid 1970s to hold more than a million shares, felt that he deserved a few years as chairman before Rayner took the post. For some years Sacher and Rayner manoeuvred around each other but most of the board felt that although Sacher was blessed with a brilliant analytical mind, he lacked managerial ability and struggled to cope with the lower orders. 'I never know what to say to them,' he once agonised to a colleague. More to the point, he was too old. The four managing directors under Sieff – Rayner, Henry Lewis, Brian Howard and Greenbury – could see no contest. 'For a company of our size and stature, it seemed to the managing directors at the time that the next chairman could not be a man in his late sixties while Derek Rayner waited in the wings,' Greenbury recalled.

The succession was finally decided at one of the board's conferences at Hambleton Hall, a luxurious Leicestershire country house hotel chosen by Sieff to which directors would occasionally retreat to discuss important matters. On this occasion, both Marcus Sieff and Sacher stayed away to enable the other directors to be objective. Rayner chaired the meeting.

The intense political manoeuvrings that characterised the M&S board-room in the closing years of family control took place within an atmosphere of elegant luxury. Retreats to spas and country house hotels had long been a feature of M&S life at the top. Before Hambleton Hall, which was also favoured by Rayner, the directors would swoop off to Chewton Glen, close to the sea in Hampshire, to confer, and when Greenbury became chairman the meetings returned there.

It was all part of a style of living that the directors enjoyed throughout the 1970s and 1980s, a style as luxurious as that of a band of medieval princes. 'Good human relations' never meant for a second that the ordinary body of M&S staff – the troops – were treated in any way as equals to the officers. For troops they had excellent conditions – subsidised staff restaurants, chiropody, dentists, free inoculations and generous non-contributory pensions – but clerical and secretarial staff were watched with hawklike vigilance by supervisors who monitored their every move. Although old fashioned clocking-in had been abandoned in the simplification of 1956, managers were sticklers for timekeeping, even for those higher up the pecking order. And no food or drink was allowed in the office, unless you happened to be a senior executive.

Not everyone felt it was a privilege to work there. 'The regimentation was frightful,' remembered a secretary who worked in Baker Street during the 1970s. 'You had fifteen minutes for your morning and afternoon break and by the time you had walked all the way from Block B to Block D where the restaurant was, it was time to come back. The supervisors even timed you went you went to the loo,' she said, 'and if you were gone more than five minutes they asked what had taken you so long.'

Middle managers had a better time of it and felt a strong sense of belonging. 'In those days,' said Walker, 'there was always a lot to laugh about. We had real fun and we often had time to go for a pint together after work.'

Directors enjoyed many privileges. They entered the building by a discreet entrance at the back, always travelled first class on trains and aeroplanes and until the 1960s, had chauffer-driven Rolls-Royces or Bentleys at their disposal. Jaguars took their place in the 1970s, with the exception of the chairman's car, and later Mercedes.

Each director enjoyed a spacious, elegant office with deep-pile carpets, paintings on the wall and decor to their own taste with the number of windows – one, two or three for the chairman – reflecting their seniority.

They were pampered in every way with armies of secretaries and administrative staff to shield them from the vicissitudes of the real world. At lunchtime they ate in the rarefied splendour of the seventh floor, and enjoyed their tea and coffee delivered by flunkies from the directors' servery. They were rarely seen in the two staff restaurants – and if they did make a visit, they would sit together. The chairman and senior directors also enjoyed the use of private twin-engine turbo prop planes parked at Leavesden aerodrome near Watford to facilitate speedy business trips to suppliers and stores. Once jets came in, M&S directors would use Northolt airport, less than an hour from Baker Street.

It was a style that had grown up with the extended family and was not unusual, although by no means universal, in public companies in the 1970s and 1980s. It had been set in train by Simon Marks, who, as 'proprietor' of the business, enjoyed the trappings of wealth, the influence it gave him with politicians and the allure for film stars and celebrities.

But money and material blessings were never his prime motivation even if he did know how to enjoy them. The Sieffs, the Sachers and the Laskis, as big shareholders in the company, came to believe that a luxurious lifestyle both inside and outside the office was their proprietorial right and the culture subsequently affected non-family directors, who adopted that same ethos when they arrived on the board.

After Simon died the perks game became more obsessively played. How many perks you had became a mark of your success. So the depth of the carpet, the quality of the curtains, size of the desk and the number of windows in your office became crucial to an executive's status. The cheap home loans that caused such a scandal in 1982 would have been regarded as just such a perk. Such comforts were so seductively enjoyable that, so long as the company prospered, no one saw any reason for change.

And so in 1982 the board repaired to Hambleton Hall – 'seriously expensive, but luxury and panache never come cheaply' in the words of one guest – to discuss who would be the next chairman. What nobody knew at the time was that Michael Sacher had an incipient brain tumour, which in hindsight may have been responsible for some of his erratic behaviour.

In any event, it was decided unanimously – even by John Sacher, Michael's son – that Rayner should be the first non-family chairman. White smoke may not have puffed out of Hambleton Hall's Victorian chimneys over the manicured gardens on Rutland Water but the man who had dreamed of becoming a cleric had become pontiff of Baker Street.

Family businesses have many virtues – the partnership with staff and suppliers, the proprietorial interest – but one of Marks & Spencer's flaws was the reluctance of the founding family to acknowledge that as a result of turning the business into a public company with outside ownership it had duties and obligations to outside shareholders. Marks & Spencer's rhetoric was full of tributes to the customers, the staff and the suppliers. The importance of shareholders was rarely considered – at least until after the share price collapsed in the late 1990s.

Much of that was Simon Marks's legacy. He saw himself as a feared but revered proprietor who controlled the ownership of the business. And while he lived, he refused to countenance enfranchising the non-voting shares held by outsiders.

Even the mighty Prudential, which put up the first outside funding and until 1996 still held around 7 per cent of the shares, found that its so-called 'special relationship' was something of a one-way street. Along with other institutional fund managers, it had its access to the company limited to twice yearly conferences at Michael House.

For much of the 1970s and early 1980s the situation had been ameliorated by the finance director, an amiable man called John Samuels, who was happy to chat to analysts on the phone and be indiscreet enough to be helpful. Intriguingly, the chairmen of the time appeared to know little of these cosy conversations. Keeping the City informed was beneath them.

The practice of informal chats with finance directors was common before Big Bang in the City in 1986, after which regulations about talking to analysts tightened up. In any event, when Keith Oates became finance director in December 1983, City analysts found him much less accessible than his predecessor and the relationship grew increasingly cold.

For many years the Pru managed a large slice of the M&S pension fund but during the second half of the 1990s some of this business was summarily taken away and given to a big American fund manager, Frank Russell, to manage. Virtually the same thing happened to Mercury Asset Management, which had also been a long-term shareholder. Such acts of arrogance, handled with zero diplomacy, did little to engender shareholder loyalty when the company's luck turned.

In the City, M&S was admired for its acumen, but disliked intensely. 'Their main problem with the City was that they didn't have any friends.

They were arrogant, pompous unworldly,' one fund manager recalled. 'They were in-turned and secretive with no network of outside supporters apart from suppliers. So when it rained they had no friends because it never occurred to them it might rain.'

Rayner, like his predecessors, regarded the City and most financial journalists with disdain. He did, however, instigate the annual conference with journalists and stockbrokers' analysts, whom he always referred to dismissively as 'spivs', following the full-year results. Not that there was much time for questions. He conducted those conferences in much the same way as he did board meetings. They would be held in Baker Street at 9.30 a.m. sharp and by 10.45 Rayner would be gone in a wave of cigarette smoke and irritation.

Occasionally he would entertain financial journalists to lunch in Baker Street on an 'off-the-record basis', but he mostly rationed interviews to the most august such as the late Kenneth Fleet, during his time as City editor of *The Times*, and Geoffrey Owen of the *Financial Times*. Stella Shamoon, a *Sunday Telegraph* and *Observer* freelance journalist, also gained the occasional 'on-the-record' access.

His distaste for public relations aside, Rayner was perfect for M&S. It was a tribute both to his professionalism and the intense loyalty of M&S staff that the press never heard any gossip about him. In London he lived at 3 Hamilton Terrace in St John's Wood with his long-term companion Kenneth Robinson, who affected the title 'Dr' Robinson. 'An outrageous queen', according to one executive, Robinson could be something of a liability and would occasionally arrive somewhat inebriated at Rayner's office to be looked after, subdued and later despatched by Elizabeth Grant, the chairman's formidable secretary. He would also borrow Rayner's Rolls-Royce and take it to tour London's gay pubs such as the King of Bohemia in Hampstead. When Rayner was ennobled the story went round M&S that Robinson had asked if he could now be called 'Lady Hamilton'. But despite the occasional embarrassment Rayner displayed total loyalty towards him and was devastated when he died.

In the political, business and royal circles (he dined with Princess Margaret) in which he moved, Rayner kept his private life private. 'On the whole he was one of those closet gay men who had his own discreet circle outside the company,' remembered one former director. In New York he had another long-term friend – a Greek called Stavros – whom he would invite to occasional M&S functions. According to Hugh Walker, Stavros could fix almost anything. On one occasion Rayner and Walker had to stay in Toronto unexpectedly overnight. Every upmarket hotel was full. Walker then rang Stavros and within minutes he managed to secure the presidential suite in one of the city's top hotels.

But no salacious gossip about Rayner ever got into the newspapers. His obituaries in June 1998 stuck resolutely to his achievements at M&S and in Whitehall. Some in the company claimed that it may have had something to do with the protection of government, but it was probably because M&S was still a family company in essence and disloyalty to the chairman was as unthinkable as disloyalty by a child to a father. Undermining the chairman undermined the whole company and, as many of those working in Michael House did not have private lives beyond reproach, who would cast the first stone?

In his business approach Rayner was not so much a breath of fresh air as a stimulating force nine easterly. Asked by Kenneth Fleet in 1986 whether it was true that under him paternalism had given way to commercialism he replied: 'Lord Sieff preached a message of good human relations to a wide audience. I won't be so available to do that.' He did, however, remind Fleet of Simon Marks's restructurings, maintaining that the family had never been paternalistic except in the care of people – 'and that is not going to change'.

Another thing that was not going to change was the power of the chairman. The chairman of Marks & Spencer was effectively God – and you didn't argue with Him. Like an army general, he made the decisions. There might be a bit of consultation with the senior officers, some robust debate even with the number two, but in the end what the general wanted was what happened. And this was true down to the tiniest detail.

David Norgrove – who became commercial director in 2000 after Peter Salsbury was fired – was taken on a grand tour of stores in south-east England in Rayner's Rolls-Royce as part of his induction to the company. Norgrove, who had been recruited from the Civil Service, observed an organisation 'almost unnaturally responsive to leadership from the top'.

First stop on the tour was the Brighton store, where Rayner exploded in fury because the oranges were displayed in the middle of the fruit counter, not on the end. 'I couldn't quite understand why anybody should get quite so livid about finding oranges on the side instead of the end,' said Norgrove.

Rayner declared that he would go upstairs for some refreshment and when he returned he expected the oranges to be on the end of the counter. And so they were. There were smiles and handshakes. At the next store on the journey, Tunbridge Wells, Rayner and his party found the oranges on the end of the counter. Norgrove asked the store manager whether they had been moved that morning. 'Oh yes,' he was told. 'And I can tell you they will have been moved in every store throughout the country.'

Like Sieff before him, Rayner was particularly interested in the food business. Every morning at 7.30 the top food executives would meet on the sixth floor in an area known as the Bureau of Standards and taste samples of all the new season fruit that had been delivered that day. 'There was always an issue,' said Stuart Rose, then a food executive. 'The nectarines were too sharp or the melon not ripe. Derek was obsessive. I remember falling out with him over the quality of the mangos.'

Rayner was not just autocratic, he had little tolerance for the debate and discussion of long meetings. Under his chairmanship the monthly board meetings would start at 9 a.m. and end, at the latest, at 10.15. He would even book his next appointment at 10.30 so that he always had a reason to bring the meeting to a close. When directors were unhappy, as they often were, feeling that policy decisions had been 'railroaded through', he was always dismissive. 'You deal with them,' he would say to Greenbury, then his deputy, 'I can't be bothered with them.'

Even so, Rayner was a moderniser. After Simon Marks's death in 1964, very little changed in the main clothing business other than the addition of more space and products. Teddy and Israel continued to do what he had done. In the words of Henry Lewis, 'Simon had continued to rule the company from the grave.' Under Marcus, whose first love was food, there had been no significant clothing competition in the middle ground to worry about. Competition was either way above M&S in Harrods or other department stores such as Marshall and Snelgrove, Selfridges and Derry and Toms, or way below in Littlewoods, where the quality did not come close. So the company had steamed on, looking neither right nor left.

During Marcus's regime there was a feeling that growth was being stifled. Many store managers complained they simply could not get enough stock to sell when it was in demand. It is clear from his memoirs that Marcus Sieff enjoyed promoting the role of the company as a national institution – a force for good in society – rather more than was good for the growth of profits. In the last years of Marcus's chairmanship there was increasing criticism of 'the family' among the growing band of non-family senior executives and there was a groundswell of opinion that a man with fewer emotional ties to the company was needed to lead it.

The bottom line, although not exactly forgotten, had become less important set against Sieff's passion for 'human relations', work in the community and supporting the British textile industry. He also spent a lot of time hobnobbing with politicians, both in the UK and Israel. The family believed – with some justification as events later showed – that it was dangerous for the company to grow too fast and to put too much emphasis on increasing profit margins. They also feared that the company's enduring values might be lost in a relentless pursuit of profits – and that along with those values might go the family's grip on the group.

Inside the company, while Sieff was obsessive about expansion in food, he refused to spend money on refurbishing the stores and growth became pedestrian. In the last five years of his chairmanship, from 1981 until 1985, the number of UK stores crept up from 252 to 265 while the square footage rose only from 6.4m to 7.2m. In Canada there were a staggering 227 stores in 1995 but Europe had just nine. In those five years, pre-tax profits rose 68 per cent from £181.2m to £304.1m on sales up from £1.9bn to £3.2bn. But inflation flattered the picture: during the same period prices rose by 40 per cent, so only 28 percentage points of the profits increase was due to real growth. In his last year, to March 1985, profits moved up by just 8.6 per cent.

Outside the bastions of Baker Street, the image of the company had become fusty and old fashioned. Professional fund managers, who by then controlled the majority of the shares on behalf of pension funds, mutual funds and insurance schemes, took note and looked to Rayner to blow away the cobwebs. They were not disappointed.

While waiting to be chairman Rayner formed a clear vision for the future of M&S. He remained loyal to the traditional ethos – value, quality and the dedication to the pursuit of excellence – but he was full of new ideas. 'My job is to manage change,' he proclaimed in his accession speech.

He lost no time about it. The day he took over, he moved into the chairman's office approached by the regal blue carpet and summoned the sixty-odd directors and senior executives to a meeting in one of the conference rooms. He sat up on a dais and straightened out a crumpled sheet of paper on the table in front of him. 'It felt as though he had been carrying that bit of paper in his pocket for the previous ten years,' recalled Alan Smith, then a hungry young executive, whom Rayner later sent to America to scout for acquisitions. Rayner listed six intentions. He wanted to internationalise the business, modernise stores, expand significantly in financial services, improve information systems, warehousing and transport, expand the food business and increase the selling space in the United Kingdom. 'And by the time he retired seven years later,' said Smith, who by 2001 was chairman of Mothercare, 'Derek had done all that.'

Rayner also recruited the first outsider at director level – the tall, quietly spoken Keith Oates, who joined after thirty-five interviews to be finance director and set about realising his chairman's ambitions in financial services.

Shortly after he arrived, Oates commissioned Robert Colvill, then a Chemical Bank fund manager, to review the nascent financial services business. And following his recommendation to expand the area, Oates put him in charge of building it. At the time it was run from Chester under contract by North West Securities, a Bank of Scotland subsidiary. NWS had developed an in-house charge card to the point where it could be tested on consumers. In June 1984 the M&S charge card was given a trial in seventeen stores in Scotland. By the end of it there were 36,000 charge-card customers and Oates and Colvill immediately saw the potential and pushed for a national launch in January 1985, although David Towell, the leading light at NWS, pleaded for more time and it was actually launched three months later. 'The target was 650,000 new accounts and we made 657,000,' recalled Towell proudly. In 2000 there were 6.1 million charge-card holders and the financial services division contributed 22 per cent of pre-tax profits – admittedly at a time of depressed profits in clothing.

Not only did Rayner bring in outsiders to M&S, he also initiated a programme of sending M&S middle managers on secondment overseas or to other companies in the UK. Having benefited from working outside the company, Rayner believed others should do the same. And as he had done in government, he implemented a programme of 'scrutinies', sending a middle manager into a department to see how it could be improved. The recommendations of the scrutineers were put into practice somewhat more swiftly and to greater effect than they had been in government, a measure of M&S's efficiency as a private-sector company and its responsiveness to commands from the top.

Rayner was a keen talent spotter. Single and childless, he loved nurturing young talent within his corporate family. He would hold regular cocktail parties for bright new management trainees, starting at 6 p.m. in his office, and pick their brains. The brightest and best would be singled out for the fast track – they were Baker Street's young elite.

Rayner's most urgent task, which he began immediately he became chairman, was to bring the stores up to date. Sieff's neglect of the stores had left them looking drab and dreary with ugly brown carpets and low counters. Rayner instantly commissioned the refurbishment of more than half the UK stores and within two years all of them had a new look. Out went the austere grey and green of the 1970s and in came pastel blues and pinks. The layout was opened out American style with wider walkways and better displays and lighting. The effect was dramatic and immediate. 'In one store, business doubled in a week when we changed the scene, but not the clothes,' Rayner told Fleet. He saw too that more casual wear was needed. 'There is a new lifestyle right through the nation. Our customers want the clothes they see on TV and in women's magazines,' he said.

In pushing for growth, Rayner had luck on his side. The heady economic boom of the mid and late 1980s created an atmosphere of aggressive consumerism. 'Shop till you drop' became the mantra of the age. He enjoyed the buzz of those times and the beginnings of a global approach to fashion in clothes, food and finance. Rayner may never have been a hands-on merchant like Simon Marks and his own successor Rick Greenbury, but according to his colleagues he had the intellectual capacity to see the big picture and understand how the economic and geographic worlds were changing. He could see how the balance of power was shifting in favour of consumers. 'After the war, when consumer goods were in short supply, the supplier was dominant,' he told a clothing design and new technology symposium in January 1985. 'In the 1970s ... supply exceeded demand and the power lay with the retailers. Now, we are seeing the increasing dominance of the consumer – the customer now calls the tune.'

Rayner had come up on the food side of the business – he and Lord Sieff both claimed credit for discovering and fostering the growth of the iceberg lettuce in Israel – so it was no surprise that he made innovations there, insisting all the time on the highest quality. Each weekend directors would take home new dishes to try out on their families, for practical reasons as well as taste. Walker recalled some kebabs he sampled one Saturday lunchtime: 'Almost immediately I stabbed my soft palate with the stick and realised it was far too sharp.' He had them taken off display immediately. By the time Rayner left the number of lines had risen to 1,300 and M&S prepared food and chilled recipe dishes began to be served not just to the family, but to guests as well.

As well as transforming the stores, Rayner pushed for more fashionable clothes, bigger food halls and edge-of-town shopping – although the first store outside a big town did not open until 1988. His understanding of the changes going on throughout the whole retailing environment resulted in sales and profits more than doubling during his seven years as chairman. Between 1985 and 1990 profits before tax rose from £304.1m on sales of £3.2bn to profits of £604.2m on sales of £5.7bn.

Even so, it was evident to journalists visiting Baker Street during Rayner's time that much of the company's psyche still looked longingly backwards. Visitors in those days would be escorted along seemingly endless, institutionally lit corridors with their closed doors on either side, by a uniformed female minder who would then transport them into the care of the white-gloved waiters on the seventh floor. Such old-fashioned ways seemed at odds with a mid-market clothing retailer whose business was to have its finger on the pulse of the modern consumer. The atmosphere reeked of imperial Britain. Similar directors' dining rooms could still be found in other big public companies such as Imperial Chemical Industries, British Petroleum and GKN, which, like M&S, had their roots in Victorian or Edwardian England. 'But it was the white-gloved waiters with their servile manners that seemed so over the top to me,' remarked one visitor.

The atmosphere was unremittingly male. Women in M&S served on the store counters, worked as secretaries and trained as selectors, some of whom became feared and powerful within their domains. But in 1990, Rayner's last year as chairman, the only woman on the board was the non-executive Baroness (Janet) Young, a former cabinet minister and the only divisional director Clara Freeman.

The shopping fervour of the 1980s benefited M&S in some ways, but it also produced the threat of real competition for the first time since Simon Marks had worried about the superior goods he found at Woolworth. Almost overnight the newspapers were full of stories about the new retailing entrepreneurs with flair and creativity. Here was Next, in its first incarnation under George Davies, Burton led by Sir Ralph Halpern, who targeted the younger shoppers with Top Shop, and Mothercare, originally started by the

Zilkha family and later bought by Sir Terence Conran's Habitat, which in turn became Storehouse when it merged with British Home Stores.

Rayner was all too aware of these threats, partly because several commentators compared him and M&S unfavourably with these new fashion icons. Rayner was portrayed as a dry intellectual with no fashion sense. In a critical review of his first nine months, the *Financial Times* wrote in May 1985 that M&S was let down 'by women's fashion wear where M&S ranges compared unfavourably with the wealth of options available from the new specialists such as Next, Principles, Options and Burton'. The *Guardian* praised the food but portrayed the clothing as floundering. 'M&S is hunting for the fashion equivalent of chicken kiev,' wrote Hamish McRae, referring to the chilled recipe-dish that set the food world alight in 1976.

The press may have viewed him as out of touch, but Rayner was working on the problem. 'In clothing, a relatively static market, the competition is particularly acute. Some clothing chains have closed down or severely curtailed their operations,' he told a 1985 clothing design symposium. 'But with the emergence of Next, Next for Men, Benetton, a rejuvenated Burton and other specialist chains, the high street is being revitalised. Each of these chains is aimed at a clearly defined portion of the market.'

These new formats, led by colourful personalities, were certainly filling space in the newspapers. Having revitalised the ailing Burton group by launching Top Shop, Halpern is best remembered for the headlines about his 'five times a night' adventures with Fiona Wright, a blonde model. When the story broke in the *News of the World* Halpern was forced to resign. Yet for a time he was a tornado on the high street, leading one of his shareholders to describe him at an annual meeting as the 'greatest living Englishman'.

George Davies initially made a huge success out of Next, which in its way was Marks & Spencer with attitude, writ small. 'I always said that M&S was the honeypot and the rest of us were like bees around it. I positioned Next somewhere between M&S and Jaeger,' he once remarked. Davies had a brilliant eye for what his customers wanted. The press at the time created an impression that Next was on the leading edge of high fashion. In fact its ranges were maybe 15 per cent sharper than the clothes M&S was selling. The garments were better defined in stronger colours and the shops displayed skirts and sweaters and trousers near each other so customers could mix and match – revolutionary at the time. Whereas M&S clothes were good value and above all 'useful', Next gave the mid-market 25 to 40-year-old 'must have' clothes at competitive prices in reasonable quality. Maybe you could not wash a Next jumper forty times but who cared?

There was a confidence about the ranges and they were sold by non-pushy staff in small well-designed shops underneath a logo designed by Sir Terence Conran. Next clothes were to be worn every day to work but they made the wearer feel sharp and snazzy. The 1986 ranges, one shopper recalled, included a Prince of Wales check two-piece suit and a glowing emerald corduroy outfit at a price substantial enough to make the purchaser feel she had bought something special without being punitive.

The sign that Next had peaked was when in the late summer of 1988, the company put on a dinner and fashion show with great razzmatazz at the Inn on the Park hotel in London's Mayfair. After the dinner, the speeches and the rapturous applause the mood of elation gradually subsided as model after model swished before the audience in their Next outfits. As a fashion show it missed the point. The catwalk demands extremes, not wearability. Next had got above itself. It had spread itself too far from its core business, accumulating vast debts in the process. Davies was ousted not long after. But he soon reinvented himself, developing his jointly owned George brand at Asda, a bee positioned a long way downmarket from M&S.

At the cheaper end of the market, Burton's Top Shop was attacking the younger market. M&S might claim that teenage girls were one of its bigger customer groups but they were a ripe target for a chain such as Top Shop with more fashion content. Teenagers would buy their underwear and tights and perhaps a few simple basics from M&S but when they wanted excitement, at least in the 1980s, they preferred M&S's more aggressive rivals. Few teenagers want to shop at the same place as their mothers.

Rayner did not ignore this new competition; if anything, he over-reacted. 'He recognised that in Next, here was somebody in the M&S market, trying to take business away,' said one supplier. To the press, directors would disparagingly claim that the whole of Next's sales – £266m in 1985 – were little more than those of the Marble Arch store. But there was also a flurry of design and buying activity to address the issue, even though there were some things Rayner could not bring himself to sell. He did, for instance, completely miss out on the boom for distressed jeans because the idea of selling something less than perfect was anathema to him and his colleagues. In 1989 M&S launched a range of stylish dresses priced at £100. It was a price point too far and many were left on the rails. There was a flurry of bad press and talk of Rayner becoming grandiose. But by the next season the company was back on form.

Then came the recession. Davies had been ousted from Next, Halpern was forced to resign from Burton and Conran's Storehouse group ran into the sand, unable to make sense of the ill-considered assemblage of Habitat, Mothercare and BHS. All three companies had been hit by the boom in retail property prices, which sent rents soaring, particularly in London. 'Our shop in South Molton Street had a rent of £4,000 a year in 1983,' said Davies. 'But when it came up for review five years later the new rent was £100,000. It became impossible to make money.'

So it is hard to know whether M&S actively saw off the competition, or whether the inherent strengths of the group – its scale of production, the unique relationship with suppliers and retail property costing less than 2 per cent of sales when Burton was paying 36 per cent – brought it through. One thing was evident, a freehold portfolio of shops in prime city sites gave the group a huge advantage over its smaller, less established competitors when times got tougher. It is no wonder M&S was so slow to see the potential of opening stores out of town – they would cost more and they would under-mine the value of the high-street properties.

On top of punitive rents, Next, Burton and Storehouse all had higher production costs than M&S, which could put the squeeze on its loyal sup-pliers. Quality overseas production, started in Hong Kong and Taiwan, was only just coming on stream.

Rayner understood what was happening and galvanised M&S to speed up its reactions to changing markets. 'Fashion changes almost overnight and this requires three things of retailer and manufacturer: swift informa-tion; flexibility; and speed of reaction,' he said. Yet he believed, like his pre-decessors, that such flexibility depended on M&S's relationship with its mainly UK suppliers. 'In many cases those relationships have developed over many years,' he said, adding the following staggering statistic: 'Forty-six of these firms have been supplying us for forty years or more.'

While Rayner remained autocratic in the Marks tradition and upheld the 'unique' UK supplier relationship, he also brought in much modernity and promoted non-family executives on to the board. He recruited two directors as well as a handful of more junior executives such as Norgrove from outside. In addition he increased the number of genuinely independent non-executive directors to sit alongside Albert Frost, the former ICI director, who had considerable influence.

By the time of the 1990 report and account there were just two members of the family, John Sacher and David Sieff, among fourteen executive directors and none among the non-executives. And among the twenty-seven divisional directors, several of whom were to move up to the main board under Greenbury, there was not one single Sieff, Sacher, Laski or Lerner.

Rayner had turned a family business into a modern, professionally managed company. But there were some areas where he found that no sooner had he rolled the rock of progress up the hill then it rolled back down again, at least most of the way.

Throughout its history M&S had believed its products needed no special marketing. 'Good goods will sell arse upwards', as Simon Marks was wont to proclaim. Rayner disagreed and set up the first ever marketing department. He frequently lectured his board colleagues on the need for marketing. 'It is the key for M&S in the 1990s,' he would tell them. Alas his words mainly fell on deaf ears, particularly those of Greenbury, the man soon to succeed him. A passionate devotee of Simon Marks, Greenbury believed in the old ways, that the right goods in the right place at the right time sold themselves and that marketing was some kind of new-fangled unnecessary evil.

So the chairman spoke and appointed a marketing director, but the culture remained resolutely against it. The culture also stayed resolute against the idea of buying goods from overseas – a principle that would cost the company dear in the decade ahead.

Rayner was almost as committed to buying British as his predecessors although his background in defence purchasing had given him a wider view of the world. 'Though we do from time to time go abroad, the core ambition is to buy British. We go abroad if we can't get the looks and styles in this country,' he told one journalist, adding tellingly, 'particularly now when people are so much more conscious of the world as a whole.'

Marcus Sieff had imbued Rayner like his other executives with his passion for employing British people to make goods for M&S, glorying in 'the 99 per cent British' claim made by the clothing division. Rayner also continued to buy from Israel where possible, taking advantage of Israel's advanced technology in growing fruit and vegetables and persuading farmers to apply the latest methods for harvesting produce. Lettuces, for example, would be put straight into the chiller within minutes of being picked.

Rayner put off expanding in the Far East, although he would proclaim that if British retailers did not trade there, the Orient would trade here. Instead, he pursued cautious expansion in Europe. Sieff established the successful store on Boulevard Haussmann in Paris and another in Lyons, but success in France had been limited. The planeloads of French who came to shop at M&S when the currency was favourable gave a false perception of how well M&S could do on the Continent.

But most important on Rayner's list of overseas priorities was his ambition to take Marks & Spencer successfully into that graveyard for so many British companies, the United States. It was a priority that led in 1988 to the one big mistake of his career, the purchase of the upmarket and old-fashioned Brooks Brothers menswear chain for nearly double what it was worth. And he did this in the full knowledge that Marcus Sieff's great error had been to buy into Canada.

For all of Rayner's chairmanship, the North American operations did not perform well. The Canadian business, the St Michael chain, which was part owned by People's Department Stores, limped along with numerous reformats. The key problem was that M&S had bought high-street stores at a time when Canadians were falling in love with 'the mall'. 'Canada was always a thorn in Derek's side,' recalled one director. Marcus paid 'a ridiculous price for it', and the shops needed a huge amount of money spending on them to make them competitive.

'We thought we knew all about retailing and that Marks & Spencer's principles and practices in the UK would apply to our Canadian operations,' wrote Marcus with the humility of retirement. 'The principles did, although it took time to establish some of them. But the practices were quite different, as we learned to our cost.'

They found that Canadians liked a much greater range of casual wear than the British, that they expected fitting rooms (not introduced in British M&S stores at the time), that they responded better to aggressive promotions than the soft sell and that they liked bright, cheerfully painted stores. When one Alberta woman was asked why she did not shop at her local Marks & Spencer, she replied that she had no wish to shop in a hospital ward.

The stores were duly painted in bright colours with mirrors and spotlights on the walls to make the atmosphere warmer. One delighted customer told Sieff: 'I just want to thank you for enlarging the store and brightening it up. I come here regularly now.' In fact there had been no enlargement, the effect was purely cosmetic.

Despite this and other initiatives, the Canadian operations struggled, never making the profits expected of them. Rayner would be openly disparaging about Sieff's mistake in buying People's but, far from putting him off trying his luck with the United States, the Canadian problems spurred him to get it right.

So in the summer of 1987 – the peak of the takeover frenzy that gripped financial markets on both sides of the Atlantic in the late 1980s – he despatched Alan Smith and a team of six executives to examine the potential for M&S in the United States. With Smith went his second wife, Joan, then a senior personnel executive, Mike Goldstone from stores, Saeed Hatteea from merchandising, Paddy Walker Taylor from finance and Gareth Williams from retail systems.

Rayner had an ambivalent relationship with Smith, viewed by many of his peers as the brightest of his generation at M&S. Rayner felt threatened by Smith's intellect, perhaps one reason why he did not back him as his successor. Much to Rayner's disgust, once he got to America Smith hired the management consultant McKinsey to do a broad study of the American market. The brief was simple: to examine whether expanding Marks & Spencer into the United States made sense; and if it did, how it should be done. McKinsey did its work and the answer came back that yes, there were potentially rewarding opportunities in the USA. But McKinsey believed that M&S did not have the necessary expertise on the type of merchandise that sold well in the USA, nor knowledge of the type of store. The conclusion was that the company – at that time Britain's most profitable retailer – should hit the acquisition trail and buy established retailers.

Smith and his team homed in on the north-east of America, partly because it was roughly the same size as the UK and partly because that was where Rayner wanted to be. After seven months of extensive research – including, according to Smith, a lot of window shopping – they came up with a list of six candidates for takeover.

Rayner went straight for the preppy upmarket Brooks Brothers chain, whose charms extended beyond its domestic stores to a small but high-profile joint venture in Japan. At the time Brooks Brothers, a 47-store chain, was a clothing icon that resonated with aspiring males throughout the Anglo-American world. The stores were legendary for their slow and courteous service, the buttondown shirts were instantly recognisable as a key part of the Wall Street investment banking uniform, about as essential as a Hermès tie. Yet perhaps Smith and his team should have seen that Brooks Brothers was just a little bit old-fashioned and a trifle too formal. Certainly they should have noticed that Ralph Lauren, a sometime Brooks Brothers employee, was about to steal the high ground in American menswear.

McKinsey also came up with some ideas for the food business and M&S selected Kings Super Markets as a company selling top-quality fresh food. In his report to Rayner and the board, Smith described both organisations as 'quality-driven in the widest sense – in relation to people, merchandise and suppliers'.

In January 1988 Rayner approached Robert Campeau, the colourful Canadian property and retail tycoon who owned Brooks Brothers, but he refused to sell it. Campeau at that stage was building a retail empire at breakneck speed and had acquired Brooks Brothers in December 1986 as part of his $3.4bn acquisition of Allied Stores. Rayner was mortified, but his luck changed in the February when Campeau made a huge $6bn leveraged bid for Federated Department Stores and decided to sell off some of the jewels in his glittering crown to help finance the acquisition.

It was a frenzied time and the M&S executives were takeover ingénues. Before Brooks Brothers M&S had never made an outright corporate acquisition, yet Rayner failed to use the best advice that Wall Street could offer. In making his bid he turned instead to Bob Pirie, Sir Evelyn de Rothschild's man in America but really not much more than a second division player in the American takeover scene. Rayner was bewitched by the fact that Pirie advised Gordon White as he built up Hanson's huge US business from scratch. Yet White was a creative genius in all his deals and he used Pirie and the NM Rothschild team mainly as technicians.

The advisor to Campeau, one of the most predatory animals in the US corporate jungle, was an altogether more aggressive investment bank, Wasserstein Perella, a breakaway from First Boston formed only a month before and a firm keen to show its mettle. The Brooks Brothers purchase was Wasserstein Perella's debut deal and Bruce Wasserstein, who led the negotiations, was determined to make it a good one.

In the event Campeau, backed up by Wasserstein, was able to persuade Rayner to pay $750m for Brooks Brothers, a sum that was about twice what Keith Oates and Alan Smith had estimated it to be worth. It was the first of a string of headline-grabbing deals in which Bruce Wasserstein persuaded companies bent on growth to pay huge prices for their acquisitions. His pitch was compelling. He would tell buyers their targets were trophy prizes for which they would have to pay trophy prices. As deal after deal was done he earned the sobriquet 'bid-'em-up Bruce', but the Brooks Brothers deal was the one that provided the best sport and he and his partners dined out for several years on how such a huge price was extracted from the ever-so-conservative Marks & Spencer.

Oates and Smith advised against buying Brooks Brothers at such a price, saying it was worth no more than $400m. But Rayner was the chairman and he was enamoured with Brooks Brothers clothing, which was in large part aimed at men of Rayner's age and taste. And while Rayner was sophisticated in many ways, finance was not his strong suit. Dazzled by the heady climate and Campeau's lavish hospitality, he lost touch with reality. What, he must have asked himself, was a few dollars more if one were buying a trophy brand recognised throughout the world as the epitome of aspirational style and one that could provide the foundation for Marks & Spencer's American empire?

There was the added excitement of opportunities on the food side through Campeau's other retail operations, for the purchase included preferential rights for five years to set up food outlets in any of Campeau's sixty malls and rights for three years to set up food outlets in more than 700 Campeau-owned department stores throughout North America. In addition, Campeau signed an agreement not to set up a speciality menswear chain in the United States or Japan for five years. At the time these preferential rights and non-competition agreements were valued at $80m, in theory bringing the net cost of Brooks Brothers down to $670m, yet when Campeau's empire collapsed they proved worthless.

Rayner was not to know that at the time, and to celebrate he invited the Brooks Brothers management and senior staff to a lavish dinner at Michael House. Equally thrilled, the Brooks Brothers directors brought with them as a present Abraham Lincoln's Brooks Brothers jacket bearing the bullet hole where he had been shot. Rayner thanked them graciously, but insisted its rightful place was with them in America, a gesture that pleased everyone.

Rayner's pleasure in pulling off the deal came through in his press statement. 'We consider Brooks Brothers to be a unique opportunity,' he said. 'I am delighted that we are now completing this very exciting acquisition. We are now purchasing in a bold and imaginative way one of the quality names in American menswear and I am confident that Brooks Brothers and its management will generate attractive, profitable growth.' Sadly this forecast was never realised.

In less than three years Robert Campeau's dreams lay in tatters as Federated Department Stores and Allied Stores – the two main planks of his domain – filed for bankruptcy. Had time been on Rayner's side he could have picked up Brooks Brothers for a song – although perhaps it would never have been a commercial success. Despite continued investment on 'in-depth refurbishments', Brooks Brothers never made a respectable return on capital and Rayner's vision of opening a Brooks Brothers store in every European capital city was consigned to the filing cabinet. The ideas about setting up food outlets never came to anything and the Kings food chain, though quite a successful operation, remained a corporate 'toe in the water' rather than becoming a bridgehead for Marks & Spencer food in America.

In the spring of 1987, the Argyll Foods supermarket group, at the time headed by James Gulliver, Alistair Grant and David Webster, spent $1bn on the British arm of America's Safeway chain, a deal that pushed the company into the first division of UK food retailing. Had M&S done the deal instead, expanding at home in food rather than setting off on an expensive but ultimately fruitless shopping spree in America, how different its subsequent history might have been.

On the day of the Brooks Brothers announcement, M&S shares fell 4p to 180p with the City unconvinced about a foray that brought the full cost of the company's investment in America, including Sieff's deals, up to $2bn (£1.3bn). Yet the great love affair with the British public and fashion press continued. The American errors were eclipsed by success at home and viewed indulgently as the escapades of an otherwise unassailable institution.

But if Brooks Brothers was initially viewed indulgently, the American push had one consequence that was to deprive M&S of executive talent in the decade that followed. The talented Alan Smith and every member of the team that worked in New York plotting the route forward left M&S of their own volition within a year of returning to Baker Street.

Smith had nurtured hopes of succeeding Rayner and even when Greenbury took the job he thought he might be appointed as a managing director. Yet Greenbury refused to give him any assurances on promotion and after a brief spell of working for his new chairman he joined Kingfisher as chief executive, working with Geoff Mulcahy, later knighted, who was then chairman. (Ironically, he then found himself in a power struggle with Mulcahy and was soon forced to resign.)

As for the others, their eyes had been opened and they could no longer tolerate the regimented corridors of Baker Street. Mike Goldstone joined the ailing supermarket group Gateway, where he lasted just fourteen months. Saeed Hatteea followed Smith to Kingfisher, where he became merchandise director of Woolworth; Paddy Walker Taylor became Woolworth finance director before joining the board of McAlpine, the building group; and Gareth Williams set up his own consultancy group. Sadly, rather like teenagers escaping from over-strict parents, they found the freedoms of the wider world more difficult to cope with than they had imagined.

# CHAPTER FIVE

# Along came Rick

Rick Greenbury became chief operating officer in 1986 – an American-style title for a job in a very British company. The title signalled to the world he would be Marks & Spencer's next chairman and chief executive – combining the roles in the tradition of the company. He had watched all the Brooks Brothers shenanigans and soon found himself robustly defending the purchase to the City and the media. But America was never his thing. Corporate acquisition was never his thing. 'I do not believe in acquisition retailing,' he told a Harvard Business School case study team in 1994. As a self-appointed disciple of Simon Marks who would regularly quote the sayings of his hero, he felt such expensive leaps into foreign countries to be at odds with the culture of the company he loved so passionately.

Snapping up retail chains abroad looked all too risky, although the fact that he was proved right gave him little satisfaction. Critical questions concerning Brooks Brothers came up at every press conference and analysts' meeting and he defended the decision as robustly as if it had been his own. Greenbury favoured the Far East as the coming market for M&S, but when he moved, he opened one or two stores at a time, testing the water every step of the way. 'We will put a store down in a local market and grow from that presence organically,' he told the Harvard team.

Behind his impatience, the power-driven argument and the tendency to speak just a couple of decibels louder than anyone else, was an innately cautious man whose idea of running Marks & Spencer was to think what Simon Marks would have done – and to try to reinterpret that into modern-day practice. For most of his career that formula, combined with drive and determination, worked like a charm.

Others saw his attitude as narrow. 'Whenever Greenbury hit a problem he always looked for the solution in the archives,' said one City analyst. One former director commented: 'Derek Rayner was a visionary and innovator.

Rick was a brilliant operational retailer but he couldn't innovate his way out of a paper bag.'

Greenbury had many of the characteristics associated with being an only child – the charm, the ego, the insecurity and the inability to take criticism. Criticism from within the company would produce a tirade that only a few enjoyed. Criticism from without would provoke a furious letter – in time these became known as 'Rickograms'. Any stockbroker's analyst who wrote a less than fulsome circular or journalist who went 'off message' in reporting on him or his company received a written salvo. In the autumn of 1996 Rufus Olins of the *Sunday Times* wrote a feature on department stores that did not include M&S. Soon afterwards, at a private dinner with M&S executives and suppliers, Greenbury complained about the article, claiming that M&S, which sold a wide range of homeware in its bigger stores, should have been included. Olins heard about his comments and wrote to him, protesting. In his reply, Greenbury revealed in full his attitude to the press. He wrote: 'Why are you so sensitive, bearing in mind that the press in general including your own newspaper consistently "slag off" members of the Royal Family, most politicians and business leaders including me, and from time to time, Marks & Spencer.'

Greenbury's motivation was legendary. He had suffered the divorce of his parents in his early teens followed by the crushing disappointment of having to give up his plans for university – events that could well account for his need to win at all costs. 'The thing you have to understand about Rick is that he will not be beaten,' said one embittered former colleague. 'He has to be the winner. He has to win every single point – that is the way he plays tennis, that is the way he plays football. His tennis hero is Pete Sampras – because he dominates all the way through. That is Rick. That is why he always saw off every threat to his supremacy.'

Greenbury was a classic example of what Jim Collins, one of America's more studious management gurus, has dubbed a level 4 leader. These have big egos, strong, charismatic personalities and do well in times of crisis. Political examples would be Churchill, Thatcher and Truman, Greenbury's great hero (Truman had a sign on his desk that read, 'the buck stops here', a sentiment to which he aspired). But they lack the distinctive quality of Collins's level 5 business leaders who 'make good companies great': sufficient humility to put the company ahead of their personal ambition. Collins cites Lee Iacocca as a typical level 4 leader. Iacocca saved Chrysler from the brink of catastrophe but then became diverted by his own fame, appearing on talk shows and taking part in commercials. Greenbury would never have dreamed of appearing in a TV commercial, although he might well have agreed to be interviewed on television if he had been asked. But he did allow himself to become diverted by personal ambition. In 1997 his twin desires to help a friend and gain a peerage led him to take on the chairmanship of a government sponsored committee on pay which not only backfired on him in a tidal wave of bad publicity but blinded him to the growing problems at Marks & Spencer. Like Iacocca he postponed his own retirement – although he always insisted that his fellow directors asked him to stay – and his dominant personality prevented possible future leaders from flourishing under him. 'Level 4 leaders often fail to set up the company for enduring success,' wrote Collins in the *Harvard Business Review* in January 2001. 'After all, what better testament to your own personal greatness than that the place falls apart after you leave?'

Greenbury was born in Carlisle in 1936, three years before the start of the Second World War. His father was from Yorkshire, his mother from Newcastle, and they lived in Leeds until Greenbury was six. Then they moved to London, where Greenbury attended Ealing County Grammar School. His parents were both blunt and forthright, classic northerners who frequently spoke their mind. They clashed often and Greenbury grew up against the backdrop of domestic battle and inherited their taste for confrontation. Rebellious, headstrong and quick to get into fights, he became the most caned boy in the school. 'I was caned about eleven times in four years and suspended three times in the fifth form. It taught me the importance of discipline,' he said.

His parents split up when he was fifteen and he stayed with his mother. Uninspired by his studies, he spent as many waking hours as he could playing football and tennis – which he played to competition standards – and was helped financially by a sponsorship contract with Slazenger. Then came a crisis over his mock O-levels – he took ten and passed two. The headmaster told his mother he rarely did any work. The riot act was read, not for the first time. But to help him, the school reduced the number of subjects he was studying from ten to seven. It must have been a hard few months but he ended up passing six subjects – enough to get him into the sixth form. His ambition was to get to university – although mainly to play sport for three years.

Then his mother was suddenly diagnosed with cancer and swiftly admitted to hospital for surgery. With his mother's life hanging by a thread – although she did eventually recover – and his father struggling for money, Greenbury had no alternative but to leave school immediately and take a job. Thanks to an introduction by a mentor at Slazenger he found a place packing parcels at Lillywhites, the Piccadilly-based sports shop. Yet it was small consolation as Greenbury saw his dreams of university and a sporting career evaporate before his eyes. 'All my ambitions were destroyed and I remember thinking to myself that life was very, very hard,' he said.

Characteristically, he soon fell out with the parcels manager and while casting around for jobs he noticed that Marks & Spencer was advertising for management trainees. Unlike most companies at that time, the retailer did not require A-levels. He applied, passed the interview and started in the Ealing Store, sweeping floors, checking stock and filling counters.

Clinton Silver liked to say that joining Marks & Spencer was like having an inoculation. If it took, you would be there for life; if it did not, you would leave very soon. With Greenbury it took. Coming from such a disrupted family background, he thrived in the structured way of life. He enjoyed the social atmosphere and took advantage of Flora Solomon's sporting clubs, where his fiercely competitive nature was allowed free rein. A few years later he captained the M&S five-a-side football team. Before the match he lectured his players to behave like gentlemen, to keep their tempers. Once on the pitch they were amused to find that Greenbury was doing all the swearing. And when they lost, he stormed off the pitch.

Outside working hours he continued to play sport avidly but suffered two slipped discs, which resulted in him being deemed unfit for national service at 18. (He turned up for his interview in a steel corset and they simply waved him away.) In the stores where he worked his energy, height and forceful personality soon got him noticed – but his hot temper got him into trouble. Once he became so angry with a difficult customer that he threatened to punch him – an incident that – as the customer turned out to have boardroom connections – resulted in a severe carpeting. Despite such incidents, he was, by his early twenties, working as a departmental manager in 'The Arch', where he was singled out by Simon Marks on one of his frequent visits.

Marks did not usually like very tall men, and Greenbury at 6ft 2in towered above him. But it is easy to see how the diminutive chairman, by that time in his mid sixties, would be attracted to this strapping young man imbued with fiery zeal for the M&S cause. Marks dubbed Greenbury 'Big Fellah' and to Greenbury he became a father figure. 'Simon was a genius, simply incredible. He would not settle for anything less than the best,' he said.

Greenbury learned the basic principles of the business at his side. One day he was showing Simon Marks round the store and explained that a popular line had sold out, but new stock was on its way. 'You idiot,' said Marks. 'What do you want to do? Put a sign up on the counter saying, Mrs Smith, come back tomorrow?' He understood then that success hung on having an item in the right colour, right style and available in the right size – now.

Greenbury, unlike many members of staff, could cope with Marks's aggressive ways; perhaps he was reminded of his own father. Although not unafraid, he did not disintegrate under the onslaught, perhaps because he was captivated by Marks's ruthless dedication to perfection. Within the company Greenbury had a reputation for enjoying conflict, so his tolerance of angry exchanges and displays of bad temper was greater than that of his colleagues. Where most people avoided confrontation, Greenbury courted it.

If Greenbury had been lacking a strong male role model, he certainly found it in Simon Marks. When Greenbury tried to impress him with tales of fantastic business with a particular line of goods Marks would retort: 'Don't talk rubbish, you "putz". Anyone can sell a pound for ten shillings.'

There were other mentors too. The manager of the Marble Arch store in 1959 was a man called Sonny Harris, cast in the hands-on, slave-driver model. One day, around 5 p.m., Harris berated Greenbury for not doing a particular task. 'Mr Harris,' protested Greenbury, 'I have not stopped since I got in this morning.' The man looked at his watch and said: 'This watch has not stopped either, but it hasn't added a penny to the takings.'

Simon Marks plucked Greenbury out of the stores and put him in head office as a trainee merchandiser and later as personal assistant to Alec Lerner, husband of Simon's daughter Hannah. 'I got under the skin of the business then. I was close to the founding family and their genius,' he told a journalist in 1996.

In the mid 1960s he moved on to knitwear, where he made his reputation. At the time, men's knitwear was undeveloped compared with women's.

Most of the time men still wore suits and jackets, but Greenbury spotted the trend towards more casual clothes, particularly for weekend wear. Critically, he formed a strong friendship with Harry (later Sir Harry) Djanogly who was running Nottingham Manufacturing, a knitwear company built by his father and uncle. The M&S–Nottingham Manufacturing relationship had started with Simon and Israel, so was well established by the time Greenbury came into contact with Djanogly. Until then Djanogly's closest contact had been Marcus Sieff, but he and Greenbury, contemporaries, hit it off. Early on they discovered they had birthdays on consecutive days – Greenbury on 31 July and Djanogly on 1 August. They began to celebrate together with a special lunch each year and during the 1980s were joined by another M&S supplier, Sir Christopher Hogg of Courtaulds, who was born on 2 August.

Together, Greenbury and Djanogly built the men's knitwear division at Marks & Spencer into a new profits powerhouse for the company. Nottingham Manufacturing, helped by the scale of M&S sales, was able to make lambswool sweaters at less than half the price they could be bought anywhere else. When, after years of trials, Nottingham unlocked the technique for making lambswool knitwear machine-washable, their progress was unstoppable. In the words of one observer: 'The partnership between them made Harry a fortune and put Rick on the board.' Nottingham Manufacturing's profits rocketed and in 1972 Greenbury was made a director of M&S at 36 – twenty years after he joined.

Djanogly was the product of a family not unlike the founders of M&S. His middle-European Jewish father and uncle had arrived in Britain in the mid 1930s after fleeing Germany, where they had built up a substantial textile business on hard work, shrewd judgement and chutzpah.

One of Greenbury's great talents was his ability to inspire people by talking. He believed he was a good listener, but he would only listen to the few people he respected – and even then he often did not act on their advice. Naturally he would listen to Simon Marks, to Israel and Teddy Sieff, to Marcus Sieff, and also to friends such as Djanogly and later Sir Denis Rooke, the chairman of British Gas from 1976 to 1989, and Sir Brian Pitman, who built up Lloyds TSB into a powerful banking force. They were, in the main, clever men with big, all-encompassing personalities, people who regarded Greenbury's forcefulness as a sign of enthusiasm and spirit.

But for the average M&S manager in the 1960s, Greenbury was already a

fearsome character. Bill Green, an M&S stalwart who managed the Folkestone store for many years, remembered when Greenbury addressed a group
of store managers in Brighton shortly after he had been made a director.
Senior executives would regularly journey out to the provinces to communicate Baker Street's message to store managers, but this particular occasion
made a strong impression. 'They always came down from head office with
an entourage and I remember he came into the room flanked by these
people,' said Green. 'They all sat at a high table in the front and all the store
managers, about thirty of us, sat in the body of the room. He started off by
saying he was not going to talk much, that he had brought others with him
who would do the talking. And then he began a non-stop outpouring as to
where we, the store managers, were going wrong, what we needed to do,
where the company was going. He was unstoppable and none of the others
with him said a word the whole meeting. In the end he paused and asked for
questions. The room went totally quiet and it was clear everyone was
nervous of asking him anything. So in the end I stood up and said I had two
questions. I asked the first – something quite innocuous. Greenbury took a
deep breath and said, "I've never heard such unadulterated rubbish in all my
life." There was then another tirade and finally he stopped and said, "What
was the other question?" You could have heard a pin drop. I said, "I don't
know, I've forgotten," and the whole room exploded into laughter.'

Throughout his career those around him found it difficult to be heard. 'It
was always hard to get your point across,' said Green. 'But they [the direc-
tors] were all like that. The place was ruled by fear.'

It was evident to anyone who met him within the company that Greenbury was on the way up. Physically imposing, with piercing dark-blue eyes,
he was always a driver, a dynamo. He had 'balls'; if he believed something
should be done he got it done even if he had to ruffle an aviary of feathers
along the way. Rival retailers took pleasure in referring to the ranks of M&S
managers as 'clones', but Greenbury always stood out. At one annual
meeting, an analyst recalled that all the directors present were wearing ties
with the M&S logo – except for Greenbury, whose tie bore a tasteful but
noticeably different design. Unlike those beneath him, he was not afraid of
taking on his superiors, even over relatively small issues.

One such issue was that of company cars. For many years Jaguars were
the only executive cars allowed at M&S – the Jewish heritage meant German
cars such as Mercedes or BMWs were unthinkable. But during the 1970s

Jaguars were notoriously unreliable. Greenbury found the continual break-downs and minor problems infuriating and lobbied hard for Mercedes and BMWs to be allowed. One day, after his car had gone back into the garage yet again, he went to see Sieff in his office, threw his keys on the table and said: 'Keep your car, I'm going to buy a BMW.' It says a lot about Sieff's regard for his abilities that he got his way and was pointed in the direction of a reputable BMW dealer. Once he had set the precedent there was a dash for German cars.

Fellow directors found Greenbury to be in a class of his own when it came to argument and debate. 'Rick always had to smash you. If you thought you had won a point, you found it had to be replayed at a later date,' said one.

Yet Greenbury had trouble recognising such a description of himself, convinced he had always been open to reasoned debate. And those who worked closely with him, such as his secretaries and PAs, all developed a strong affection for the highly emotional, endearing character beneath the aggression. 'He could be so kind and understanding if you had troubles in your personal life, but he had absolutely no idea of how he affected other people,' said one. He was also known to be a 'total softie' when it came to his four children, whom he adored and who failed to recognise many of the less flattering descriptions of him they read in the newspapers.

While Greenbury thrived on combat most of his colleagues backed off, retreating to the personally chosen decor of their offices, the luxury of the seventh-floor dining rooms and their chauffeur-driven limousines. One who coped with his combative style more than most was the property director Roger Aldridge. 'It was difficult to get your point across with Rick because he was very accomplished. He had worked in all areas of the business and if someone was not 100 per cent sure of their facts he would spot it. He also worked very hard. Some directors would send him a thick document on a Friday in preparation for a meeting on the following Monday. They would hope he would only have time to skim it, but by Monday he would have crawled all over it and there would be underlinings and question marks everywhere. And it is true he was very competitive; he would exploit weakness so people were nervous of countering him, particularly in the boardroom in front of their colleagues,' said Aldridge. 'I don't think people were frightened of him, but they were nervous about the confrontation and Rick of course, really loved a good argument.'

Robert Colvill, the finance director, would also argue with Greenbury – most frequently over the wording of results statements. Colvill, a neat, precise man who could eat a crusty baguette without a single crumb falling on to his suit, would advise moderate wording, while Greenbury would want to play up the success of the results as much as he could. But arguing with Greenbury could be a wearying exercise and adversaries found he would quickly escalate a clash of views to a resigning issue.

Greenbury enjoyed his reputation for toughness, believing it to go hand in hand with openness and honesty. He was fond of quoting President Harry Truman: 'They say I give them hell. I don't – I give them the truth and it feels like hell.' Because he was more competitive and more focused than his peers he moved swiftly through the ranks. And he developed an instinct for what 'she' – the Marks & Spencer customer – would buy. He could spot the lines that would sell.

'He was one of the best merchandisers I have ever met – brilliant, decisive, confident,' one senior M&S selector said. And like Simon Marks, who is reputed never to have passed a working day without visiting one of the stores, Greenbury relentlessly walked the aisles talking to staff and to customers just as his mentor had. Within M&S he was seen as an outstanding merchant with a gut feeling for goods; a star retail operator who, when he became chief executive, excelled at running the business in a hands-on, visceral way. 'He was the best chief executive we ever had,' said one former director, adding sadly, 'and the worst chairman.'

Despite its insularity, M&S sent him to Oxford University Summer School in his twenties and to the London Business School Executive Programme in his thirties, but he never had much time for formal learning. City types who had been educated at top public schools and Oxbridge intimidated him and he often said that he had learned at 'the university of life'. He believed hard work and commitment were more important than education. He even said once that these were 'every bit as important as genius'.

Greenbury absorbed the M&S principles of quality, value and service along with everyone else, but above all he believed that the three keystones of the business were – product, people and property. 'Lord Marks was obsessed with the product he was selling and the service he was giving. So am I,' said Greenbury in 1996. 'There was no amount of detail he would not go into. I am the same. If you get the product and the service right and have

95

good staff then you will have satisfied customers and eventually satisfied shareholders.' Greenbury's attitude was identical to that of the founding family, putting this reference to shareholders right at the end. He was not, as he put it, 'prepared to spend my life or even any of my time on buffing up the company's image or its share price'. Yet by 1996 M&S was just like other big public companies with its shareholder base widely diversified among pension funds, insurance companies and individuals. It was as if he simply refused to acknowledge that M&S was no longer owned by the family he hero-worshipped, even though his mentor had died more than thirty years before.

While other companies concerned themselves with mergers and acquisitions, corporate image, branding, the price of their shares, corporate governance and making their customers' lives easier, M&S wanted to plough its own furrow, resolutely refusing to take outside credit cards and only grudgingly putting costly fitting rooms and toilets into the bigger stores.

Despite Greenbury's appetite for hard work he found plenty of time for sport and family life. He had met his first wife Siân Hughes while he was a junior manager in the main M&S store in Edinburgh. She was a student at Edinburgh University, but had taken a holiday job in the store and Greenbury spotted her there. Compared with Greenbury she was cultured, enjoying music and the theatre. Initially she had no time for this aggressive, sports-mad tearaway and rebuffed all his approaches. Then the newspapers announced that Laurence Olivier was shortly to appear in *The Entertainer* in Edinburgh. Within a day every ticket was sold. But Greenbury, through his contacts, managed to secure two tickets and used them to entice her out on their first date. They were married in 1959 and had four children over the next few years.

They were still together in 1978, when at 41 Greenbury was made a managing director, having by that time worked in every area of the business including food, property, womenswear, menswear and lingerie. Clothing, though, in particular knitwear, was his first love.

At that stage it became clear to M&S suppliers such as Christopher Hogg and Harry Djanogly that Greenbury was the coming man. Marcus Sieff clearly thought so and passed on his views to Derek Rayner, who, although a very different personality from Greenbury, got on well with him.

But Greenbury was not everybody's choice for the next leader. Shortly after becoming chairman in 1984 Rayner decided he should signal to the group and the world outside who he thought should be his heir apparent by appointing Greenbury to the new post of chief operating officer. But first Clinton Silver, whom Sieff had promoted to the board in 1974, was asked by Rayner to sound out the executive directors about the next chairman.

Alan Smith and Andy Lusher were two of several directors who voiced reservations about Greenbury's suitability for the role. 'A group of us got together and metaphorically held hands and said nervously that although we admired him as an operator, we did not think he had any strategic vision at all – and vision was necessary if he was to be the next chairman,' said one.

This dissension on the board caused Rayner to take the unprecedented step of calling in an outside consultant. Through Albert Frost, the former ICI man who had become a non-executive director, Rayner had met John Harvey Jones, chief executive of ICI, who had in turn introduced him to a consultant called John Broadbent Jones, a former headhunter who had developed his art into advising chairmen on company boardroom structure.

By 1985 there were three managing directors under Rayner – Greenbury, Brian Howard and Henry Lewis. Lewis had been asked by Rayner to stay an extra year but was on the point of leaving. Brian Howard was too close to Rayner in age to take over, apparently leaving Greenbury with the field to himself. Other directors who might have been in the frame were Marcus's son David, who spent most of his career in personnel, and John Sacher, son of Michael, the family director, who had lost out to Derek. But by then nobody wanted a chairman from one of the founding families, so neither of them was viewed as a serious contender against such a clear favourite.

But there was one non-family director who felt that he should at least be considered for the top job. Alan Smith had been born in Leeds in 1941, making him five years younger than Greenbury. Like him he was an M&S lifer – unlike him he had the benefit of a university education, a dry sense of humour and a lightness of touch that some mistook for frivolity. Yet, behind his affable exterior Smith was an ambitious man with an ego only slightly smaller than Greenbury's. He had his backers – M&S directors were constantly dividing into camps about this and that – but others viewed his motives as suspect. 'The trouble with Alan was that, like Keith [Oates], you felt he cared more about his own progress than he did about Marks & Spencer,' remarked one former director.

When Broadbent Jones did his research, spending time with every director, he unearthed similar negative views on Greenbury to those found by Silver. But there was insufficient backing for Smith or anyone else to override the wishes of the current and previous chairmen. Whatever Broadbent Jones had come up with in his talks with M&S directors was insufficient to prevent Greenbury from being anointed as the heir apparent.

To neutralise any negative feelings, and possibly to ease any hurt pride, Alan Smith was duly despatched to America on the acquisition trail in the summer of 1987, when Greenbury was made chief operating officer in preparation for becoming chief executive. Smith cannot have been too upset. Some months later, while he was enjoying life in New York, Sir Terence Conran tried to recruit him to join Storehouse, the company he had put together from Mothercare, Habitat and British Home Stores, but Smith turned the opportunity down.

If Rayner's big sin of commission had been to buy Brooks Brothers, his big sin of omission was not to take M&S out of town earlier. He inherited his reluctance from Sieff and the other family directors, who by the 1980s had lost Simon Marks's pioneering spirit. Marks & Spencer's success in trading in the high-street made them slow to see the spoils to be had in out-of-town and edge-of-town retailing. John Sainsbury, head of another great dynastic company, used to urge Sieff to go out of town, but Michael Sacher and Teddy Sieff were set against the idea, seeing it as a fad that would soon fade away. The idea went against the ethos of serving the community in the high street where M&S would be a magnet to other retailers, creating prosperity for the whole town.

Out-of-town shopping was perceived as a threat to the high street and M&S was reluctant to damage its traditional patch. True there was an M&S in the Brent Cross shopping centre in north London and Rayner also put M&S into the Metrocentre in Gateshead when it opened. But fully fledged shopping centres were perceived differently from edge-of-town – they were regarded as high streets recreated in separate locations.

The first tentative moves had come in 1985 when Henry Lewis had an informal discussion with Leslie Porter, then chairman of Tesco, about developing a joint venture with M&S on an edge-of-town site. The moment was right and Lewis was able to set up a meeting between Rayner and Porter, who later handed over negotiations to Ian (later Lord) MacLaurin, Tesco's chief executive.

Initially the idea of having a joint venture with a major rival must have seemed strange to the board of M&S, but in reality it worked extraordinarily well. Eventually, in February 1988, M&S unveiled its first edge-of-town store next to Tesco on the outskirts of Cheshunt in Hertfordshire – and announced its intention to invest £350m in a dozen or so out-of-town ventures.

The new store had 69,000 square feet of selling space all on one floor. This dwarfed the typical square footage of most of the other 281 stores, which ranged from 10,000 in Pinner to 25,000 in Cheltenham. The new format enabled the company proudly to display its furniture ranges in a dozen different room settings. Cheshunt rapidly became one of M&S's best-performing stores.

By that time the supermarkets were well entrenched away from the high street. In contrast to M&S, Tesco already had 140 of its 380 stores located out of town by the time of the joint venture. Greenbury handled the announcement for M&S and for the first time was interviewed by the press. The *Sunday Times* carried a tactfully written piece designed to keep both M&S and Tesco sweet, and a picture of a smiling Greenbury with MacLaurin, who was by then Tesco chairman. One small event hinted at trouble ahead for Greenbury and his press relations. The photograph emphasised his double chin and he personally rang the *Sunday Times* picture editor to demand that the picture be removed from the files and destroyed. It says a great deal about his force of personality that the picture editor agreed.

Within months it was clear that the Cheshunt experiment was a success and for many years the most profitable food departments in M&S stores were the ones next to Tesco. Customers went to Tesco for their bulk shopping and topped up with exotic foods, chilled recipe dishes and luxuries from M&S.

The first out-of-town store also introduced another innovation – fitting rooms. Since the early years M&S had allowed customers to exchange goods or to get their money back for garments they took home and found were the wrong size, or simply did not like. But at every annual meeting for several years shareholders would ask why there were no fitting rooms when so many of the competitors had them. Logic decreed that fitting rooms would reduce the number of goods returned – the lack of them was also attracting a considerable amount of criticism. In his day, Simon Marks would never have dreamt of allowing them and Greenbury was against them – they cost money and filled space that could be used for selling clothes. But Rayner rightly saw them as a necessary if costly part of modernisation. (Intriguingly – and irritatingly for the management – the subsequent introduction of fitting rooms into all larger M&S stores never reduced the number of goods returned.)

By the time Greenbury became chief executive in 1988, Rayner had shaken off most of the earlier criticism of his era. His track record looked good. From 1984 to 1988 profits before tax rose from £279m to £502m on sales up from £2.9bn to £4.6bn. Earnings per share kept pace, up from 6.3p in 1984 to 12.2p in 1988. Dividends moved slightly more conservatively from 3.1p a share to 5.1p. By that time food sales accounted for 38 per cent of sales, homeware and furniture 13 per cent and clothing 49 per cent.

That year Rayner's review in the annual report noted that 'sales of our growing range of ladies' leisurewear made a buoyant start to the Spring' and 'a hundred of our stores now have sections set aside for [men's] tailored garments where we offer a specialised service'. Food sales that year rose by 12 per cent – well ahead of the national average. 'We continue to widen customer choice with the further development of fresh chilled foods particularly in prepared and snack foods,' he wrote. Fish sales were expanding and the range of wines was being developed. Not only did M&S enable working women to lay on food for a stylish dinner party in an hour or so, it also provided champagne and table wines of good quality that the male of the house was not ashamed to serve, despite the high-street label.

In 1988 the newly extended Oxford Street store near Marble Arch was unveiled. 'The Arch' now operated on four floors with 157,000 square feet of selling space, making it larger than many traditional department stores. Once again homeware and furniture were given display space while the new food hall occupied the whole of the basement. Rayner also noted: 'In three years we have increased our selling space by 17 per cent to 8.5m square feet, an addition of 1.3m square feet, nearly half in the form of new stores or satellites. In the same time we have modernised 4.75m square feet of existing footage.'

The slow, store by store, expansion in Europe was going well. The fourth Paris store had just been opened and there were eleven stores altogether across the Channel and Irish Sea – in France, Germany, Spain and southern Ireland. Sales in 1988 rose by 13 per cent while profits jumped by 50 per cent to £19m, partly helped by currency fluctuations.

Greenbury showed his strategic thinking in the Far East, where he presided over the opening of the first store in Hong Kong – a tester for the rest of the region and aimed at a higher-spending, more sophisticated customer than in the UK.

But North America presented a gloomy picture with Canadian sales falling from £211m to £180m, producing profits of £2.5m against £3.7m. Hopes for success rested in the newly acquired Brooks Brothers.

For the next three years Greenbury worked as chief executive under Rayner's chairmanship. Both were full time, but despite their wildly different personalities the relationship worked. The directors remained divided about whether Greenbury had the vision to be chairman but he had his own way of dealing with the mixed support he had from the board. One by one he would summon his colleagues to his office and ask if they were for him or against him. No one faced with his imposing figure and determined demeanour ever had the courage to say they had reservations. To do so, they feared, would have been tantamount to resignation, or at the very least relegation to a job on the sidelines.

It was often said of the Rayner/Greenbury partnership that Rayner possessed the intellect and vision while Greenbury had the dynamism and operational skills. This used to irritate Greenbury, who would declare that 'Derek was also an extremely good detailed shopkeeper'. Privately, Greenbury felt he knew enough about strategy to continue to develop the company.

Greenbury summed up their relationship thus: 'I got on well with Derek because we respected each other. That's where it started. If he respected you, you could have an argument with him. I used to have terrific arguments with him. He knew I thought the world of him. We would bow to each other's view on subjects where we knew the other one was strong.' Greenbury admired Rayner's intellect. Rayner recognised Greenbury as a true merchant.

They would occasionally have huge arguments over policy. One area of contention was fresh food. Greenbury believed, strongly advised by the senior food executive Mike Taylor, that M&S should sell loose fruit and vegetables in the stores as well as ready packaged. 'Derek used to say I was talking through the back of my hat, that it would never work.'

Yet the moment Greenbury became chairman he sent for Taylor and said, 'right, press the button'. New tills with weighing machines had to be installed. One of the lines they introduced was loose potatoes. Rayner, by then retired but retained as a consultant, said, 'Don't be ridiculous, nobody is going to buy potatoes one at a time.' But within weeks the stores were selling as many loose potatoes as packaged – and a wide variety of fruit and vegetables then became available loose.

Rayner was generally seen as the 'foodie' – but although for most of his career Greenbury had been involved in the clothing side, he gave the food team headed by Mike Taylor its head, and by the time he left in 1999 the number of lines had more than doubled to 3,000.

When Rayner retired in March 1991 he left behind a company expanding in the UK and overseas. Suddenly the recession loomed – and that is when Greenbury's instinctive retailing skills came to the fore. Cometh the moment, cometh the man, and for the next four years he did not put a foot wrong.

# CHAPTER SIX

# *Suppliers*

It was often said that Marks & Spencer was Britain's biggest manufacturer without owning any factories and that its suppliers were retailers with no shops. For decades this symbiotic relationship provided low prices and flexibility for M&S and security for the supplier. The huge volumes M&S would order – always by the hundred dozen – enabled manufacturers to produce goods way below the cost of others, giving the customers both quality and value. It seemed a shining example of what later became known as stakeholder capitalism, a method of doing business that benefited customers, suppliers, staff and shareholders in equal measure. Yet the progress of globalisation in the 1990s and rising manufacturing and design standards in developing countries, where skilled as well as unskilled workers were paid just a fraction of what their counterparts demanded in Britain, were too powerful for the 'made in Britain' philosophy, most loudly proclaimed by Marcus Sieff, to be sustained. Like King Canute, M&S directors might claim they could hold back the tide, but in the end, the tide of globalisation swept over them as well-designed, high-quality goods sourced from overseas and sold by their rivals hacked into their market share.

For years M&S seemed like a beacon in the night to the hard-pressed textile regions of Britain as they fought against the influx of cheap fabrics and finished goods from abroad. In 1985 Lord Rayner could boast that M&S bought a fifth of all clothing made in the UK and that almost half the entire home production of shirts carried the St Michael label. The number of people employed in the UK clothing, knitwear and hosiery industries fell from 400,000 to 300,000 between 1979 and 1984, but the number involved in making St Michael goods rose by 12,000. In short, M&S was helping to keep the UK textile industry alive.

M&S had always been famous for its unique relationships with British suppliers – something that Peter Salsbury set about destroying when he became chief executive in 1999. In some quarters the relationships were viewed as far too cosy. Yet from the moment Israel Sieff achieved his clandestine breakthrough with Cecil Coleman, production director of Corah, persuading him secretly to leapfrog the wholesalers and supply socks direct in bulk, a relationship with M&S became too mutually beneficial to abandon. By the 1960s M&S was a cornerstone of the British textile industry and companies such as Dewhirst, Foister Clay and Ward, Charnos, Nottingham Manufacturing and William Baird thrived.

Israel, Simon, Teddy and Marcus achieved this through close personal relationships with individual manufacturers, who would often invest millions of pounds in a new factory or technology simply on the basis of a conversation and a handshake. For the small garment makers there were short-term month-long contracts for orders, but there were no long-term contracts. David Suddens, who was chief executive of William Baird when Salsbury terminated the relationship with six months' notice in 1999, said: 'Nobody had contracts longer than six months. I am sure if I had gone to Andrew [Stone] or Rick and asked for longer-term contracts they would have said: "We have done business with suppliers for more than 100 years on the basis of trust and loyalty and mutual benefit. If that is not good enough for you then we are obviously not the kind of people to do business together".'

Until Peter Salsbury became chief executive in 1999, UK based manufacturers were treated as partners, albeit junior partners. In 1982 the *Financial Times* described how Peter Wolff, an ex-M&S executive who left to set up the clothing group SR Gent, would patrol the women's counters of the Marble Arch store to see how his blouses, skirts and nightwear were selling. On one occasion, through talking to customers, he discovered a flaw in the sleeve binding of one of his nightdresses. 'I rushed to the manager's office, phoned the factory and got them to change the sleeve binding to a frill. We rushed the redesigned items down to London over the weekend and they sold like a riot,' reported Wolff, who described his relationship with M&S as 'almost like a marriage'.

Like a marriage, it was for better or worse. When the going was good, the suppliers reaped the benefit and acquired for themselves Rolls-Royce cars, trophy wives and villas in Spain. When the going got tough they were expected to cut their margins and 'make a contribution'. Relationships were based on trust and there was one extra dimension that until the mid 1990s set M&S apart from so many other large companies – top management clearly enjoyed seeing their suppliers prosper with them.

Sir Harry Djanogly, who built up Nottingham Manufacturing into a world-class supplier of knitwear and fabrics, put it like this: 'M&S was not jealous of others making money. They wanted us to prosper. They knew if suppliers made money they would service them better.'

He was not alone in thinking this. In the 1980s a joke went round the food manufacturers about how they perceived the difference between M&S and the rest of the big chains: 'Marks & Spencer wanted their suppliers to make a profit, Tesco didn't care whether they made a profit or not, Sainsbury didn't want them to make a profit and Asda didn't know whether their suppliers made a profit or not.'

The three Harvard Business School studies gave a clear idea of the importance of supplier relationships to the company. The first page of the 1989 study lists the five operating principles laid down by Lord Marks. Two are about suppliers.

1. To offer our customers a selective range of high-quality, well designed and attractive merchandise at reasonable prices.
2. To encourage our suppliers to use the most modern and efficient techniques of production and quality control dictated by the latest discoveries in science and technology.
3. With the co-operation of our suppliers, to enforce the highest standard of quality control.
4. To plan the expansion of our stores for the better display of a widening range of goods and for the convenience of our customers.
5. To foster good human relations with customers, suppliers and staff.

The culture of strong relationships started by Israel and Simon continued until 1999, even if meetings took place in offices rather than in family homes. Longstanding suppliers felt that M&S was different from other customers. The top executives were more involved, the standards were higher and it was a continuous process. Once you were in, you usually stayed in, and despite being asked to suffer in tough times, there was a feeling that M&S wanted to share the good times.

Yet it would be foolish to pretend that every manufacturer enjoyed the rigours of being an M&S supplier. One of the penalties was dealing with the buying team, the selector and merchandiser, who wielded great power. Some of the middle-aged women selectors who had worked their way up the company were fearsome characters who almost breathed fire. They could be arrogant, and in some cases downright rude, towards suppliers. 'It was quite clear they liked to lord it over us,' said one.

Lord Rayner, on a train to visit a new factory in the north-east of England one morning, was horrified to overhear a group of selectors in a neighbouring carriage disparaging the chairman of the company they were going to see and joking about what a hard time they would give his managers. Rayner avoided a confrontation at the time, but later that week summoned the culprits to a meeting where he lectured them on the damage arrogance could do to M&S's long-term relationships with suppliers.

The selectors and merchandisers were also wooed aggressively by certain suppliers, as happens in most retailers, and would be regular recipients of soft bribes and lavish presents at Christmas.

Rayner aggressively addressed this practice (which was hardly unique to M&S), banning selectors from receiving presents and luxurious perks tagged on to buying trips. Greenbury also tried to enforce the rule, but it was never easy to do so. Djanogly was well aware of what went on, although he believed he kept his own company clean. 'Nobody at Nottingham Manufacturing ever bought a present for anyone in M&S,' said Djanogly. 'If you can't get business in the proper way on value, price and quality, you shouldn't be in business.'

In the beginning most suppliers were small, because M&S was small. Some suppliers grew with the company. Isaac Dewhirst, the wholesaler, was the first and his company, having evolved into a maker of shirts, blouses and later men's suits, survived everything – the war, the end of family control and even M&S's profits collapse. After Coats Viyella severed its relationship with the post-Greenbury regime in 2000, Dewhirst became M&S's largest clothing supplier after Courtaulds Textiles, which in the same year was taken over by Sara Lee, the American consumer goods combine that made Playtex bras and Pretty Polly tights as well as the cakes Marcus Sieff liked so much.

Others stayed small and the problem for M&S was that it was loath to terminate orders from longstanding suppliers. Often, too, the best and brightest ideas came from new, smaller companies, which would beat a path to Marks & Spencer's door. In the 1970s Jennifer D'Abo introduced a range of soaps to M&S and soon began importing baskets from the Far East. It took months for her to get her first order, but a lucky chance social encounter with Derek Rayner eased her path. Once she was in, life became easier and the kudos palpable. 'There is nothing like the buzz of walking into Marks & Spencer and seeing your goods on the shelf,' she said.

Buying goods directly from UK manufacturers had many advantages. The lines of communication were short – a phone call or a visit could sort out a problem. Quality control was easy to enforce and local sourcing also offered greater flexibility. The long runs that M&S gave its manufacturers enabled them to produce goods that could sell at stunning value, yet still yield a profit for both supplier and retailer.

For decades the relationship gave M&S an advantage over competitors that did not provide such big or reliable orders. Whereas every other retailer ordered garments by unit, as in 5,000 units, M&S ordered them by the dozen – as in 5,000 dozen. And, as long as products were both made and sold in the UK, there was no currency risk. Only later, when M&S developed its own international business, did currency become a problem. In the late 1990s the costs of its British-made products – high both relative to those from emerging markets and because of sterling's strength – decimated the profits of its Continental stores so much that in 2001 they were closed. German, French and Spanish customers had found the goods just too expensive.

M&S developed a policy of co-operating wholeheartedly with suppliers on design and technology. That meant sending in designers and technologists – at a time when no other retailer even employed technologists – to advise on yarn and fabric and dyes. It also meant carrying out stringent tests such as washing garments several hundred times and putting up with M&S hygiene and workplace personnel throughout the factory. Some saw it as intrusive and resented the senior partner/junior partner relationship. But most of the bigger ones welcomed it with open arms. It was, after all, free consultancy and advice from a major customer with unparalleled expertise and experience. 'If I were parachuted into a factory I would be able to tell within minutes whether it was an M&S supplier or not,' said Baird's David Suddens. 'I would know by the canteen and toilets, the physical state of the equipment, the way the management dressed and the way the whole place looked and smelt. There would be a quality about it. M&S did a tremendous amount for the UK clothing industry.'

Nottingham Manufacturing became one of M&S's most important suppliers of knitwear and remained so for several decades. The company had been started by Harry Djanogly's father, Simon, and his uncle Jack, who fled Nazi persecution in 1937. Like Michael Marks, their parents left Russia to escape the pogroms, but unlike him they settled in Germany, where they built a successful cotton trading and manufacturing company. In a classic tale of pre-Hitler Jewish enterprise in Germany they became big manufacturers of lisle stockings and began reaching out into export markets. In 1925 they set up a selling office in Gresham Street in the City of London and began supplying stockings to shoe companies such as Lilley & Skinner and Dolcis. They noticed Marks & Spencer and its growing presence in high streets and sought a meeting with Israel and Simon.

'My father and uncle spoke mainly German so most of the conversation was conducted in sign language,' said Harry. 'Simon and Israel said that M&S did not sell hosiery. My father responded by saying that they should sell it.' In the end the brothers offered them 100 dozen pairs of stockings on a sale or return basis. They appeared on sale in the Kilburn store on a Friday and by the Monday morning 'they were screaming for more goods'. It was the start of a personal trading relationship that lasted until Djanogly sold the business to Sir David Alliance's textile group, then known as Vantona Viyella, although under that ownership it continued to supply M&S until 2000.

The two brothers continued to export stockings from Germany to M&S for the next twelve years. Prosperous and busy, for many years they dismissed Hitler as merely a lunatic, failing until 1937 to realise the seriousness of his threat to the Jews. By that time, life had become so dangerous that they decided to flee Germany, leaving their business and most of their wealth behind.

They headed for England and asked their contacts for the area with the best mines – their idea was that mining areas always had a good supply of female labour, which they needed to work in their textile factories. They were told that Nottingham, coincidentally the home of UK lacemaking, was the place. Simon and Jack Djanogly bought an eight-acre site at £40 per acre on which they could build 34,000 square feet of factory space per acre. They started with 8,000 square feet and by purchasing some old machinery from Bear Brand were able to start producing very soon and so they could continue to supply Marks & Spencer.

When Harry joined the company in the 1950s he took it away from hosiery into knitwear. Until then finely made lambswool sweaters had been the almost exclusive preserve of ladies who shopped at Harrods and other upmarket department stores, buying brands such as Pringle. Djanogly developed two-ply lambswool jumpers and cardigans at less than half the price of the branded goods. 'We sold millions and millions every week,' he said. By the 1960s Nottingham Manufacturing had moved even further to develop machine-washable lambswool.

During the post-war years the relationship with M&S was close and familial. 'We would have dinner with them, they would talk about their plans, we would talk about ours. It was a close, honest, open relationship. There is no question in my mind that we and many of the suppliers played a significant role in the development of M&S,' he said.

During the immediate post-war years many suppliers were also Jewish firms, particularly the garment makers. Clearly, Simon and Israel felt at home with fellow Jews and there was also a sense of communal responsibility following the Holocaust. Yet there were great tranches of the British textile industry, such as Corah and Courtaulds, that were solidly Anglo-Saxon and that also developed strong relationships with the company. What counted was being able to deliver good quality at the right price. 'It was not so much that M&S wanted to do business with Jews,' said Djanogly. 'It was more that the young Jewish companies were aspiring, hungry and eager to produce the type of goods they wanted.'

Once a trusting relationship was established and proved so mutually beneficial it tended to endure for many decades. Most of the longest-lasting suppliers were clothing manufacturers operating in what was traditionally a fragmented industry. Often owned by their founders or their families, they received help from M&S as they grew. The chain paid on time, helped with any cash-flow problems, but in essence ran the show. But from the 1960s, the start of a long period of decline for the British textile industry, manufacturers began to consolidate into bigger companies. The two major predators were Courtaulds and Coats Viyella, the creation of Alliance, scion of an Iranian textile manufacturer, who had arrived in Manchester aged 17 in the early 1950s. Lord Kearton of Courtaulds was the consolidator during the 1960s and Alliance took up the baton in the 1980s.

During the 1970s, when there was still a shortage of product – in other words, the balance of power was still tilted in favour of the manufacturer –

M&S used more than 100 different suppliers in clothing alone. Many of them were typical 'cut, make and trim' companies churning out the garments in small factories in the East Midlands and Scotland. According to Greenbury they made little contribution to the development of the product. 'We bought the raw materials and allocated them, we decided what designs would be made, what colours, what fabrics, everything,' he said. 'We really organised their production facilities. They were all making a few hundred thousand items a week and it meant that the good, innovative suppliers could not grow, because these guys just collected their contracts every month, because they always had. It just grew and I remember at one point we had nearly forty suppliers of ladies' blouses.'

Food production, with the exception of that made by speciality niche players, was concentrated mainly in the hands of a few major suppliers that started to do business with M&S in the 1970s. Although M&S's custom helped build their businesses, the food manufacturers rarely became as dependent on the company as the small garment makers. At Northern Foods, which supplied chilled meals, sandwiches and other M&S staples, the longstanding chairman, Lord Haskins, gave the credit for much of his company's transformation from a small dairy producer into a multimillion pound group to M&S. 'They made us what we are,' he said. 'I was running a dairy in Northern Ireland twenty years ago and they needed some fresh cream, which they couldn't bring from the mainland because of their standards – bacteriological standards that everybody has now but nobody had dreamed of then.' But he recognised the dangers that closeness to M&S could bring, particularly in clothing.

'I remember the first time I went to one of their meetings of suppliers,' recalled Haskins. 'It was around 1973 and there was a line of at least a dozen Rolls-Royces owned by the textile and garment suppliers queuing up outside. At that time there were only three food companies and we came in our Fords, or whatever, and I remember thinking: "Boy these guys have got it coming to them." because they were completely and utterly beholden to Marks & Spencer.'

An example of this vulnerability came in June 1979 when Geoffrey Howe, then chancellor of the exchequer, put up VAT in the first Tory budget of the Thatcher era. M&S adjusted clothing prices accordingly with the result that customers simply held off buying. M&S took drastic action, rang all its suppliers and told them they would have to cut their profit margins forthwith.

A press release was duly issued saying that Marks & Spencer, in co-operation with suppliers, was fighting inflation.

Martin Taylor, a former *Financial Times* journalist, joined Courtaulds in 1982 and began helping Sir Christopher Hogg, his chairman, to modernise the group. Four years later he became managing director of Courtaulds Textiles. Then in 1990 he led a demerger from its parent company and set about managing a swift decline in UK manufacturing and an increase in overseas production. In 1992 he became chief executive at Barclays Bank, but in 1979 he was still writing the Lex column of the *FT*. Years later he remembered the announcement clearly. He rang a number of M&S suppliers to ask about the proposed margin cuts, but they all refused to comment. Such pain sharing was typical as was the unwillingness of the suppliers to talk for fear of damaging their precious M&S business. 'M&S could be savvy, ruthless and hypocritical, yet everyone there believed that what they did was virtuous by definition,' said Taylor, who in 2000 became non-executive chairman of WH Smith.

By 1980, when Greenbury was moved from running property and stores to take charge of clothing, the supplier base had become unwieldy. He quickly saw there were far too many suppliers for the sort of business M&S was becoming. M&S needed bigger companies that could produce long runs of what were called 'power ranges' – bras, knickers, nightdresses, skirts and his favourite lambswool sweaters. Greenbury persuaded Sieff, then his chairman, to allow him to start a cull. It was a delicate operation, given the longevity of the trading relationships.

Some suppliers were dropped altogether, although those with long-term links were given as long as two years' notice. Others were asked to reduce their capacity. 'We would say: "Look, we can't fill three factories, but we can fill two. So if you close one, we will make sure the other two are fully used",' said Greenbury.

However delicately M&S directors may have thought they were managing the process, some manufacturers, after decades of working with M&S, reacted to what was effectively losing all or part of their livelihood with anger and bitterness. The wife of the founder of one company appeared in Greenbury's office one day and berated him: 'She gave me a piece of her mind and was pretty unpleasant. But she was a remarkable woman,' he said.

Greenbury also began to encourage mergers and acquisitions so that the small suppliers were grouped together as bigger, stronger businesses. He recognised that too many M&S resources were going into the suppliers and thought that they needed to build their own product development departments. 'Not all the brains could reside in Baker Street,' he said. The idea was to create bigger, more profitable suppliers that could afford to invest in design and innovation. In practice the process caused huge upheaval and much heartache, although few of the owners lost out financially. Observers dubbed the mergers shotgun marriages – if small suppliers did not agree to be taken over their custom would be terminated.

Alliance was the most aggressive consolidator. He started by buying a company called Thomas Houghton in 1956 when it was on the brink of receivership, a tactic he would often repeat. He built up a private company, R. Greg, which he reversed into the publicly quoted Spirella. Using Spirella as a bid vehicle he bought Vantona, Carrington Viyella, Nottingham Manufacturing, Coats Patons and finally Tootal to become Britain's leading textile businessman, his company overtaking Courtaulds in size along the way. After a myriad of name changes it was finally called Coats Viyella.

It was a decade of turbulence and takeovers – whenever one M&S supplier came up for sale it would usually be bought by another – or in the case of Corah and Textured Jersey by a financial buyer. By the early 1990s there were just ten big clothing manufacturers supplying two-thirds of M&S clothing – and twenty companies supplying 85 per cent. 'So instead of forty companies making ladies' blouses we now had six, but they were six very powerful, capable ones,' said Greenbury.

They were all, however, still British. Greenbury, like Sieff, was intensely committed to the 'buy British' philosophy and had in true M&S tradition developed strong personal links with his bigger suppliers. Sir Christopher Hogg first met Greenbury in 1976 when he was running Courtaulds' clothing business. He rapidly identified Greenbury as the coming man and when he became Courtaulds' chairman in 1980 Hogg set about repairing a relationship that had been damaged by his two predecessors, Lord Kearton and Sir Arthur Knight. Kearton had run Courtaulds in the heyday of man-made fibres and made few concessions to customers still struggling to get enough product to put in the shops. 'Courtaulds at the time was run by chemical engineers interested in fibres for tensile strength, not beauty. Kearton wanted to make oceans of pink acrylic, which was not exactly what M&S wanted,' said MartinTaylor. 'But Chris realised that the product mattered and he met

Rick half way. And Rick could see the growth potential for M&S if it had suppliers of a similar size and scale to itself.'

In the same way as Greenbury had built up men's knitwear with the help of Djanogly, he and Hogg, who became chairman of Reuters in 1985 and Allied Domecq in 1996, rapidly expanded the underwear and lingerie range using Courtaulds as the major supplier. These chairman-to-chairman relationships would set the tone throughout the two companies. At Courtaulds Textiles a dedicated team of executives was set up to interact with the M&S buying departments. Colin Dyer, ultimately chief executive of Courtaulds Textiles but in 1994 the director in charge of M&S operations, explained to Harvard Business School how they co-operated: 'Along with our own fabric suppliers and the M&S buying departments, we move in like a vortex on product solutions. It is like a spider web of communication between their merchandisers and selectors and our designers and sales staff. Their technologists work closely with our factory production staff, designers and material suppliers.'

Dyer also spelt out the symbiotic closeness of the relationship: 'There are important nods and winks between us. It takes three-quarters of an hour for a message to move through the Marks & Spencer hierarchy and, because of our connections at every level of the organisation, we hear the exact same information in an hour and a half.'

Derek Rayner recognised the benefits of such close relationships, but he had a wider vision. His more international approach meant that when he became chairman in 1984 he began to look around the world for both food and clothing suppliers. Rayner was a frequent visitor to America and the Far East, particularly Thailand. Although he continued to preach the 'made in Britain' message he was less wedded than Sieff had been to the idea of British suppliers at all costs and felt that UK manufacturers had become too inbred. He even went so far as to declare that, for some of them, M&S was a soft touch.

So he brought in the idea of overseas competition. Just as Simon Marks had been driven by pragmatism – the rise of Hitler and the Second World War – to concentrate sourcing at home, Rayner was driven by necessity to begin shifting the balance overseas. For many years the company had believed that its unique relationships with its suppliers, relationships that enabled it to put the squeeze on margins in time of need, also gave it a cost advantage its competitors could never match. But a combination of low-cost labour and high technology turned the tables – and those in power took too long to realise it. Rival companies such as Burton, now Arcadia, and Next were buying quality knitwear from Mauritius and jeans from the Far East in the early 1980s – way before M&S ever contemplated buying finished garments from overseas.

Toward the end of the 1980s it became difficult to source basic cotton and wool fabric in the UK because the industry had virtually disappeared. In his book *From Empire to Europe*, Sir Geoffrey Owen, a former editor of the *Financial Times*, wrote of Courtaulds: 'In the mid 1980s, 90 per cent of the products that Courtaulds Textiles sold were made in Britain, and 90 per cent of its sales were in Britain. The objective, over a period of a decade, was to reduce the first of these two figures to 40 per cent, by sourcing more goods in cheaper overseas locations, and the second to 50 per cent, by exporting more British made products and by overseas acquisitions.'

Yet it was not until 1996 that Courtaulds Textiles' last remaining Lancashire spinning mills were sold to Shiloh, an old established firm run by Edmund Gartside, whose family had controlled the business since 1874. 'Shilo's survival,' Owen wrote, 'was based on flexibility, service and the ability to respond quickly to a wide variety of customer demands ...'

The Far East was beginning to manufacture fabric in bulk and improving quality all the time. Japanese companies, meanwhile, began to produce new man-made yarns that mimicked silk, but at a fraction of its price.

Greenbury followed the trend unwillingly. It was inconceivable for such an emotional and loyal character to contemplate replacing any of his bigger UK suppliers with faceless companies from overseas. He also feared for the image of M&S with customers if he began ditching UK manufacturers. When Peter Wolff at SR Gent told him he was setting up a factory in Sri Lanka in the late 1980s, Greenbury expressed severe reservations about the move. But gradually he came round and allowed his UK suppliers to educate him when they set up factories in developing countries. One mentor was Sir Donald Parr, onetime chairman of William Baird, who with his wife used to go on holiday with Greenbury to the Caribbean island of Barbuda each winter. But although Baird moved some production abroad relatively early, it proved ultimately to be less than enough to protect it when Salsbury took the axe to UK suppliers in 1999.

Steeped in the Marks and Sieff tradition of supporting the UK textile industry, Greenbury knew the world was changing, even if his heart held him

1. *Michael Marks, founder of Marks & Spencer*

2. *Tom Spencer, partner of Michael Marks*

*3. Store front: Manchester, 1898*

*4. Store interior: 1930s (fancy goods)*

5. Simon Marks, Lord,
M&S Chairman
1916–64

6. Israel Sieff, Lord, M&S Chairman 1964–7

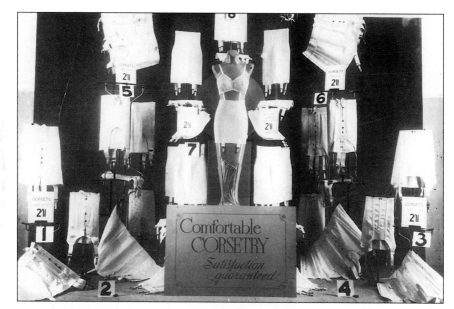

7. *Window display 1930*

8. *Window display 1937*

*9. Edward Sieff, M&S Chairman 1967–72*

*10. Marcus, Lord Sieff of Brimpton, M&S Chairman 1972–84*

*11. Derek, Lord Rayner, M&S Chairman 1984–91*

*12. Sir Richard Greenbury, M&S Chairman 1991–9*

13. 'The Arch', M&S's flagship store

14. Boulevard Haussmann, the largest M&S store in France

15. *Peter Salsbury*

16. *Clara Freeman*

17. *Keith Oates*

18. *Luc Vandevelde*

19. *Roger Holmes*

*20. Men's wear department in the new-look stores of 2001*

*21. George Davies's Per Una range*

back. Executives down the line, however, remained adamantly against the gradual move overseas. 'There was always a degree of schizophrenia at M&S about buying overseas. Derek and Rick would say it was something that had to happen, and to an extent it did happen. But the rank and file of the company was so set against overseas sourcing, it did not happen fast enough,' said Baird's chief executive David Suddens.

Greenbury saw that what was already happening in fabrics would soon happen in certain 'commodity' garments such as shirts and T-shirts. His dilemma was how to increase the amount of imported goods without destroying the UK suppliers. 'We could not afford to see them in severe financial difficulties because we still needed them. In fashion items you want most garment factories to be as close to your customer as possible because it gives you flexibility and turnround time,' he said. 'If you have got a problem with a contract in the UK, you get on the phone to the suppliers and say: "Look, these are not selling as well as we thought, can we come up and talk to you about it next week?" And it gets sorted out. But when you have a conversation with someone 8,000 miles away he says: "So sorry, I have just finished making them, they are on the high seas." So it is not all beer and skittles, sourcing abroad.'

But by the early 1990s some clothing suppliers had followed the lead of SR Gent and Baird and had set up manufacturing plant abroad. Greenbury was torn between the clear evidence that in some ranges China and Indonesia could produce the requisite quality at far cheaper prices and his loyalty to traditional suppliers. If the competition was going there, then so was Marks & Spencer, but, as ever, it was going carefully and, as it turned out, too slowly. 'By 1993,' he said, 'I was starting to travel, taking some of our top people with me looking at overseas manufacturers in China and the Far East.' He also explored the Continent further, in particular Italy.

One result was the Italian collection of women's suits, jackets and trousers, which by the mid 1990s was turning over £250m a year. But Greenbury stuck to the view that the preferred solution was for British suppliers to set up their own production overseas. 'The important thing was to get them investing and developing and getting into bed with some of the very best suppliers abroad – those making for The Gap and Ralph Lauren because you got ideas from that,' he said. 'You couldn't copy them identically, but you could see what look they were pushing.' Gradually Greenbury increased the amount of goods sourced overseas.

Moving production abroad meant that the British holding company may have been saved but much of the workforce was sacrificed. Courtaulds, Coats, Dewhirst and Baird all had to close numerous factories. At first, the unions protested, threatening industrial action, but the message was simple. They could settle for one factory closure or face the entire company going out of business. Greenbury personally negotiated with textile union leaders such as John Edmonds and Alex Smith and even John Monks, head of the TUC. During the whole time there was never a strike of any significance.

But this approach had one big disadvantage, according to Brian Godbold, M&S's former design director. 'M&S selectors and merchandisers got little experience in running around the world sourcing direct from suppliers. They were like babes in arms,' he said. Buyers from rival retailers would meet M&S representatives in the Far East and be amazed at their lack of sophistication. 'I remember meeting some M&S people in Hong Kong in 1996 and they were like I was twenty years ago,' said one.

At the end of the 1980s the amount of M&S goods made in Britain had been around 80 per cent but by the end of Greenbury's chairmanship in 1999 that figure had fallen to 60 per cent, including goods manufactured by British-based companies abroad. This proportion was not enough to make M&S thoroughly competitive, but those who criticised Greenbury for not sourcing overseas were only partly right. He may not have enjoyed buying from abroad, but he recognised that it had become a necessity if M&S clothing was to stay competitive.

Others in M&S, as Suddens pointed out, were not so convinced. Paul Smith, who ran the Far East operation for five years, recalled setting up a meeting in Hong Kong with Peter Salsbury, after he became chief executive, along with other UK executives to meet a group of suppliers. To his astonishment he found that the then head of buying, Joe Rowe, had failed to attend. 'We were very slow,' said Smith. 'There was an inbuilt resistance to buying offshore.'

Life was less painful for the food manufacturers – they were different animals and had come on the scene much later in M&S's history. Simon Marks had only grudgingly developed the food side, urged on by Marcus Sieff. But Sieff was determined that M&S should supply customers with the very best and newest fruit and vegetables – selling grapefruit, avocados and other 'exotic' specimens for the first time in the UK along with little leaflets explaining what to do with them, and it was under his chairmanship that

Henry Lewis pushed at the boundaries of technology, developing chilled, ready-made dishes requiring little preparation.

In the early days some of these dishes would be tested in the kitchens in Baker Street, although most of the work was undertaken by the suppliers. One of Lewis's early successes was chicken kiev, which he originally developed with the help of a small Midlands company called Alveston Kitchens run by John Docker, nephew of the flamboyant Lady Docker and her husband, Sir Bernard. It proved a runaway success despite considerable scepticism within the food industry. Chris Haskins of Northern Foods recalled Lewis taking him into the Manchester store and showing him the first chicken kiev: 'I thought: "That will never sell." But it did. In fact, it rapidly became a top seller.

Seasonal fresh-produce suppliers could not be other than British owing to the perishable nature of their product. Yet if M&S was to pioneer non-stop fruit and vegetable sales throughout the year it had to scour the world for supplies so that its customers could have raspberries in winter and avocado pears all year round. Executives made a point of ensuring that even when they used a British company such as Hunter Saphir to import exotic fruit and vegetables, high standards were set where the produce was grown. Directors would fly off to Spain, the Dominican Republic or remote parts of Thailand to make sure that the sources of supply had good standards and that they were produced in an ethical way.

M&S had no compunction about making well-established companies comply with their ways in order to be suppliers. One young executive who worked on the developing wine side recalled her embarrassment at approaching centuries-old vineyards in France and insisting the staff should wear hairnets. 'But we did it because we had the power of the company behind us, and, to be honest, that made us incredibly arrogant,' she said. 'And what was amazing, after their initial disbelief, most of these companies complied.'

Although many of the UK food suppliers began small, they soon became big. The rapid expansion of chilled foods, sandwiches and recipe dishes turned companies such as Northern Foods, Hillsdown and Unigate into large enterprises during the 1970s and 1980s. Like the clothing manufacturers, they snapped up their smaller competitors to form bigger groups.

Wherever possible, M&S gave unwavering support to manufacturers that endeavoured to innovate on their behalf. M&S wanted to sell trifle, which was notoriously difficult. It had to taste absolutely fresh but on the other hand all the layers had to stand firm and remain separate for a specified number of days. Unigate tried and abandoned the idea, while Haskins at Northern Foods had his chefs working on it for ten years before it was perfected. 'M&S were determined to persevere,' he said. But the result was a best-selling product.

M&S developed chilled recipe dishes at a time when supermarket freezers were full of frozen TV dinners. The problem was that chilled meals were regarded as extremely high risk. 'Chilled meals were microbiologically dangerous; then they decided they wanted to sell fresh chicken – another potentially dangerous route. They went down all these dangerous routes and encouraged suppliers to go with them,' said Haskins admiringly.

M&S started producing sandwiches during the 1970s. At the time the idea was revolutionary and, like many great ideas, it came about by accident. Henry Lewis was involved in an ultimately unsuccessful scheme to open more coffee bars in the stores. 'It turned out to be fast food for slow customers. They would sit there for hours with a cup of tea,' he recalled.

The first one was to be in the Croydon store, but the builders, as ever, took longer than scheduled to complete the construction, which left a number of staff trained and ready to make a new line of sandwiches for sale at the coffee bar. Rather than leave them idle, Lewis decided to sell the few dozen sandwiches they made every day to the public through the store. They vanished off the shelves at such speed Lewis realised he had a winner on his hands. By 2000 M&S was selling 85 million sandwiches a year.

The companies that developed the chilled recipe dishes, fresh chicken, desserts and sandwiches learned to live with the constant supervision of M&S personnel, partly because it ensured their market but also because they felt they were getting good advice – once again it was free consultancy. The most famous technologist in the company was Nathan Goldenberg, who had escaped Nazi persecution and was brought in by Marcus Sieff to ensure the highest possible hygiene standards. Goldenberg was known as 'Dr No' within the company because of his refusal to compromise. He worked particularly closely with suppliers in Israel and for decades Israeli food factories had a white line on the factory floor known as the 'Goldenberg line' past which no equipment could go.

Sir Harry Solomon, who chaired Hillsdown Holdings until 1993, explained how the partnership worked. 'The food technologists had three roles. The first was to ensure that all the health and hygiene standards were being met and they were very, very thorough. Secondly, they would work with you developing new lines, which was very much a joint enterprise. Sometimes we would come up with an idea, sometimes they would. And thirdly they would advise you on what you should be doing to develop the business. In some factories such as the smoked salmon business, M&S people would be there all the time – it was sometimes difficult to differentiate M&S people from our own it was such a joint enterprise. It was a good arrangement.'

It was not particularly easy but the rewards made any difficulties worthwhile. 'They were difficult, they were pernickety, they could be very tough and hard,' said Solomon. 'But we built up a close relationship and we felt there was a bond. There was a certain amount of honour and decency and you felt a personal need to give them your best. If you had a problem you could always go to them and they would always help you.

'We always felt very proud to be a Marks & Spencer supplier, it was like a stamp of credibility. To be one of their major suppliers was a very good thing, not just with other customers, but with the City and analysts. It meant that your standards were high, that you could comply with stringent conditions and that you were innovative.'

The main problem for the fresh and recipe dish suppliers in dealing with M&S was that directors were jealous of other corporate customers. New products may have been developed in partnership but M&S would be very proprietorial over those products. As the good companies grew, they needed to sell to Sainsbury and Tesco to fill their capacity, but M&S disapproved. 'Rick would accuse companies of stealing their ideas and selling them to others,' remarked one supplier.

'They reckoned they had a proprietary right over everything and this caused problems,' said Solomon, who had to refuse to supply Sainsbury with sandwiches because of pressure from M&S. 'I remember one of the Sainsbury directors throwing things around and shouting: "Marks & Spencer didn't invent the sandwich."'

The reply may well have been that while the men from Michael House did not invent the sandwich they certainly helped develop specific types of fresh, interesting and microbiologically safe sandwiches that could be mass produced. M&S was meticulous about the quality and cleanliness of ingredients – and the amounts of filling were specified down to the last prawn.

Sandwich factories were hymns to hygiene with constant handwashing and disinfection of gloves and shoes. When staff went abroad they had to give stool samples before returning to work to avoid contamination. It was repellent but necessary. 'If you picked up something like typhoid on holiday and you started making sandwiches, you could kill half the population,' explained Solomon.

M&S was very demanding in all respects. As with the clothing companies, a strong relationship between the chairmen was crucial – even though the majority of the work was done by executives down the line. The respective chairmen would lunch or have meetings a few times a year. And then there would be 'royal visits' to the factory, after which a posse of directors from each company would repair to the dining room to sample new dishes.

Most of the nitty-gritty negotiating was done by divisional heads, who found M&S tough bargainers. Having insisted on food being prepared a certain way – often not the most cost-effective one – M&S executives would argue ferociously over pricing – although once something was agreed they never went back on their word. But the advantage and kudos of being an M&S supplier were so great that few suppliers fell out permanently with their biggest customer.

One way round the possessiveness was to build dedicated factories exclusively to supply M&S. And what seems remarkable is that Hillsdown or Northern Foods would spend more than £5m building a brand-new factory without a single contract or document changing hands. Hillsdown built one new factory solely to make chicken kiev. 'It was done on trust,' explained Solomon. 'There was no risk that they would switch to another supplier, it was inconceivable. The only risk we took was whether the product would keep on selling.' Haskins at Northern Foods would do the same. 'We have dedicated factories because I always treat supplying M&S as though I'm sharing in a brand of food,' he said.

M&S would also use the power of its custom to protect a long-term supplier under threat, as Haskins discovered. Towards the end of April 1988 Haskins was alerted by his stockbroker that Hazlewood Foods, an aggressive company built up by quickfire takeovers, had acquired a 3 per cent shareholding in Northern Foods, where profits had been marking time. Behind-the-scenes detective work left Haskins in no doubt that Hazlewood was planning a takeover bid for his company. On Sunday 1 May following a briefing, the *Sunday Times* business section revealed the Hazlewood stake and carried a Marks & Spencer statement that read: 'We value Northern Foods very much as our major food supplier. It has invested £40m on our behalf and we would like it to remain independent.' Hazlewood had been planning to make the bid the following week but the story killed the planned bid stone dead. Such was the power of the men from Michael House.

# CHAPTER SEVEN

# The glory years

Rick Greenbury stepped up to be chairman of the company he loved on 1 April 1991. Britain was in the middle of the second worst recession since the war. At 54, he was as fit for the job as a racehorse trained to its peak ahead of the big race. He had been chief operating officer for a year and chief executive for two, he knew all aspects of the business backwards – with the exception of financial services. His personal life looked sublime. He was happily married to his glamorous second wife Gabrielle, while still remaining friends with Siân, mother of his four children. He and Gabrielle had bought an extensive 1930s-style house in ten acres of landscaped grounds in Berkshire, which they had turned into a plutocrat's home. There was a bar, a gym and sauna for Gabrielle, tennis courts for him. From there Greenbury could monitor the newly built Camberley store – a one-storey edge-of-town joint development with Tesco. He played his beloved tennis twice a week and attended every Manchester United match he could – occasionally using a private plane for European games, when he could fit in a business meeting as well.

In Rayner's last year as chairman, the twelve months to 31 March 1991, profits had risen by a pedestrian 2 per cent from £604.2m to £615.5m. The recession had started to bite just as he had allowed his ambitious selectors, still riding the designer-dominated wave of 1980s high spending, to take women's clothing a little too far upmarket. Customers let it be known they did not expect to spend £100 on a dress in M&S. This would never have happened under the founding family, they said. There were mutterings that M&S was losing touch with its core customer – but not for long.

If Rayner had been concentrating on £100 dresses and expansion in the New World, Greenbury focused on everyday operations. 'It was as if Derek had been floating off in all directions and then Rick hit the ground running and pulled everything back to the centre again,' said one director.

Greenbury's first significant act was to sack 850 people – 300 from head office, the rest from stores. He also encouraged some 'natural wastage'. By the end of the financial year to March 1992 the number of people employed in the stores was down by more than 5,000 to 51,442 while the head office payroll was 559 souls lighter at 3,748.

His second act was to call in the heads of all those suppliers he knew so well and persuade them once again to accept cuts in their margins. It was time once more for them to make 'a contribution', he told them, this time a substantial one. They agreed, because, painful though it might be, they knew that selling goods through M&S was the best shot they had. Simon Marks would have approved – if ever there was a time to bring back better value into the business, this was it. In November Greenbury had to admit to his shareholders that half-year profits had fallen by 7 per cent, the first profit decline in a decade. It was enough to bring out the knives in the unforgiving City and the press.

On 28 July 1991 the *Indpendent on Sunday* published a perceptive and finely written article by James Buchan, grandson of the author John Buchan and a former *Financial Times* journalist. Buchan described M&S as a company under siege from the fashion retailers in clothing and the big supermarkets in food. The fashion retailers had been seen off, he wrote – Storehouse, Burton, Next and Laura Ashley were fighting for their existence under the weight of high rents, high mortgage rates and a severe business downturn. But in foods, 'the big guns of Sainsbury, Tesco and Safeway kept up a heavy fire'.

Buchan had spent several weeks talking to everyone from the sales assistants upwards and discovered a common thread – uncertainty. 'Britain's most successful business is suddenly unsure of itself. All sorts of uncharacteristic things are happening,' he wrote. 'A company that prided itself on looking after its staff has just fired several hundred people. The pragmatic Jewish idealists who ran the business for three generations have been replaced by Gentile professionals. The big shareholders are no longer Markses, Sieffs and Sachers but the men from the Pru. The finance guy has never worked in a store. In the food business, buyers and merchandisers are suddenly scared of the big supermarkets. Overseas, Marks has moved into unfamiliar markets, either on tiptoe or head first.'

Buchan accused the management of making three mistakes: first the failure to move faster into edge-of-town sites while Tesco was leading the stampede followed by Safeway and Sainsbury. 'Marks should have been out there, slugging away on the bypass, even if this meant borrowing a lot of money. Instead, the company didn't open an out-of-town store until 1988,' he wrote.

The second mistake he cited was the Brooks Brothers acquisition: 'Brooks was profitable, well managed, extremely expensive to buy and desperately in need of a lick of paint. Immediately it passed into Marks's ownership, its business fell off a cliff.' The third mistake was the recent sackings, which Buchan believed went against the principles of Simon Marks.

Buchan was spot on about the first two, but misguided about the third. He had ignored the precedent of Simon and Israel's great simplification of 1956 and the subsequent loss of 5,000 people in the stores and 1,900 from Baker Street. Since then, the fat had been allowed to pile on and by 1990 M&S had been overstaffed for two decades. If anything, Greenbury did not sack enough people.

The article brilliantly caught the atmosphere of Baker Street: 'You can get quite fed up with these people: the grey suits repeated endlessly, the women like Stepford wives, the touchiness, the obsession with figures, the uninterrupted lowbrowness of the place. But you end up admiring them simply because of the way they concentrate on the job.' He then quoted Martin Taylor, at the time chief executive of Courtaulds Textiles, as saying, 'There's something over there which kills complacency.'

But the piece, which had taken six weeks of solid research, irritated Greenbury sufficiently for him to call in suspected contributors and carpet them. Northern Foods boss Chris Haskins, who had been quoted in the article, was one; Martin Taylor another. Taylor was summoned to Baker Street and accused, to his astonishment, of being behind some of the more negative anonymous remarks in the article and subjected to a long berating. Finally, he managed to calm Greenbury down, pointing out that the article was generally friendly towards the company and, at the end of the meeting, the two men strode amicably along the long corridors and down the grand staircase to the main exit. Yet Taylor might not have been totally convinced when Greenbury looked him sternly in the eye, shook his hand and said loudly: 'Remember, I never bear a grudge.'

A few months later Greenbury was again on the defensive, announcing a fall in profits before tax from £607m to £589m in the year to March 1992. There followed a steady drip of critical articles and bearish brokers' circulars. Then, in February 1993, the tide turned. Profits started to recover marking the beginning of the Greenbury glory years.

Buchan's article had ended on an upbeat note, yet what he and many others had failed to recognise was the extent of Greenbury's talent as an instinctive retailer and a dynamic leader. Needled but resolute, he put his shoulder to the wheel and by that spring his measures could be seen to be paying off. Overseas, he bit the bullet of Canada and sold People's Department Stores. It cost M&S £14m, but it was a huge relief all round.

In reality the turnround had started in the autumn of 1992. With the help of the suppliers, M&S launched an 'outstanding value' campaign and Greenbury was able to boast in his chairman's statement the following June that '25 per cent of all selling prices were lower than in the previous year while the balance remained the same'. After the high spending of the 1980s customers were craving simply cut, good quality clothes that did not break the bank. They also wanted vibrant colours to cheer them up as mortgage payments soared and disposable income declined. M&S delivered both. 'I put it to the board that we should streamline the product range, we should go for classic wearable clothes in high quality raw materials and that way we would kill the High Street,' said Greenbury in typically graphic language.

Brian Godbold, the divisional director in charge of design, and his team were given their head. The clothes in the 1992 ranges duly came in clean simple lines in primary colours. The autumn collections included a post-box red women's blazer, canary yellow leggings and jewel coloured knitwear. After the excesses of the 1980s M&S lived up to the promise of outstanding value – all-wool skirts for £25, pleated wool trousers for £30, 100 per cent cotton shirts for £15. Customers flocked to the stores and as sales rose so did the confidence of the buying departments.

The fashion press took notice. In September 1993 the *Sunday Times* magazine carried an entire fashion spread exclusively devoted to St Michael clothes, quoting Brian Godbold as saying, 'We aim to make definitive pieces rather than watered-down versions.' Shortly afterwards Godbold was featured in *Face* magazine as one of the most important people in British fashion. Then *Vogue* put a model wearing an M&S silk shirt on the cover. In 1994 Andrew Stone, then in charge of clothing and advised by Gillian Wheatcroft, head of fashion public relations, hired Linda Evangelista to model M&S clothes for publicity shots. 'For a while,' wrote *The Times*, 'Patrick Demarchelier's photograph of her in thigh-length black socks, a black mini-skirt and polo-neck came to symbolise the new Marks & Spencer.'

Merchandising lay at the heart of the growth. During the course of his career Greenbury had done every job in the buying department and he understood the psychology of the task better than most. 'Buyers are like football centre forwards, when their confidence is high they get more right than wrong,' he said. 'When their confidence is high they buy large quantities of a few lines – when it is low they buy a little of everything.' He got behind the selectors, urging them to buy long and deep, and they performed like stars. He was omnipresent in Baker Street and in the stores, where he would turn up with only a few moments' warning.

One group of people he stayed close to were the suppliers. Most of the heads of the longstanding regular M&S suppliers liked and admired Greenbury for his straightforward ways and underlying warmth. Like his predecessors, he treated them like partners; with most he lunched and dined, with some he played tennis, with others he went to the movies and with a favoured few he went on holiday.

In business he prided himself on being tough, fair and above all honest. 'I never lie,' he told Stella Shamoon, who interviewed him for the *Observer* in November 1991. 'No matter how hard the truth I am straightforward and do not try to hide or cover up the reality.' He might be defensive, excitable, irascible all within a few minutes – but at least what you saw was what you got.

But many felt he could only ever see anything from one point of view, that of Marks & Spencer, which was always on the side of the angels. One example of this was when M&S produced a line of skirts in a pattern that bore a startling resemblance to the famous Burberry check. Burberry called in the lawyers and in the ensuing meeting with executives from both sides it was plain to the lawyers present that the M&S camp could not understand what all the fuss was about. 'It was almost as though they felt Burberry should be flattered,' remarked one lawyer who was present.

Even so, Greenbury's imposing, forceful manner all too easily gave way to reveal a man of warmth and endearing lack of worldliness. Despite his power in business and his ability to pick up the phone to business and political leaders, Greenbury remained at his core almost childlike. After he was knighted in 1992 his burgundy Bentley bore the personalised numberplate SRG – for Sir Richard Greenbury. And like a child he was vulnerable, prone to tantrums. Naïve and irritating though such behaviour might be, close colleagues and suppliers alike responded emotionally to it.

At his London flat close to Baker Street, the shelves in his cosy sitting-room were crammed with pictures of his four children, at play, on holiday, getting married. There he would on occasion hold informal meetings, relaxed in his monogrammed Brooks Brothers shirt and casual shoes, drinking instant coffee from a Father Christmas novelty mug.

When he made the obligatory tour of a supplier's factory he may have lacked the showmanship and style of Sieff, but neither was he cold and aloof like Rayner. 'You got the feeling Rick was genuinely interested in the process, in what people were doing. He recognised their contribution,' said one supplier.

He was also totally loyal to people he trusted and, as was seen in the defence of Northern Foods against takeover threat, he would take action on their behalf. Another example came in February 1991, just before he became chairman, when a stock-market bear raid on Hillsdown's shares sent them into free fall. The rumour fuelling the collapse was that Marks & Spencer was unhappy with Hillsdown as a supplier.

Hillsdown's chairman Harry Solomon rang Greenbury for help but was told by his secretary Celia that he was in a board meeting. Solomon hesitated only a moment. To bother the chief executive of M&S in a board meeting would have seemed unwise to many, but Solomon knew his man. 'Celia,' he said, 'I would not normally ask this, but would you take a note in to Rick saying I need to speak to him urgently.' Within minutes Greenbury was on the phone. Solomon told him of the rumours regarding M&S and asked for assistance. Greenbury instantly summoned a press officer and instructed him to issue a denial of the rumour, stating that Hillsdown was one of M&S's most valued suppliers. 'It killed it and the shares started to recover,' recalled Solomon. 'I don't know how many other chief executives would come out of a board meeting to help a supplier; it was quite something.'

Greenbury's style in the boardroom was markedly different from Rayner's. Out went ninety-minute board meetings where debate was actively discouraged. In came board meetings that would run on and on, sometimes into the afternoons. 'I felt that the boardroom is where you make decisions and create policy,' said Greenbury. 'So when we made a decision in the boardroom, that is what we would get behind. Therefore everybody had got to speak their mind. On some issues I would force people to give their views.'

But there were problems with such a stance, problems that were later to prove so destructive to boardroom unity when trading began to deteriorate. Many of the executive directors did not say what they really thought. There were various possible reasons – many had been promoted by him and were weak or frightened or just could not see the point of subjecting themselves to the inevitable tirade.

Many of them too would have been canvassed ahead of the meeting. 'Rick would summon you to his office or ring you over the weekend to make sure you were onside over an issue he cared about,' said one former director. In reality, most issues were sorted that way with the executives before a board meeting – a practice that became more common as problems began to loom later in the decade.

One director put it this way: 'Rick had as much air time as we gave him – every time we were silent he would fill it. And people were reluctant to express their views; it was part of the culture.'

Greenbury disliked people coming to him after the board had voted an issue through and complaining. 'If they came to me and said they were worried about something I'd say: "Well, you had your chance to speak, the vote has been taken. You must either get behind it or leave the company."'

Greenbury described the first half of the 1990s as the happiest time in his career, and as the company shook off the malaise of the first two years it seemed he could do no wrong. In City lunchrooms where businessmen, bankers and analysts met to chew the fat, Greenbury's name was heard everywhere. He appeared to be refreshingly frank about almost everything, he played sport, enjoyed football, and had worked his way up the corporate ladder from a difficult start to the very top – in short, he was a man's man, a chief executive's chief executive. By 1993 his was the name on the business community's lips. In the summer of 1993 he came out well ahead of anyone else in a poll conducted by the *Independent on Sunday* asking top business-men who they most admired. A month later an analysis of press coverage showed M&S as the most favourably reported company. In the following January, NatWest Securities named Greenbury 'retailer of the year' for 1993.

Greenbury may have been feared within the confines of Baker Street – but in this he was no different from every chairman before him. As one of the non-executive directors put it: 'Most successful retailers are run by gifted dictators, and Rick was a dictator. The problem came when, after years of success, the company began to operate only to please Rick, not the customer.'

Behind his back his directors complained endlessly. 'We suffered years of brutalisation in the boardroom,' one grumbled to an analyst over lunch one day. 'So why stay?' asked the analyst. 'Well, there is the prestige of being a director of the best loved retailer in the land,' replied the director. 'There is a comfortable financial package, wonderful pension, great lunchrooms, a car and a driver, company tickets to the opera and first-class travel wherever and whenever you want it without questions.' To those who had escaped, M&S directors were like birds in a gilded corporate cage.

But to Greenbury's FTSE 100 index peers, many of them also dictators, he was a hero. If, in this clear blue sky, there was a cloud, no bigger than a man's hand, it was that of corporate governance. When Greenbury became both chairman and chief executive in 1991, Sir Adrian Cadbury was still nearly two years away from reporting his findings on how boardrooms should be run. When the report was published in 1993, Cadbury's committee recommended that the roles of chief executive and chairman should be split. The idea was to diffuse the power in order to prevent such rogues as Robert Maxwell, Asil Nadir and George Walker from wrecking public companies.

Yet even in 1991 the trend towards separating the roles was already apparent and there was some discontent from the more trenchant institutions at Greenbury combining the roles. David Rough, head of investment at Legal & General, was quoted as saying he preferred the roles of chairman and chief executive to be separated and a number of big fund managers agreed with him.

Such mutterings were summarily dismissed by an M&S spokesman who said: 'We have never subscribed to the view that the chairman takes care of strategy while the chief executive runs the business on a day to day basis. Our chairman has always taken a hands-on role.' Greenbury himself told one journalist, with typical directness, 'The idea that chairmen do the long-term stuff and the chief executive does the short-term stuff is rubbish, business school rubbish.'

At M&S, the tradition was firmly laid down that all powers resided in the chairman and this formula had proved so successful that in 1991 it barely occurred to anyone there that it should change. A couple of days before the announcement of the succession was due to go out, the company secretary popped into Greenbury's office to check the details of the proposed statement. 'Are you going to stay as chief executive as well,' he asked, 'or should we just drop it?' Greenbury told him to leave it in. 'That is how casual it was,' Greenbury later recalled.

The subject would come up periodically with the non-executives, but if Greenbury were to cease to be the chief executive and be chairman only, who then would be chief executive? The non-executives did not trust the aloof Keith Oates, the director of financial services, who was the obvious candidate, nor did they rate anyone else highly enough. So they backed off like a flock of ostriches burying their heads in the sand to avoid seeing the truth – there was no capable successor.

Rayner had advised Greenbury to appoint a deputy chairman he could trust, with whom he could talk any problems through. 'Marcus had me,' he told Greenbury, 'I have had you. There needs to be someone you can trust.' Rayner recommended Clinton Silver, who, already in his sixties, would never threaten Greenbury for the succession.

Silver was regarded as one of the great merchants of M&S and had been influential both in clothing and in building the food side. He came to the board in 1974, and he and Greenbury liked and respected each other. Although he was regarded by some as a corporate 'yes man' who slavishly followed his master's wishes, he inspired great affection among most of his colleagues and served as a valuable sounding board for Greenbury. Above all, Greenbury trusted him and valued his knowledge of the business – had they not both sat at the feet of Simon Marks in their youth? Although Sir Martin Jacomb was later to take on the role of confidant, as a lawyer turned investment banker he lacked Silver's deep understanding of the business.

Rayner, who had been well aware of Greenbury's egocentric character, was thinking of the greater good for the company when he made this suggestion. A couple of years before Greenbury took over, Rayner had twice summoned David Sieff to his office and warned him that when Greenbury became chairman, someone would 'need to watch Rick'. It is likely that suggesting Silver become deputy chairman was Rayner's way of making sure Greenbury had a balanced confidant at his side to guide him.

In his first year Greenbury promoted two divisional directors, Chris Littmoden and Paul Smith, to the board – both of them had formed strong relationships with him early in their careers. They were viewed as 'his boys'. Sir Martin Jacomb, a respected City figure who was chairman of Postel Investment Management, a director of the Bank of England and a former chairman of the investment bank Barclays de Zoete Wedd, was appointed a non-executive director in 1991. Jacomb brought with him considerable City credibility. Such was his reputation that when he later became non-executive chairman of the Prudential, M&S's biggest shareholder with around 7 per cent of the stock, nobody even brought up the possibility of a conflict of interest.

In 1993 the Cadbury Report recommended that where the chairman was also to be the chief executive there should be not fewer than five non-executive directors. Advised by Jacomb and John Broadbent Jones, Greenbury was already working on the issue and in the 1993 annual report there was a whole page devoted to the subject of corporate governance. The casual attitude was gone. 'At the specific request of the board, Sir Richard Greenbury is the chairman and chief executive of the company,' it stated, adding further on: 'As recommended by the Cadbury Report for cases where the chairman is also the chief executive, there are five experienced non-executive directors, who represent a source of strong, independent judgement.'

Jacomb had joined the former Tory cabinet minister Lady Young, Denis Lanigan, who had been chief executive of the advertising group J. Walter Thompson, and David Susman, one of the family members. Sir Ralph Robins, chairman of Rolls-Royce, was appointed in 1992, bringing their number to the requisite five. Yet Susman actually retired in 1993 and, as the fuss about Cadbury and corporate governance died down, there were for the next two years only four non-executive directors.

Then as the City mutterings about Greenbury splitting the roles grew louder again in 1996, two more heavyweights were added to the board – Sir Michael Perry, the astute former joint chairman of Unilever, and Brian Baldock, who had witnessed the near destruction of Guinness by Ernest Saunders from his vantage point as a director there. Intriguingly, both Perry and Robins came from companies where the roles of chairman and chief executive had also been combined, and they themselves had held both jobs.

During Greenbury's glory years such premier-league corporate heavyweights, with their busy portfolio careers, had little to do at M&S other than attend the monthly board meetings, enjoy their shared spacious offices in Baker Street, the delights of the directors' servery at lunchtime, a personal secretary and a chauffeur-driven car whenever they needed it. Brian Baldock, who had his own office, was the only one to be permanently based there, as he had promised Greenbury two days a week of his time.

None of them had any experience of retailing. The corporate governance guidelines decreed that non-executive directors had to have no conflicts of interest such as working for a competitor. This brought objectivity, but also lack of deep knowledge about the business they supposedly served. But Perry, Robins and Baldock did know about the importance of the brand and consumer marketing. Perry, in particular, had witnessed the furore over Persil Power, a brand of washing powder that, although it washed clothes wonderfully white, was proved to be less than beneficial to them.

The non-executive directors were paid between £25,000 and £50,000 for a ringside seat from which to watch the nation's most successful retailer in action. Lulled by the music of unceasing accolades and seduced by easy living, small wonder they failed to hear the distant ringing of alarm bells.

More questioning non-executives might have asked why Lord Rayner was given an office, a secretary and a car with a driver for a full five years after he had retired. Rayner stayed on as 'consultant' for Greenbury to chat to occasionally. When Silver retired in 1994, he too stayed on as a 'consultant', also with an office and a secretary. They might also have asked why directors' wives had the use of company cars, or why, until he became too ill to be moved, Marcus Sieff would be picked up in a company Bentley of an afternoon to be taken for a drive. If they did wonder, perhaps they told themselves that these were just the paternalistic quirks of a family business, and one that was doing very well indeed.

The first year of recovery, 1993, contained one incident that hinted at the nature of the trouble ahead. Keith Oates was a governor of the BBC and in March he had opposed the bizarre proposal that the BBC's new director general John Birt should be employed – for reasons that suited Birt – as a 'freelance' and not be on the payroll. The issue got banner headlines in the press. Yet it was not long before the media spotlight turned on Oates. The *Daily Mail* discovered that Oates, whose previous job as finance director of Thyssen Bornemisza was based in Monaco, had £80,000 of his M&S £400,000 salary paid into a Monaco bank account where it was not liable to UK tax. Oates still had a home in Monte Carlo – a famously sunny place for shady people – and the *Mail* labelled Oates as 'one of the Great Avoiders, the mega rich or middling rich people who escape much of the 40p in the pound tax burden on higher earners'. The paper carried a full-page story complete with a picture of the concierge at his Monaco home. The inference was that M&S was party to a tax dodge.

Greenbury reacted with typical fury and ordered an information blackout. All anyone, including Oates, was allowed to say was 'no comment'.

132

Oates's deputy, Robert Colvill, rang Tony Good, a public relations consultant who acted for the financial services arm, and asked him to go to Baker Street urgently and meet Oates. Good arrived to find Oates's office in chaos with secretaries fending off calls from around the world. He was desperate for help.

Oates explained to Good that when he joined M&S the Inland Revenue had said that provided he spent half his time outside the UK and maintained his Monte Carlo home, which as head of international operations as well as finance was not difficult, a fifth of his salary could be paid in Monaco. Good advised him to put out a statement saying just that to every newspaper and news agency. 'By the weekend it will be dead news,' he predicted.

Oates prevaricated. 'The chairman said we must make absolutely no comment,' he said. Good insisted Oates ring Greenbury to discuss it. A few minutes later Greenbury came storming into the room and before hearing Good's plan began threatening to sue the *Mail* if they carried on with the story. Good explained that suing newspapers generally cost a lot of money and achieved little. He asked Greenbury to read the statement. 'Is putting this out your considered advice?' enquired Greenbury, his mood changing. Good answered that it was. 'All right then, that is what you had better do,' said Greenbury and left the room.

After the statement duly went out the *Mail* and the *Telegraph* ran small articles on the affair and as Good had predicted, the story died by the weekend. The incident showed that Greenbury could listen and take advice from others, when it was obvious it made sense.

Greenbury's policies paid off. Pre-tax profits rebounded to £736m in 1993. By 1994 they were up at £851m. Greenbury, ever ambitious, could see that the magic £1bn was in sight during his chairmanship. 'Rick became obsessed with getting to the £1bn,' commented one former selector. 'Costs were constantly being hacked back. There were silly things like only being allowed to use one type of hanger to put everything on. You can't hang a T-shirt and a cashmere jumper on the same hanger, it just doesn't look right.'

In 1992 Alan Smith and Andy Lusher – whose son was married to Gabrielle Greenbury's sister Bernadette – retired as executive directors. Smith left to become chief executive to Geoff Mulcahy's chairman at Kingfisher. Greenbury said he warned Smith, who was later ousted in a power struggle with Mulcahy, not to go. But he refused to give Smith what he wanted – the assurance he would be promoted to managing director level. Twice Smith walked along the royal blue carpet to Greenbury's office to ask – and twice he was told he was merely in the running along with several other contenders. Opinion in M&S is divided about the talents of Smith. Those who worked directly for him found him to be extremely able – 'the most talented man we had', said one. Some of his fellow directors were in awe of his agile intellect while others considered him a little too keen on his own advancement. He was viewed as 'not a team player' and having worked at M&S for twenty-nine years, he soon fell foul of Kingfisher's more worldly corporate politics and was ousted in a boardroom clash with Mulcahy in 1995. In 1996 he took on the chairmanship of Storehouse which owned BHS and Mothercare, and in 2000 sold BHS on to Philip Green, while staying on as chairman of Mothercare. He also became a director of Colefax & Fowler, the upmarket furnishing company, and several smaller companies.

Rather than allow the boardroom to become smaller, Greenbury increased it, bumping up three divisional directors to the main board. They were Roger Aldridge, who ran property and store development, James Benfield, an arch corporate politician who oversaw the unlikely combination of childrenswear and home furnishings, and Joe Rowe, who had joined after a brief career at Unigate, and who was put in charge of foods.

Certain new 'powerhouse lines' emerged during the recession. Women's leggings was one. Classless, utilitarian but sexy, they came in cotton, velvet and satin mixed with the essential ingredient of Lycra, Du Pont's wonder yarn that gave stretch and cling. Well-off women tipped them into their baskets three or four pairs at a time at £20 a throw, while even those of modest means could afford one pair.

Then there was 'the body', which M&S described in 1993 as the biggest phenomenon since tights. The body was a garment that resembled a blouse, shirt or jumper but which fastened under the crotch with a row of poppers. Originating in America, it also used Lycra mixed with other yarns to create a lean, smooth line, putting an end to blouses 'riding up', bunching or billowing out. The growing confidence of Greenbury and his team is evident in the 1994 report and accounts, which devoted more space to new products and services than ever before. In a section on the body, M&S paid tribute to one long-term supplier, Textured Jersey, which had invested £1m in new machines to produce the fabric, Claremont Garments and Du Pont.

It was also a time of innovation in food, where, despite relatively high prices and huge expansion by the supermarkets, sales held up. In 1993 M&S began providing high-quality fresh meat, using only Aberdeen Angus beef for steak. Through its Scottish salmon subsidiary, Hillsdown began selling more smoked salmon and produced a smoked salmon mousse ring that became an instant best seller. At Northern Foods, forty-seven ingredients went into the Cantonese-style menu for two, including mushrooms and water chestnuts from China along with egg noodles made by a Chinese firm in the UK. New technology and growing techniques enabled British growers to supply fresh strawberries from April through to November.

Each weekend directors and executives took home food boxes to sample some of the 3,000-plus food lines. It was part of the all-enveloping culture at M&S. If you didn't eat M&S food all weekend and visit at least one store on a Saturday, your career would be blighted.

Another big change during the mid 1990s was the move to edge of town. As Buchan had pointed out, M&S had been left behind by the supermarkets, which had been much faster to spot the advantages of having a big selling space combined with easy parking. But Greenbury, having seen the success of the Cheshunt joint venture with Tesco, was determined to catch up. In 1991 three new stores were added, another four in 1992, one more in 1993 and another three in 1994 bringing the total to twelve. During these years capital spending was running at £300m a year, most of it going on the new stores as well as extensions to the biggest and best town-centre stores. Much less talked about was the quiet closing of smaller, non-profitable stores, often in depressed areas. From 1991 to 1998 the amount of selling space in the UK rose from 9.5 million square feet to 11 million and the number of edge-of-town stores to twenty-two. In 1999, in Greenbury's mistimed dash for growth, selling space jumped to 12 million square feet.

When critics later claimed that Greenbury had under-invested in the company and run it for short-term profits, he would always point to the capital expenditure figures, which rose dramatically towards the end of the decade, and the increase in square footage during his time. In 1995 capital spending jumped to £367m, retreated to £300m in 1996, then rose dramatically to £426m in 1997. In 1998 the Littlewoods acquisition pushed it up to £740m and the repercussions from that left it at £683m in 1999. Over Greenbury's nine years as chairman spending averaged £412m.

Some directors would point to down-at-heel stores, such as those in Kilburn or Rugby, filled with drab merchandise having not seen a penny of the spending for the previous nine years. Baldock frequently complained about his local store at Newbury and the non-executives would regularly relay their wives' complaints. Yet Greenbury, who was said to monitor the heartbeat of the Camberley store, near his Berkshire country home and naturally one of the brightest and best, appeared to ignore their comments. In order to get to his desired £1bn he knew he had to put maximum resources into the most profitable stores, and he had to push return on sales way above the 10 per cent his mentor Simon Marks decreed was the maximum for sustained profits growth.

Those new edge-of-town stores and big city-centre stores were the ones that made the most money. Not only did they attract higher sales, they had lower costs. Staff costs in those emporia ran at around 6 per cent while in the small to medium stores they could be as high as 12 per cent. By the late 1990s the twenty-two edge-of-town stores accounted for £2bn of sales or a quarter of the total – an astonishing figure out of a total of 290 stores. Greenbury drove this expansion hard, partly because he could see that M&S was trailing the competition and partly because these stores made huge profits. To his surprise, Greenbury discovered that the edge-of-town stores had little effect on the major city-centre stores to which they were close – so he embarked on adding extra footage to city-centre stores such as Newcastle, Edinburgh and Cardiff.

By 1998 the forty big city-centre stores, including 'The Arch' and the Pantheon, turned over another £2bn. In short, the top sixty M&S stores were making half the group's money.

About half the sales in the big stores came from clothes and furnishings from the growing homeware business, which only the bigger stores could display to proper advantage. In a big city-centre store such as Glasgow, sales of clothing and homeware would account for 80 per cent and only 20 per cent would be on food. But in the smaller high-street stores the reverse was true – only 20 per cent of sales would be on clothing while 80 per cent was on food. This in itself made the high-street stores less profitable, as the profit margin on food at 6 or 7 per cent was less than half that on clothing. Bigger stores with state-of-the-art systems and tills could also be managed by relatively fewer staff, also increasing their profitability.

There was also a second tier of provincial city stores that were expanded under Greenbury and each clocked up sales of £30m to £40m a year. But there were 160 smaller and medium stores that did little better than break even. 'We tried everything with those stores,' said Greenbury. 'We tried having food and basic women's clothing, or food and women's and children's clothing, but whatever we did never worked. We were in a mess. We could not sell them off and they were too big to make food only. We didn't spend on them, because we were not going to make money out of them.'

So Greenbury spent on the stores that made money, failing to understand the impact of the lack of spending on other stores. And, so, as the 1990s progressed, the image of the group became blurred. Was a Marks & Spencer store a spacious, gleaming, brightly lit emporium with all the latest bestselling lines, Italian suits, satin lingerie and cunningly designed homeware? Or was it some drab little shop on a provincial high street with the same boring old lambswool sweaters they had been selling for twenty years, but a useful selection of recipe dishes, fresh fruit and vegetables? Greenbury had made it clear where he thought the future lay.

Like Rayner, Greenbury also spent money overseas, but cautiously. His preferred target was Asia rather than America and by 1995 M&S had seven highly profitable Hong Kong stores as well as franchised operations in the Philippines, Singapore, Indonesia, Malaysia and Thailand. In Europe there were twenty-nine stores in France, Spain, Holland and Belgium and, despite sluggish growth, Keith Oates, who was by then in charge of international as well as financial operations, continued to push for more stores. Germany was added in 1996.

There is one other ingredient that fuelled the growth of the early 1990s: that of financial services – based coincidentally next to Keith Oates's former school in his home town of Chester. Overseen by Oates who was chairman, Robert Colvill the managing director and David Towell the day-to-day executive in charge were building a substantial business on the back of the Marks & Spencer brand. Financial services had its first significant mention in the chairman's statement in the annual report in 1994, when profits jumped by 40 per cent to £40m. Account-card business rose to 20 per cent of sales and nearly 4 million cards were in circulation. Oates oversaw the entry into personal loans and unit trusts and the following year he launched the company into pensions and life assurance. For longstanding customers who loved M&S for its reliability and quality it was the obvious choice.

Since its formation in 1985, financial services had been able to operate with little interference from Baker Street. Whenever Greenbury was in the area he would always visit the Chester store, but only occasionally pop into the financial services headquarters. Housed in an imaginatively designed building with many nautical features reflecting Colvill's passion for sailing, the airy open-plan offices with their communal eating area must have seemed like an alien world. And finance was not where Greenbury's heart or intellect lay. 'The further Rick was away from a knitwear checking list, the less comfortable he was,' commented one colleague. It is hard to say whether the team there felt unappreciated or relieved that they could get on with their job without interference – and they continued to advise against the company accepting outside credit cards without fear of opposition.

By 1994 Marks & Spencer was back on top as the retailer that would never let you down. So besotted were its customers that one woman was heard to remark that if she bought an M&S prepared meal and it was not as good as she expected, she felt she had done something wrong in heating it up. If a jumper did not emerge from the wash in perfect shape, well, the blame must lie with the washing machine. The belief within the company that every-thing it did was virtuous by definition had spread to the customer base. Career women delighted in buying an Armani lookalike suit for a fraction of the price and boasting it came from Marks & Spencer. Few middle-class dinner parties did not contain some component from M&S. Where else could you get a soup or ratatouille you could pass off as your own? Even top businessmen who still patronised Savile Row tailors stocked up on socks and underpants and even started buying a few cheap, but sound quality, shirts.

Innovation continued with a new range of classic, low-priced costume jewellery and in food new lines of low-fat and vegetarian dishes. The acco-lades flowed in. By 1994 the group had received the Queen's Award for Export Achievement four times.

There had been a moment in 1993 when Sainsbury, historically M&S's most fierce rival, snatched the title of 'most profitable retailer' from M&S when it lifted pre-tax profits to £733m. But a week later M&S trumped it with profits of £737m. Although both Lord (David) Sainsbury and Green-bury were ostensibly friends and would have denied it, the race was on to see which company could hit the magic £1bn first.

And so Marks & Spencer entered 1995 with its reputation and share rating higher than ever before. And as business school textbooks tell us, a company is most vulnerable at the point of its greatest success. Very gradually, that small cloud drifting in the clear blue sky was joined by others. The biggest, darkest cloud of all was labelled succession, one that contained its very own storm system. But even those who noticed it could never have predicted the mayhem that lay waiting just three years further on.

# CHAPTER EIGHT

# *Storm clouds*

In July 1994 Clinton Silver retired as deputy chairman after forty-two years' service with the company. He was 65. Greenbury kept him on as a consultant with an office near his on the first floor of Baker Street, ostensibly to give guidance to the younger directors, but Silver was officially no longer part of the business. He became chairman of the British Fashion Council in early 1994 and from then on most of his energies went into revitalising it. The following October, Marks & Spencer received the British Fashion Council's award for the top retailer of classic clothing – the first time a chain store had been so honoured.

Greenbury lost the last person on the board that he truly respected, a man whom he would always describe as 'a great merchant', someone as steeped in the Simon Marks era as he had been. He lost his safety valve, the colleague with whom he could talk contentious things over and thus vent his anger harmlessly. He lost the last person he trusted always to put the interests of Marks & Spencer before his own. In turn, the company lost the man who, in his own gentle way, had been 'watching out for Rick'.

At 57, Greenbury had seen off his senior contemporaries and all of his fellow executive directors were in their forties or early fifties. Six of those directors had been promoted on to the board by him – Jim Benfield, Clara Freeman, Derek Hayes, Chris Littmoden, Joe Rowe and Paul Smith. Many of those who remained at the divisional director level just below the board claimed the new directors were selected for their perceived loyalty to Greenbury rather than their talent. Even allowing for some sour grapes, it was true that none of them posed a real threat to his leadership. Most of them would have liked his job – who would not want to head the land's most loved retailer? – yet none appeared cut out to do it successfully.

The two remaining family directors, David Sieff, then 55, and John Sacher, then 53, were too close to Greenbury in age to succeed him and in any case had realised, not without some bitterness, that they were not considered chief-executive material. Paul Smith, Nigel Colne and Don Trangmar were considered too close in age to succeed him, leaving a bunch of relatively young men – the Young Turks – as contenders for the succession.

The M&S board began to resemble a medieval court, with Greenbury as king surrounded by ambitious barons each hoping that he might claim the throne. In many ways that was how things had been since Simon Marks's day, but there were two crucial differences. First, the bloodline had been broken after Lord Sieff had retired and second, for the first time in the company's history, there was no obvious successor, no heir apparent. Greenbury was all too aware of the potential problems. 'The succession had been bothering Rick since around 1992. I remember him talking about it then and saying it would be difficult – but nobody realised how difficult,' said one director. But he fudged and never effectively addressed the problem.

One disastrous mistake Greenbury and the non-executive directors made was to underestimate the intensity of Keith Oates's ambition. Oates was the man who most passionately would be king. After joining the company in 1984 he built up the financial services business, but once that was established he lifted his eyes to the next mountain top, which to his annoyance was already occupied. Tall, dark and aloof, Oates even looked the part of a conspirator, although in the end he would see himself as a victim. Ultimately his overweening ambition would drive him to try to overthrow Greenbury in November 1998.

When Clinton Silver retired that event was four years away, but Oates's ambition already burned bright. On Monday 23 August 1993 Greenbury hosted a long lunch meeting in his office to outline to his key directors his plan for a new board structure. The plan was designed in part to address the succession and pacify Oates, whom Greenbury knew had aspirations to be chief executive under his chairmanship – as he himself had been under Rayner. Having previously discussed it with the non-executive directors, Greenbury told the executives round the table that he had decided to create three new joint managing directors and promote Oates – currently joint managing director with Silver – to deputy chairman on Silver's retirement the following year. This plan – rather like a sports contest – was devised in the hope that, given new responsibility and power, one of the four would come through as the clear successor. In reality it was a plan that created huge tension and acrimony between the four men and their supporters, distracting them from their primary purpose of running the business.

Oates was delighted when Greenbury told him that he was now deputy chairman elect. Greenbury expected opposition from some board members, as Oates was not a 'merchant retailer' as Clinton had been. But according to those present, he doused Oates's pleasure by making it elaborately clear that his role would be merely to chair board meetings in his absence, and that this did not put Oates in line to be chief executive or chairman.

Oates remained in charge of finance and international operations as he had been while simply joint managing director, but Silver's area of general merchandise was divided into three. The business had grown so huge, Greenbury argued, that it would take three men to cope with it.

Andrew Stone, whom Greenbury regarded as the most talented merchant in the company, at 51 became joint managing director in charge of merchandise. Despite his creative talents, Stone, who had started his career on a market stall and had been plucked out of the ranks to be Marcus Sieff's assistant, was viewed as too undisciplined to head the company. Greenbury and Stone would have heated arguments. 'Half the time Rick just didn't understand what Andrew was trying to say. They were so different from each other they had huge problems communicating,' said a friend of both. 'Rick bullied Andrew unmercifully, he would humiliate him publicly,' said another. 'But Andrew was like a little puppy dog who would come bounding back for more.' Yet Greenbury would say he had huge respect for Stone: 'Some of Andrew's ideas were so off the wall they had to be curbed but he was a true creative spirit.'

Peter Salsbury, the youngest at 44, headed personnel, store operations and development, while the charmingly ineffectual Guy McCracken, 45, was put in charge of food. 'Guy was lovely, but he was overpromoted,' one of his juniors remarked. 'He just could not take tough decisions.'

There were some – including Oates, it is said – who believed the new structure was simply a tactic by Greenbury and the non-executives to block Oates. Even then Salsbury, who had been made a director by Rayner but with Greenbury's support, looked the most likely to succeed. 'There was never any chance that Keith would get it,' said one supplier. 'It was always going to be Peter.'

Oates wasted little time before making his feelings clear. A few days after the lunch he paid Greenbury a visit in his office. It started pleasantly. He thanked Greenbury for his confidence and assured him of his loyalty and determination to continue helping the company to expand successfully. But then his tone changed. He declared that he would never be happy to work for any of the new managing directors. They lacked his experience and maturity, he argued, claiming he was much more capable than them.

Greenbury would have none of this. He again made it clear that being appointed deputy chairman did not put Oates in pole position to succeed him. Oates retreated, appearing to accept his lot, but then called for another meeting a couple of weeks later. This time he did not prevaricate. To Greenbury's astonishment, he demanded to be made chief executive immediately, claiming that people both inside the business and outside – referring to his friends in the City – were expecting that to happen.

Once again he expressed his lack of confidence in the abilities of the three new managing directors.

Greenbury was horrified and told Oates: 'There is no question of you becoming chief executive in the near future.' He added that he had no intention of making a recommendation for anyone to be chief executive until a year or so before his retirement, which although officially still scheduled for 1996, was in Greenbury's mind several years away. When Oates protested that Greenbury had been chief executive for the last two years of Rayner's chairmanship, Greenbury angrily accused him of pushing him into early retirement and threatened to take the matter to the board.

At that point Oates could see that, if it came to that, the board would back Greenbury and his career at M&S would be over. So he retreated and apologised. But this was just a tactical retreat – a withdrawal from a battlefield to which he would later return with, he hoped, suitable reinforcements.

Perhaps to soften the blow, Greenbury explained to Oates that no non-merchant had ever headed M&S. If Oates seriously aspired to the leadership he would have to win over the bulk of the directors, including the non-executives and the suppliers. He would need to get out of his offices in Baker Street and Chester and start breaking bread with the suppliers. He had to visit more stores and talk to staff and customers.

Greenbury believed he was putting Oates off, giving him a clear signal that he would never run Marks & Spencer. Oates, on the other hand, took Greenbury's words as a sign of hope.

Beneath the veneer of civility Greenbury and Oates thoroughly disliked each other. The Lancastrian Oates viewed the Yorkshireman Greenbury as insular and ill educated, the product of an era when business was far less complicated. Greenbury, ever mindful of his own lack of higher education, felt threatened by Oates's financial expertise and his academic prowess as a graduate of the London School of Economics and Manchester University. Their only common ground was football, and every now and then they would go to matches together, Oates supporting Chelsea, Greenbury, his beloved Manchester United. They rarely argued about company matters, because although Greenbury loved an argument, he preferred to pick his own ground where he could win. He knew little about finance and so there were hardly ever confrontations between him and Oates on that.

In private, Greenbury dismissed Oates as a mere 'bean counter', a view shared by many on the board. Oates was unpopular with many of his fellow directors, who disliked his air of superiority. His critics claimed he would take the credit for successful projects leaving others to take the blame for failures. But those who worked closely with him, such as Robert Colvill and Paul Smith, and who therefore saw behind his taciturn façade, rated him highly. 'He was good to work with,' said Smith, who reported to him when based in the Far East. 'He had a clear brain and was a good delegator who let you get on with the job. He told you soon enough if he thought you were making mistakes, but on the whole he left you alone.'

If Greenbury believed Oates would get the message, he was to be disappointed. One friend outside the company remembered Oates talking optimistically about the new structure: 'Keith had been made deputy chairman, his package was well above that of the other managing directors and his office was just along the corridor from Rick's on the first floor. He believed he was in line for the top job.' People outside the company also believed he was destined for the top, something suggested by the invitations he received to join the boards of Guinness (later Diageo) and British Telecommunications as a non-executive director.

Oates still fondly believed that Greenbury would retire in 1996 on his sixtieth birthday, as had been stated in the official announcement when he was appointed. Oates, who by then would be 54, was a suitable age to succeed him. In this he was naïve. Even a cursory reading of Marks & Spencer's history, and in particular the volume of Lord Sieff's memoirs that David Sieff gave him within days of his arrival, would have shown him that no previous chairman had ever retired before reaching 65. And Greenbury had always said that, in an ideal world, it was his dream to be like his predecessors and to stay on as chairman until he was 65.

So the king of Baker Street initiated a policy of divide and rule among the barons and, like many a medieval court, the board of Marks & Spencer broke into factions. There was the 'let's keep Greenbury in power, he is our best shot' faction, the 'Keith Oates is intellectually superior and should be chairman' group and the 'let us back Peter Salsbury, the Young Turk for chief executive' band. Salsbury had formed a close alliance with Clara Freeman, who had been made a director in 1995 following increasingly vocal pressure at annual meetings from shareholders to have a woman executive on the board. She was put in charge of personnel under Salsbury, although her history had been in buying. The dapper James Benfield headed the Salsbury supporters. He had been given the task of defending M&S against the 1996 *World in Action* programme that accused one of its suppliers of using child labour.

Andrew Stone filled the role of court jester. Charming and witty, he was known as much for his fertile mind and creative ideas as for his inability to manage people. He was also the most conspicuous womaniser since Marcus Sieff, whom he had witnessed in action as his personal assistant, with a reputation for flirting outrageously with pretty young selectors keen on promotion.

Although Greenbury had made him a managing director, it was never clear that Stone actually wanted to be chief executive. 'He liked the idea of it, but he knew he was not chief executive material,' said one colleague. 'The responsibility would have made him miserable.' Like many who are blessed with great charm, Stone's egocentric behaviour went against him. 'He was a loose cannon,' one colleague said simply.

There were three directors who backed Oates in the succession race, believing that, as an international businessman, he had superior credentials to the M&S lifers to lead what had become a complex, global business. These were Robert Colvill, the finance director whom Oates had recruited, Paul Smith, in charge of the Far East, and Chris Littmoden, who headed the United States operations. All three reported to Oates and all three had seen enough of the outside world to believe that a lifetime education in Baker Street might not be enough to equip someone for modern business. 'I genuinely believed that Keith would make a good chairman,' said Colvill.

Oates complained later that most of his colleagues treated him as an outsider – yet they felt he made little attempt to integrate. He rated himself above his fellow directors, but he lacked the common sense to see that winning over Greenbury was the route to the top. He might have cultivated those close to the chairman such as Clinton Silver. Yet Silver remembered that Oates never once sought his counsel about business. 'It was always clear he held the culture of M&S in contempt,' he said.

Oates rarely walked the corridors or visited colleagues in their offices. He had decorated his own office with dark murals and there he would stay, summoning others to his lair. Colleagues recognised his financial ability, international experience and agile intellect, but most didn't feel at ease with him. 'You could never get a straight answer out of Keith,' said one. 'You never knew what he was thinking.'

Oates's hope that Greenbury would go soon after reaching 60 in 1996 received a rude jolt in the summer of 1995 when the following communication from the company secretary, John O'Neill, arrived on his desk. Addressed to the members of the board it was headed 'The Office of Chairman' and read:

> When Sir Richard was appointed Chairman he agreed to serve in that role until the age of 60. For a Chairman of Marks and Spencer to leave office at 60 is a departure from the long established custom of the Company and it is inconsistent with the 1988 Hambleton Hall discussions ... which declared that the Chairman would normally be expected to serve until 65. In fact no Chairman in the Company's history has left office earlier than the attainment of that age.
>
> Following recent discussions with the Non-Executive and Executive Directors, the Chairman has now agreed to serve until his 65th birthday – subject to his health permitting it. Additionally he has proposed that from and after his 62nd birthday his position should be reviewed by the Board on an annual basis and to assist that review the Board should have the benefit of recommendations from the Non-Executive Directors as to whether his role as Chairman should continue to be Executive. It is now proposed that the outcome of these informal discussions be formally noted by the Board and recorded in the minutes.

To Oates, the memo must have read like a death knell to his ambition. The stark truth hit him – if Greenbury stayed on until he was 65, Oates at 59 would be too old to succeed him. The non-executive directors had finally woken up to the uncomfortable truth that none of the managing directors would be ready to take over as chief executive in 1996, when Greenbury would be 60. They could also see that Greenbury showed no inclination to leave. At the time he was at the peak of his powers – the business leader *du jour*. Marks & Spencer's reputation had rarely been higher. Under Greenbury the group had not only weathered one of the worst economic storms of the century, it had 'killed the competition' – although many had aided their own destruction – and profits had risen by 50 per cent from £615.5m to £924.3m in the four years to the end of March 1995. This jump in profits had been achieved on sales up by only 18 per cent. The warning signs that the company was squeezing profits out of cost cutting were already there, but there had been plenty of costs to cut and nobody at the time complained. Certainly the City did not, reaping the benefits of a rising share price, and neither did the independent non-executive directors.

And so, faced with the idea that this miracle worker – the best chairman since Simon Marks – might disappear in 1996 leaving the group in a much less experienced pair of hands, the board voted to keep him on. The preparatory memo from John O'Neill gave a wonderful insight into how things were done. In line with boardroom protocol Greenbury left the board meeting before the formal discussion, but in fact he had orchestrated what would happen.

Greenbury had the best job in town – he could pick up the phone to international business leaders and heads of state and be confident of getting through. Wherever he went he heard nothing but praise for himself and his company. But there was still one ambition which was unfulfilled. All of his predecessors had been honoured with peerages – and so far that ultimate accolade had eluded him.

As indicated by the memo from O'Neill, Greenbury had discussed the idea that he stay on with most of the executives. As was his custom, he summoned directors to his office or rang them at home in the evenings or at the weekend to sound out their views. 'Are you behind me or not?' he would ask. And on this particular issue, no one would ever say, 'No, Rick, I think it is time for a change.'

At the board meeting the business was quickly despatched. The board minutes of 2 August 1995 read thus: 'Sir Martin Jacomb reported that the non-executive directors had discussed the matter with the chairman, who had expressed a willingness to serve in his present capacity until the age of 62 and the board expressed its intention that this should be the case.'

The minutes continued: 'Any period of office thereafter would be reviewed by the board on an annual basis, such a review to be initiated by the then serving non-executive directors arranging board discussions of the nature noted in this minute.' Greenbury had objected to the insertion of an annual review – on the grounds that it made him look as if he were on trial – but the non-executive directors persuaded him of its correctness.

*Board asked him to stay*

From then on Greenbury would confidently declare to anyone who accused him of hanging on to power that 'the board unanimously asked me to stay'. The reality was that the board could see no viable alternative to Greenbury within the company. 'I do not recall him ever actually being asked to stay on,' said one director who was there at the time. 'Rather it was a case of him gathering support ahead of board meetings and nobody daring to oppose him.'

The board's mistake was to believe that an alternative leader would mysteriously arise from the mists like a young Arthur to pull the sword from the stone. For this the non-executives must take responsibility. 'We should have started looking outside at that point,' said David Sieff. 'But to be honest I did not believe the company was ready for that much change at the top.'

Following the board's decision Oates became a man obsessed. 'He did become a little strange after that,' remarked a friend. But it was not just blinding ambition that gripped him. Oates told friends he felt it was his duty to rid Marks & Spencer of Greenbury – that Greenbury had become a force that was out of control and therefore ultimately bad for the company and its shareholders.

As for Greenbury, it seems the success of his early years as chairman gradually blunted his antennae. 'All the family chairmen if they met you in the corridor would always ask the same question: "What is new?"' recalled one director. 'Rick stopped doing it. It was a part of the family history he had forgotten.' Greenbury loved to visit M&S stores but he rarely visited his rivals – in fact he found it distasteful even to contemplate that they might be doing something worth copying. Travelling always by chauffeur-driven Bentley, Concorde, private plane or first-class rail, he began to lose touch with ordinary people – the customers of Marks & Spencer.

There was also a good deal more on his mind in 1994 than the succession. One subject that preoccupied him was the quandary of how to build on the success of the past four years. One solution would be to engage in a corporate merger to form a dynamic new force in British retailing and find a new road to growth.

Marks & Spencer had never made a corporate acquisition in Britain – it

148

had never been that type of company. The takeover boom of the 1980s may have spurred Rayner to overpay for Brooks Brothers in the United States, but at home M&S had grown organically, expanding the square footage in its existing stores, opening new stores and extending into different geographical areas. In his day, Lord Sieff had been great friends with Lord (Victor) Rothschild of NM Rothschild, the investment bank – and together they had orchestrated mergers between suppliers. But once Sieff retired the relationship weakened – although Bob Pirie at NM Rothschild did advise Rayner on the Brooks Brothers deal.

In the 1990s M&S listed Cazenove as its stockbroker but did not retain any one investment bank as its official financial advisor, a fact that encouraged bankers to pound on the company's door for business. One of them was an American called Bob Hamburger, who in the 1980s worked for Goldman Sachs, a Wall Street firm that had set up in London and was infuriating the UK banks with its un-British aggressive wooing of clients. Hamburger had first come into contact with M&S in Rayner's day when the bank had created the first sterling commercial paper note, a form of borrowing, for the company, working with the former M&S finance director John Samuel. In the late 1970s Goldman Sachs also helped M&S to attain the much-coveted tripple A credit rating from Standard & Poors and Moody's – a first for a British company – which it lost in 2000 after the profits collapse.

By 1985 Hamburger had moved to become head of European operations at Smith Barney, another American bank. He kept in touch with Greenbury, sensing he would be the next chief executive of M&S, and also courted Lord (Leonard) Wolfson at Great Universal Stores, founded by his father Sir Isaac Wolfson and a major force in mail order clothing. GUS, or Gussies as it was affectionately known in the stock market, dominated the mail order scene in Britain rather as M&S dominated the high street. But like M&S it was a mature business and Wolfson was well aware of this. In fact his father, concerned for the economic future of Britain, had begun courting Sears Roebuck, the powerful American mail order retailer, as far back as the 1960s and Wolfson junior had carried on the courtship for some years. But the Chicago-based company had eventually backed away, fearful of the commercial climate in Britain in the 1970s when Labour was in government.

But as the takeover boom of the 1980s gathered momentum Wolfson began to cast around once again for a suitor for the company. A former colleague at GUS recalled: 'Leonard, like his father, wanted a home for GUS and he had come to the conclusion that it should be M&S.'

Hamburger rang Greenbury and arranged to see him at his Baker Street office, where he set out a scheme to merge GUS with Marks & Spencer.

At the time Rayner was still chairman and the idea did not get off the ground. But in 1994 Hamburger again made the journey to Baker Street and once more spelled out his detailed plan for an agreed merger between M&S and GUS to Greenbury. Hamburger thought the two companies would make such a good marriage that he codenamed the proposed deal Project Heaven.

Indeed, in many ways the idea seemed inspired. GUS was the market leader in mail order, M&S was the clothing market leader in the high street. M&S had Brooks Brothers while GUS owned Burberry, another classy international brand. Wolfson and his team at GUS saw that this could be a winning combination for expansion in the United States. In addition, GUS owned a property company and CCN, the leading credit-card creditation company, a business that was extensively used by M&S Financial Services.

Both companies had similar histories – created by one entrepreneurial genius and family dominated in their culture – with one important difference. While the Wolfson family had kept an iron grip on the majority of the voting shares through a series of trusts, once the M&S shares became enfranchised in 1966 the family shareholdings became diluted and dispersed.

Both companies had ambitions in the United States – they wanted to use Brooks Brothers and Burberry to build serious businesses there. Most compelling of all was the financial synergy. GUS had invested heavily in developing state-of-the-art mail order and delivery systems and was years ahead of M&S on new technology. Merging the two companies could have saved up to £2bn, not to mention the huge operational gains a merger would achieve.

Wolfson and Greenbury already knew each other well from the corporate circuit. They would also meet up sometimes in Venice, where they both spent a week's holiday every spring at the Cipriani Hotel across the lagoon from the main island.

At the beginning of the talks Greenbury and Wolfson met several times for lunch at Claridge's in London's Mayfair to discuss the merger. They got on well and both saw the exciting potential for the giant retailing empire they could create. The combined group would have been worth around £20bn – big money in 1994 – making it far and away the biggest UK retailer by market value and on a par with the biggest groups overseas.

One of the key issues was the respective roles of the two men. Wolfson, who was nine years older than Greenbury and who indirectly controlled the ownership of GUS through a number of trusts, favoured becoming non-executive chairman to Greenbury's chief executive.

But once the discussion was extended to include the M&S board problems soon emerged. The main opposition came from Keith Oates who, according to those present at the meetings, believed that M&S could not handle such a big acquisition and that the two cultures would clash. He felt that M&S would not be able to take advantage of the GUS operations and would end up imposing the home culture on everything, thus losing the benefit. There were a number of meetings with Oates, Clinton Silver and Greenbury together with Hamburger, Wolfson and other key executives. To the GUS camp Oates seemed to be set on over-analysing the situation and putting obstacles in the way of the deal.

There may have been a more personal reason for Oates opposing the merger. He still believed he was in line to be chief executive of M&S and he must have feared that it would be impossible for him to rise to the top of a combined group. But there were, in fact, few M&S directors who supported the idea. GUS had always operated with a very small holding board of directors, where M&S had sixteen executives plus five non-executives. Part of the plan was to slim the board of the new company down to around nine – so a vote for the deal was, for many, effectively a vote for their own demotion. M&S directors were also opposed to the idea of Wolfson becoming chairman – even though the role would have been non-executive – because M&S had always had an executive chairman. An alternative would have been to make him life president, as Marcus Sieff had been. But in the end the enclosed world of M&S could not entertain the idea of so much change.

Hamburger and his team worked long and hard on the logistics of the deal. Agreed mergers are more complicated than straight takeovers, as the needs and egos of both sides have to be considered. As talks progressed, Greenbury became concerned that M&S had no knowledge of mail order and would be entirely reliant on GUS for all expertise in that area. He was also worried by the competition from the new breed of slicker, high-fashion mail order companies that were growing rapidly. In the end, his nervousness and the strong opposition from M&S directors who feared for their positions in the new entity, led a disappointed Greenbury to write to Wolfson telling him the board had decided against going forward. Although discussions lasted a number of months and involved directors from both companies plus Hamburger's corporate finance team, there was never even a hint of the talks in the press. Project Heaven was mothballed without the shareholders ever knowing how close they had come to the pearly gates.

An even bigger distraction from the main business of running Marks & Spencer came from John Major's government. On 20 November 1994 the *Sunday Times* broke the story that British Gas had given its chief executive, Cedric Brown, a 75 per cent pay rise from £270,000 to £475,000. Coming at a time when many homeowners were still struggling with negative equity and many people were out of work following the recession, the newspapers played up the story for all it was worth. The picture of Brown in a shapeless anorak at the gate of his country house was one of the enduring images of the decade. He was dubbed a 'fat cat' and the term soon spread to describe any public company executive who received a pay increase higher than inflation. Fuelled by Gordon Brown, then shadow chancellor, yards of column inches were devoted to scathing articles about 'fat cattery' in an orgy of judgemental journalism that harked eerily back to the 1970s when businessmen had been viewed as social pariahs. For a while, it was as if Margaret Thatcher and her rampant capitalist ethos had never existed.

The prime minister was quick to act in an attempt to quell the hysteria and to deflect pressure on him to legislate to curb salary rises. Major seized on an initiative by the Confederation of British Industry to set up a committee of top executives to design a code of practice for companies on executive pay. The man he chose to chair the committee was Greenbury. Once again a Conservative prime minister, like Heath and Thatcher before him, turned to an M&S chairman to solve the nation's problems.

When first approached by Michael Heseltine, then Trade and Industry Secretary, Greenbury baulked. He had his hands full and he knew it. But he and John Major had become friends. Marks & Spencer was a regular if modest contributor to Tory party funds and Greenbury would attend high-profile dinners for business leaders at Downing Street – the subject of scathing attacks by Labour. He and Major found they had much in common. Both men had scaled the heights of their respective careers from modest backgrounds and both had been influenced by strong mothers in their childhoods. Both had left school with only O' levels and shared an enthusiasm for sport, particularly for cricket and football – Major supported Chelsea, Greenbury Manchester United. They both had young adult children of similar ages, although one of Major's seemed more accident prone.

In 1993, Major's son James joined M&S as a management trainee at the Cambridge store, where he soon became attracted to his supervisor, Elaine Jordache, some thirteen years older than him. Her husband, Michael Jordache, reportedly first noticed their closeness at a pyjama party at his house, when he found Major junior and his wife entwined. Jordache subsequently divorced Elaine, citing James Major in the action. He then told the tabloids how the prime minister's son had 'ruined his life'. The tabloids had great fun trailing the couple, at one point following them on holiday to the South of France, before James Major broke off the relationship.

But perhaps more than anything else, Greenbury and Major shared the loneliness of high office and during the recession-hit early 90s they would spend evenings together at the Downing Street flat, talking through their various problems over informal suppers.

So when Major appealed to Greenbury for a second time, he felt he could not refuse. Duty called and he might also have hoped that such an act of public service would produce the coveted peerage. It is tempting to speculate what his personalised number plate on his Bentley might have read had it been forthcoming – just LG or perhaps TLG – but it was not to be.

At that point the non-executive directors of M&S might have complained that such an exercise would be too time consuming and forbidden him to do it. Alternatively, they could have insisted he become non-executive chairman at that point on the grounds that compiling the report would take up most of his time for the next six months. But, surprisingly, they actively encouraged him to do it. 'It got him out of everyone's hair,' said one pointedly. 'And we felt it would allow acorns to grow into trees, which they could not under such a big personality.'

On 16 January 1995 the official announcement that Greenbury was to head a special group on pay was released. Greenbury was joined by a heavyweight cast of business leaders including David Simon, then chief executive of British Petroleum, Whitbread chairman Sir Michael Angus and Sir Denys Henderson, then ICI chairman. The deadline was tight for such a group of busy men – the report had to be ready for publication by July.

Meanwhile problems began piling up in Greenbury's personal life. His marriage to Gabrielle was showing signs of stress. Greenbury liked to work, play tennis, have dinner with colleagues or suppliers and work some more. Gabrielle, a vivacious, stylish woman twenty years his junior – who would arrive in the office dressed in her leather biker's gear after a fast ride to work on her Harley Davidson – liked to party, to ski, to have fun. Although she was more involved with Marks & Spencer than Greenbury's first wife Siân had been, she found living with a man she hardly saw, and with whom she had little in common, increasingly difficult.

The chasm opening up between them grew as Greenbury's health deteriorated. He was beginning to pay the price for being an active sportsman, with his right hip causing him pain. A consultation with William Muirhead-Allwood – a leading specialist who had operated on the Queen Mother – showed he needed a hip replacement. (Later the surgeon would make tabloid headlines when he announced his intention to have a sex change and be known as Sarah.)

But the operation would require a three-month recuperation period, and, faced with having to produce the Greenbury Report by July, he decided to defer. It was a mistake. By the late spring he was nearly crippled and in extreme pain, despite taking very strong painkillers.

Fellow guests at a Tory Party fundraiser hosted by Lord and Lady Harris at their country house one perfect summer day in June were struck by the change in him. The guests, a mixture of entrepreneurs such as furniture king Graham Kirkham, later Lord Kirkham, top corpocrats and senior politicians, sipped champagne on a terrace enjoying one of the finest views of the Kent countryside. But Greenbury, who had been walking with great difficulty aided by a stick, was forced by the pain to sit on the low wall surrounding the terrace. Major was soon at his side, comforting him and attempting to take his mind off it. 'They obviously had a deep friendship and it was clear that Major was really worried about Rick,' said one observer.

It is unclear whether it was his hip problem or the Greenbury Report that proved too much for his relationship with Gabrielle, but by the time the summer was over, so was their marriage. Greenbury returned to the comforting embrace of his first wife Siân, whom he remarried in 1996. Generously, she moved into the Berkshire home he had bought with Gabrielle and put her own stamp on the house, most significantly transforming Gabrielle's spacious gym into a music room complete with piano.

154

During its six-month investigation the Greenbury committee received 3,000 pages of advice and the august members found it difficult to agree on almost anything. When the report was published on Monday 18 July it sparked a row over the recommendations regarding share options. Martin Taylor, the public relations voice of Lord Hanson (not the former journalist who became chief executive of Courtaulds and then Barclays), contributed a guest article for the Personal View column of the *Financial Times*. In it he pointed out that the recommendations to treat profits from share options as income, rather than capital gains, and to make employees pay the tax at the time of exercise, rather than when the shares were sold, would hit middle and junior managers hardest. It would mean that many would be forced to sell their shares to raise money to pay the tax on their notional profits, rather than hold them for the longer term. Taylor made an all too valid point: 'Taxing individuals when they do not have the resources out of which to pay the tax cannot be a fair way to proceed and will foster the sort of short-termism the government is anxious to avoid.'

The point was taken up by commentators throughout the business press and viewed as an inexcusable blunder. Perceived as the personification of fat cats themselves, the members of the Greenbury committee were fair game. On Friday 21 July Greenbury himself was summoned to appear before the House of Commons employment select committee chaired by Labour's Greville Janner, who clearly relished every moment. Almost immediately Greenbury revealed that he personally, along with Sir Michael Angus, had expressed reservations about the share option proposals, distancing himself from the very committee he had chaired. 'Did you want everyone to be taxed on share options, including those low down?' asked Harry Greenway, a Conservative MP.

'No,' replied Greenbury. 'It is no secret that I personally had reservations about this recommendation.' In answer to further questioning he added, 'We didn't think it through because we made a recommendation that was obviously too broad and I accept that was a mistake.'

Then in classic style he poured out his heart, declaring: 'My personal life has been affected to an unbelievable degree. My son, who is a school teacher, has been telephoned on numerous occasions, my present wife has been subjected to harassment and for reasons unbeknown to me, my first wife has been pestered on her doorstep by photographers.'

He also stressed the difficulties of achieving consensus. 'Nobody agrees with anybody else, which makes it extremely difficult to steer a sensible course. I can't begin to solve the problem of pay and rations in the UK.'

The formal proceedings over, he opened his briefcase. There on top lay a red apron, which he had received that morning from the Harry Truman Society in America, to which he subscribed. A bright spark in the gallery spotted it and asked to have a look. In an ingenuous gesture wholly typical of the man, Greenbury held up the apron for everyone to see. 'Put it on,' called someone, so he slipped it over his head to popping flashbulbs. The words printed in large letters on the apron read: 'If you can't stand the heat get out of the kitchen' – the motto of his hero Truman. There was a ripple of laughter, but the picture went around the world, a prophetic image of things to come. Within a week there was an emergency meeting between the committee members and Treasury and Inland Revenue officials and the option clause was changed. But the row over various details rumbled on for the rest of the year.

Greenbury later described 1995 and 1996 as 'the unhappiest two years of my life'. As a result of the Greenbury Report he became public property, something he might have foreseen but that caused him immense emotional pain. Greenbury had always struggled to handle criticism of any kind, and the gratuitous personal jibes that now came his way made him furious and miserable.

The episode highlighted his lack of worldliness. He had gone, with no professional advice, into the public arena, and his reputation had been torn to shreds by the wolves of Westminster and Fleet Street. In some ways he never recovered his confidence. 'He became edgy and paranoid after the Greenbury Report,' commented one friend. 'He never seemed quite as relaxed and gung ho.'

In the late summer he had his operation and was effectively out of action for six weeks. Did he take his eye off the corporate ball during that time, fuelling Oates's resentment? In some ways he did. Already myopic in his focus on the business, he paid even less attention to the outside world than usual.

But in other ways he became more obsessive and his already volatile temper grew even more unpredictable. Spurred on by the prospect of £1bn profits he pushed ahead with opening more edge-of-town footage and encouraged his directors to pare costs even further. Always hands-on, particularly in the buying departments, he now became even more controlling.

One small incident highlighted the way things were. At the time Jock Green-Armytage was chief executive of William Baird, a major M&S supplier. In that summer the company had produced a particularly stylish line of polka-dot dresses that were flying off the rails so fast they were in danger of selling out. Green-Armytage and his team attempted to get an increased repeat order at various levels of management from directors James Benfield and Barry Morris downwards. But they spent weeks being put off on the grounds that no decision could be made because Greenbury was recovering from his hip operation. It was a small incident but symptomatic. Decisions were Rick's thing – others preferred not to make them for fear of a verbal tirade if they wrongly second guessed him.

Peter Salsbury and Clara Freeman continued to trim the store staff and related costs. Freeman, the daughter of an ICI executive, was an Oxford graduate married to Michael Freeman, who created the property group Argent with his brother Peter. Her father-in-law was David Freeman, a powerful City lawyer.

Freeman had joined M&S straight from university and had spent most of her career in the buying department. Despite her obvious intelligence, she did not endear herself to all her colleagues – particularly those just beneath her. 'Clara was married to a multi-millionaire, had a fleet of nannies and the only shop she knew anything about was Harvey Nichols,' said one junior executive scathingly. Freeman espoused feminist principles, and in the late 1990s headed the Opportunity Now campaign to promote more women in business. Not surprisingly she soon ran into trouble with Greenbury, who, although he got on well socially with powerful women, had, it seemed, never quite come to grips with the idea of women as equals in business – at least not in his business.

Whether pure male chauvinism was to blame or merely bad chemistry between them, Greenbury gave Freeman an exceptionally hard time and she retreated. Greenbury found Freeman's attitude as head of personnel puzzling. Freeman tended to put the staff's point of view in a way that reminded Greenbury of a trade union leader. He found it necessary to remind her several times that now she sat on the board they were on the same side – that of the management. Never very subtle, Greenbury put her right in a way she found deeply upsetting. 'Clara could not withstand the torrent of abuse she got from Rick,' said one fellow director. 'Having promoted her on to the board, he harangued her almost constantly, either over the telephone or in his office. She became a control freak. Nobody apart from Peter [Salsbury] could tell her anything.'

Nearly all the capital spending went on new stores, or existing big city store expansion. Out in the smaller provincial stores life was becoming increasingly desperate. One store manager who spent thirty-three years with the company found the constant cutting almost unbearable. 'They constantly hacked away at the numbers,' he said. 'Nobody ever listened to us. They were never supportive.'

As well as staff numbers, training was pared to the minimum so that those who survived were less able to do their jobs. Another way of paring costs was to slash maintenance budgets. 'It became impossible to get someone to change a light bulb,' said one store manager.

David Sieff, the lone family member left on the board, feared for the old values. 'Nobody talked to the young trainees about the principles of the business any more,' he said. But his voice went unheard – drowned out by the noise of the gathering storm on succession. Nobody was listening; nor were they watching the marketplace.

Outside the company, in the retail jungle, the competition that had been shattered in the recession was beginning to regroup. By 1995 Next, which had almost collapsed after its founder George Davies was ousted in 1988, had recovered strongly under the leadership of David Jones and Lord (David) Wolfson, nephew of Isaac, the founder of GUS.

In January 1996 when Next reported a 13 per cent hike in second-half profits Jones was quoted in the *Financial Times* as saying: 'People buy value and they buy quality'. Such a phrase should have sounded eerily familiar to M&S executives, but success had blunted their perceptions. 'The company had lost that immigrant insecurity,' said one supplier. Unlike the first time Next appeared on the scene in the early 1980s, they paid little attention.

Burton too was gathering strength in the capable hands of John Hoerner, a witty, dog-loving Nebraskan who turned the company round, eventually renaming it Arcadia. Selfridges was taking on new management, although recovery was still some way off

And there were some new boys and girls on the block. Angus Monro, a former M&S man, had set up a discount clothing group called Matalan in 1985 in the north of England and it had grown like a magic beanstalk. The company floated on the stock market in 1998 and was briefly valued at more than £2bn before falling back. The cheap designer lookalikes and commodity items such as T-shirts and trainers that had proved so popular in the north of the country began to make an impact in the south too.

A number of foreign invaders had made it past the beach into the interior. From Sweden came Hennes & Mauritz, a company set up in 1947, which developed a successful global retail strategy. Hennes set up in Britain in 1976 after expanding in Scandinavia and provided stylish high-fashion clothes at knockdown prices. Growth was initially slow but took off during the 1990s and by 2000 it had fifty stores. Zara, from Spain, was cast in a similar mould but with the advantage of having a vertical structure – it manufactured its own garments, something that gave it huge flexibility. Like Hennes it provided high-fashion clothes aimed at the young. Neither of these groups had enough outlets to take serious amounts of business from M&S – but they were perceived as the young, hungry retailers with interesting shops, against which the seemingly endless rails of garments in M&S looked increasingly dull.

A host of smaller home-grown groups jostled for attention in the prime high streets and shopping centres – New Look and River Island catered for the country's youth, while Oasis, Jigsaw, Phase Eight and French Connection aimed at fashion-conscious thirty- and forty-somethings. The supermarkets had also embraced clothing as part of their offering, most noticeably the George range at Asda, which even by 1996 had captured 1.6 per cent of the total clothing market; Tesco was not far behind with just under 1 per cent.

The customer's eye was changing and so were styles of living. People were becoming a little bit greener, a little less formal and, at the lower end of the market, more interested in brands. Then from America came The Gap, purveyor of good-quality classic casual wear. The Gap gained momentum at a time when Britain was learning about dressing down, particularly at work. Suits went out and smart casual came in – even in the City of London, where 'dress-down Friday' became de rigueur and in some departments it was dress down every day. The trend caught M&S completely on the hop and it was very late in the day in its often feeble efforts to catch up.

What all the stand-alone formats, with the possible exception of Matalan, had in common was small, welcoming shops. Next and Gap had well-trained sales assistants while M&S staff had become increasingly unhelpful – if you could find them. Over the second half of the decade all these new formats encroached on M&S's market share, Next and Arcadia being the biggest gainers with The Gap, Monsoon and Matalan all making small, but cumulatively significant gains.

Greenbury was later to liken M&S to a charging bull elephant. 'It is so big that nobody can stop it charging. But if enough individual warriors with spears run round the side and spear it in the back, eventually they will bring it to its knees,' he said. Yet as late as 1996, when according to Verdict, the retail research firm, Next already had 3.4 per cent market share, The Gap 0.7 per cent and Matalan 0.7 per cent, nobody senior at M&S had apparently even felt a pinprick. After all, Marks & Spencer still dominated the market-place with 13 per cent of women's clothing according to Verdict and 16 per cent according to M&S's own calculations.

Despite the reaction to the Greenbury Report, the chairman of Marks & Spencer, the most profitable retailer in the land and second most profitable in the world next to WalMart, still had huge pulling power among his peers. In both 1995 and 1996 he appeared in the top ten of a survey of most impressive industrialists conducted by MORI. While he was recuperating from his hip operation a steady stream of the great and good beat a path to his bedside along with suppliers and hordes of fawning directors bearing gifts.

Once back in action, he organised a string of monthly seminars for what he called his development group – a mixture of directors and senior executives – inviting the same great and good to speak. Politicians who came to speak included John Major, Michael Heseltine, Leon Brittan, Geoffrey Howe, Chris Patten and Peter Walker, all of them Tories. Of the fellow captains of industry, most were predictable enough choices: Lord Simon and Sir Michael Angus, both of whom had served with him on the Greenbury committee; Sir Denis Rooke, former chairman of British Gas, where Greenbury had served as a non-executive director; his old friend Sir Christopher Hogg, by then at Reuters and Allied Domecq; and Martin Taylor who, after leaving Courtaulds Textiles, had gone on to head Barclays Bank. But there were also some surprises. Michael Green, who had built up Carlton Communications, the television and media group, spoke as did Marjorie Scardino, who had become the first woman chief executive of a FTSE 100 index company when she took over as chief executive at Pearson in October 1996.

These events, which began in the boardroom at 5 p.m. and continued over dinner in the directors' dining room, often told the speakers as much about M&S as the executives learned from the speakers. Michael Green had the unusual experience of speaking twice – and the difference between the two occasions was palpable. His first presentation was made around 1995 when the company was at the peak of its success. Green greatly admired Greenbury – 'He was a star, a wonderful leader'. During and after his talk, he was struck by the youth and intelligence of his audience, the quality of the questions and the dedication of everyone he met that evening: 'There were thirty people for dinner all happy to spend their evening working. I remember I went home feeling that I at last understood why M&S was the most successful retailer in Britain.'

Four years later, in 1999, Greenbury invited him to speak again. The outside world had moved on. Technology had invaded every office, staff dressed more casually, management structures had become flatter and less hierarchical. Not so at Marks & Spencer, where Green was struck by the formally dressed waiters, the heavy crystal glasses at dinner and the fact that there was still a directors' car park with reserved spaces. Possibly he noticed these things because by then they were in such contrast to every other company he visited, but also because, this time, there was little sparkle from his audience to distract his attention. There were fewer people and the whole atmosphere was more subdued. 'I left feeling they had lost the plot – they were stuck in a management style better suited to the 1970s,' he said.

Martin Taylor's appointment to speak fell in January 1999, following his abrupt resignation as chief executive of Barclays Bank and the day after Peter Salsbury had been named chief executive of M&S. Salsbury was present, but Greenbury had been held up returning from a trip to Brussels and Taylor had almost finished speaking by the time he arrived. Greenbury greeted Taylor warmly, gave his heartfelt apologies for being late and sat down. 'I just wound up my talk and then asked for questions,' said Taylor. 'And I remember there was absolute, total silence. Nobody dared ask a question before Rick.'

The evening John Major spoke he found himself exposed to the stresses and strains between Greenbury and Clara Freeman at dinner afterwards. According to one M&S executive present Freeman rounded on Greenbury in response to a remark made by him and exclaimed: 'Let's face it, Rick, you are a Jekyll and Hyde.'

But back in 1997, the cracks had not yet begun to show. In the twelve months to 31 March 1997 Greenbury's dream of heading the first British retailer to break through the £1bn profit barrier came true. In May, M&S announced annual pre-tax profits of £1.1bn – a rise of 14 per cent on 1996. Over the previous five years profits had risen 87 per cent, earnings per share by 98 per cent on sales up by only 35 per cent.

Highlights of the year mentioned in the annual report published in July included overseas profits up by 23 per cent to £103m, financial services profits up 28 per cent and a recovery in house prices fuelling a rise in the home furnishings division's sales. The chairman's statement thanked directors, staff and suppliers as usual and mentioned the departure of Nigel Colne, one of Greenbury's promotions to the board, after thirty-seven years of service, David Sieff's switch from being an executive to being a non-executive and the retirement of John O'Neill. All three were safe hands – loyal, steadying influences. He also mentioned the retirement of Denis Lanigan and Baroness Young as non-executives. They were to be replaced by younger, more streetwise blood – Brian Baldock, formerly at Guinness; ex-Unilever chairman Sir Michael Perry; and the former director general of MI5, Dame Stella Rimington.

Greenbury concluded his statement with the following words: 'Looking ahead, the outlook is challenging but I am confident that the group will continue to flourish and grow profitably as it has in the past, thus justifying your investment.'

That year Greenbury was voted Britain's second most impressive industrialist according to the MORI survey of the chief executives of Britain's 500 largest companies, winning 21 per cent of the votes. On 3 October 1997 the shares hit an all-time high of 664½p, valuing the company at £18.95bn and making Marks & Spencer Britain's ninth largest company and by far the largest UK retailer. Tesco was the next largest at the time, valued at £9.97bn – not much more than half M&S. There was little to hint that the shares had peaked, or that the next two years were to be a nightmare for Greenbury and M&S.

# CHAPTER NINE

# The challenger

On Sunday 6 April 1997 a full-page profile of Keith Oates appeared in the business section of the *Observer*. Written by Ben Laurance, the City editor, it carried the somewhat contrived headline: 'The man who fits in the M&S suit'. Contrived or not the message was clear. It became even clearer in the picture caption, which read: 'Keith Oates is tipped to be St Michael's choice to fill Richard Greenbury's shoes.' The article made much of Oates submitting himself to thirty-five separate interviews with M&S personnel before taking the job of finance director in 1984, although it failed to mention his special Monaco arrangement with the tax man, made so much of by the *Mail*. Laurance made a point of contrasting the personalities of Oates and Greenbury. Oates was placid, Greenbury was volatile, Oates was a 'smooth operator' where Greenbury came across as 'the chippy warehouse boy'; Greenbury was forthright, Oates diplomatic. He mentioned their mutual love of football and support for different teams and then declared: 'right down to their St Michael woollen socks, they are M&S men through and through'.

Oates presented himself as someone imbued with the M&S culture, someone who had thoroughly gone native – a picture of him that nobody at the company recognised. While charting his success with financial services and on the international side, Laurance quoted Oates as a man who would get out into the retailing trenches: 'I am involved in clothing reviews; the chairman has reviews; we have food reviews. We are looking all the time at what's coming. We literally do eat, drink, use, wear the products. I don't think that's wrong.'

Laurance described how Oates reeled off facts about his own areas of success. 'Within the next four years there will be 120 M&S franchise stores in 32 countries. More than 5.5 million people hold a charge card. If the group's financial services business were a stand-alone operation, it would be in the top 150 quoted companies.' And so on and so on.

On the succession issue Oates did not allow himself to be quoted but Laurance appeared sure of his ground, reporting that certain M&S staff referred to it as 'the general election'. He went on: 'But Oates remember is the man most likely to lead M&S into the next millennium ... Outsiders certainly believe that when Sir Richard Greenbury retires, Oates, now 54, will be a front runner to step up from deputy chairman to take the top job.'

The article set off alarm bells through the higher echelons of M&S. Pushing yourself forward in the press was something as alien to the company ethos as wearing a shirt from Asda. However the article portrayed Oates, the mere fact he had agreed to be interviewed for such a piece without any prior consultation with colleagues showed him as a man completely out of touch with the culture of the company of which he was deputy chairman. When all those 'lifers' who had been with the company from school or university picked up the *Observer* that Sunday they had to pinch themselves in disbelief.

Greenbury was said to be incandescent with rage. Oates's rivals in the race for the top job – Peter Salsbury, Guy McCracken and Andrew Stone – were furious. 'It was an insane thing for Keith to do,' said one director. 'The article alienated everybody.'

The piece appeared seven weeks before the 1996–97 annual results were announced on 20 May – just outside the sensitive six-week 'close period' ahead of financial news when directors are warned not to speak to the press or analysts. But Oates was careful not to cross the legal line and talk about trading at the time or expected profits.

Reading between the lines, Laurance's conclusion made it pretty clear that he either knew of or sensed the struggle between Oates and Greenbury: 'The two men could hardly be more different. And perhaps that is the moral: only an organisation as robust and successful as M&S could happily accommodate two such disparate characters.'

Clearly Oates was positioning himself in the eyes of the outside world to become chief executive in July 1998, when, according to the decision made at the 1995 board meeting on succession, Greenbury was due to step down as chief executive while continuing as chairman. But it seemed that none of the non-executives wanted Oates as chief executive though Denis Lanigan, the former head of the JWT advertising agency, could imagine Oates as a good non-executive chairman. But to put him in that role would have meant going against the tradition of having an executive chairman at the head of M&S.

Greenbury asked the non-executives to meet him just before the next monthly board meeting, where he told them he believed Oates might have the support of several – even a majority – of the executive directors. If they, the non-executives, were set against Oates, then the company was heading for a damaging boardroom split.

As a result of that meeting, Brian Baldock volunteered to conduct a survey of the executive directors to find out their views so everyone would have a clear reading of the situation. Sir Martin Jacomb, generally regarded as the senior non-executive, was ill at the time, so Baldock was largely helped in his interviewing by new board member Stella Rimington. They discovered that Oates's supporters included Robert Colvill, Paul Smith and Chris Littmoden – although Littmoden himself had ambitions for the job – but that the rest of the board did not view Oates as the correct choice for chief executive. However, just who would be the right man was not clear. Some, such as James Benfield and Clara Freeman, backed Peter Salsbury, others felt that there was no candidate of sufficient maturity to take on the job.

The Baldock /Rimington interrogations appeared to take for ever. Directors were seen twice, sometimes three times, and each interview lasted a couple of hours. Baldock took copious longhand notes of each meeting. Not only were directors quizzed about the succession, they were also questioned about a whole raft of issues. They were asked for their views about the future, the structure, the relationship with the outside world and so on. There were a few wry jokes about being grilled by the former head of MI5. Not everyone made themselves available at Baker Street. John Sacher was travelling at the time, yet Baldock even rang him in Burma to question him over the telephone.

The soundings went on throughout the summer. Finally, a clear consensus emerged. Everyone felt it was time for Marks & Spencer to separate the roles of chairman and chief executive. The company had become too big to be ruled by one man and the directors could see they were not addressing the outside world. 'We don't spend enough time with investors', 'We don't take the press seriously', 'We do not meet our international partners often enough' were frequent comments.

As the comments reached Greenbury, he began to gear himself up to relinquish the role of chief executive and even discussed how the story should be handled in the press. Having made the decision, he wanted to move quickly, even if that involved announcing his plans to retire as chief executive before a successor had been chosen. He was beginning to think of 'going plural' by taking some other non-executive jobs. He was not short of offers. Sir Bryan Nicholson, the chairman of BUPA, had sounded him out about taking on the presidency of the CBI while Sir Robin Ibbs had approached him to become non-executive chairman of Lloyds TSB once Sir Brian Pitman retired.

Yet even then the board, with Jacomb taking the lead, decided to move at a snail's pace, fearing that an announcement by Greenbury that he was set to give up the role of chief executive without news of his replacement would destabilise the business. The directors decided the roles of chairman and chief executive should be split – but not until July 1999 at the earliest, and possibly not until 2000.

As Baldock conducted his interviews the atmosphere had grown progressively more poisonous and at one point Greenbury found himself on the receiving end of bizarre accusations of impropriety.

In July 1997 the Inland Revenue wrote to the company to say it had received an anonymous letter that accused Greenbury of having a large extension added to the back of his substantial Berkshire house. The Revenue said it had been told that he had not been charged for that work. As the builders that did the extension were Bovis and Yeomans, the chief builders of M&S stores for decades, the implications were serious. What was even more extraordinary was that this allegation, made in 1997, related to work done in 1989.

As someone who prided himself on his integrity, Greenbury was stunned that anyone could suggest such a thing. Yeomans had since ceased to trade, but fortunately Bovis had retained all the paperwork, showing that Greenbury had paid a full commercial price for the work at the time. In fact, they had overrun the original budget and Greenbury had ended up paying considerably more than the first estimate. The investigation took several months but was duly wound up with the Revenue writing to Greenbury to say 'we have found nothing of concern in your income tax affairs'. The source of the allegation was never discovered but it was a disturbing incident that continued to prey on Greenbury's mind – and indeed on the minds of the small band of directors who knew about it. All Marks

& Spencer chairmen since Teddy Sieff had to live with threat of terrorist attack because of M&S's longstanding support of the State of Israel and close links with its leaders, but within the company they felt totally secure. Now Greenbury faced an uncomfortable question as those under him jostled for advantage. Had one of them tried to sink the knife into his back?

Ironically, considering the frustration he must have felt about his own slow progress, Oates chaired the board meeting on 3 September 1997 where the decision to split the roles was formalised. The minutes referred back to the 2 August 1995 meeting that had confirmed that Greenbury should continue to hold office as chairman and chief executive 'at least until July 31, 1998', and after that his position would be reviewed on an annual basis. Now that was to be changed. The minutes of the September meeting read: 'The conclusion of the non-executives following discussions with all executive colleagues was that "Sir Richard be asked to continue to serve the company:

1. As its chairman and chief executive until the conclusion of the AGM in 2000 (shortly before his 64th birthday) or, if otherwise determined by the board until the conclusion of the AGM in 1999 (shortly before his 63rd birthday).
2. As its non-executive chairman from the date he ceased to be chief executive until the conclusion of the AGM in 2001 (shortly before his 65th birthday)."'

Both these items were once again to be subject to annual review and the proposal received the unanimous support of the board. In short, instead of standing down as chief executive in July 1998, Greenbury would stay in both roles until July 1999 or even 2000. Whatever Greenbury's true feelings at the time, it was a decision he later came bitterly to regret.

One can only speculate as to the pain this caused Oates, who – short of resigning on the spot – could do nothing other than vote with the rest of the board. A less ambitious person might at that stage have realised that his dream would never come true. He could so easily have discreetly put his name out with headhunters and secured a high-powered chief executive's job elsewhere. But according to friends, heading the icon of British retailing had by then become too dazzling a goal for him to relinquish – nothing less would do. Obsession had set in.

Greenbury still allowed Oates to hope. And on the surface Oates continued to play the part of the loyal subject, writing to his chairman on 27 November, eleven weeks after the fateful board meeting, pledging to put past conflicts behind him. 'Under your leadership,' he wrote, 'I would like to play my full part with the MDs and Directors to ensure our continued success.'

Yet the handwritten note, in an immature almost schoolboyish scrawl, spoke volumes of the tensions between the two men. It followed a letter to Oates from Greenbury containing 'explanations' about board policy. Such was their lack of rapport that the two men, whose offices were after all just a few yards from each other, could communicate only by letter.

In his note Oates wrote of his 'considered view ... that there is nothing further to be gained in holding meetings about the past' while expressing optimism that the future board structure would 'take care of itself through the Annual Review process' outlined in the September board meetings.

What also came across from the letter was his impatience to overhaul the company, partly in response to pressure from M&S's big investors who were pressing for the company to enhance shareholder value. The accounts to March 1997 had shown cash in the bank and easily tradeable securities of more than £900m, a big sum for a company of M&S's size and a possible sign of the lack of attractive investment opportunities within its business. The fashionable nostrum of the day was that not only should Greenbury spend the money on store openings and acquisitions, he should also gear up the balance sheet further through returning the capital to shareholders by way of share buybacks or special dividends.

Such ideas were clearly being floated in the meetings between Oates and his friends in the City. In pushing for a debate about 'the strategic direction' of the company, Oates was quick to say: 'This is, of course, not to imply that we take our "eye off the ball" in any way on meeting short term plans and es- timates and running the business.' But the implication of his letter was that, unless M&S produced some plan to enhance shareholder value, the board might find itself facing an investor revolt. 'Our priority', he wrote, 'would seem to be to answer fully the question posed by most of our large share- holders in the meetings held with them in the last few months. The question is what are our plans to improve shareholder value further with all its ram- ifications including our cash balances.' The letter ended 'Yours ever', some- thing that may have produced an ironic smile on Greenbury's lips in the light of all the tussles between the two men.

Oates's strategic push to enhance shareholder value had begun in earnest the previous summer with the acquistion in July 1997 of nineteen large city-centre stores put up for auction by the privately owned Littlewoods group. M&S paid £192m, a tidy £10m a store.

It went against the grain for M&S to make an acquisition, and particularly one that involved bidding against others in a public arena. But then Oates, as chairman of the capital expenditure committee, was the driving force behind the deal. When Littlewoods had first put its entire 135 high-street stores up for sale that June, Oates saw it as an opportunity to solve the M&S shortage of space at a stroke. He rang Greenbury, who was at the start of a two-week visit to Hong Kong and the Far East, to tell him about it. He recommended that he set up a small committee in Greenbury's absence to examine bidding for some or all of Littlewoods. Greenbury agreed. Shortly after he returned to the UK this committee, which included Robert Colvill, the finance director, and Roger Aldridge, the property director, presented their ideas, first to Greenbury and then to the full board. Their recommendations were to bid for the nineteen largest stores, not the entire portfolio. As might be expected from a board that comprised twenty-three people – sixteen executive directors including the chairman plus seven non-executives (although two of them retired that July) – not everyone thought it was a great idea.

'Some of us wondered aloud just what we would put in these stores, especially as some of them were so near existing M&S stores. But Keith seemed very gung ho about it,' said Paul Smith, the director in charge of the Far East. 'He seemed to believe he could persuade the buying departments to source more from overseas; but even Rick, who had the best relationships, could not persuade them to buy more from overseas, so it was unlikely Keith would succeed.'

Greenbury's view of the Littlewoods deal was tempered by reservations about cities where, as a result of the acquisition, there would be two M&S stores near each other. On the other hand he conceded that in certain cities, such as Edinburgh, where the existing store was unable to meet demand, it would instantly solve M&S's problems of space.

All the directors knew that M&S had reached the point where there was little more profit to be had from the existing floorspace – and they were running out of time. Far from complacent, Greenbury had been warning his colleagues that the competition was becoming more intense

– and producing the 14 per cent return on sales of the previous two years was not going to be possible. The Littlewoods deal brought 600,000 square feet in London and major provincial high streets without the headaches of planning permission and building from scratch. It seemed an elegant solution.

Sales were buoyant and if M&S were to sell more goods, then it needed more space. Despite some reservations, when the directors were asked to approve the deal, nobody voted against it. Greenbury put his worries behind him. True to his policy of thrashing out strategic decisions in the board-room, then backing them to the hilt once the plans were voted through by the directors, he backed Oates's plan to expand out of trouble.

In the spirit of the time, when the deal was announced at the 1997 annual meeting on 17 July it met with universal praise from the City. The analysts were not to know – and by all accounts nor was anyone at M&S – that by the time the stores had been refurbished, and the nearby M&S stores had also been upgraded to bring them to a similar standard, the total bill would be almost £450m, more than double the purchase price.

Pleased with the public reaction, Oates now swung into full empire-building mode and pushed for a big spending drive including more stores overseas, particularly in Germany, and for yet more footage at home. Perhaps Oates was doing his best to show the non-executives just what a clever fellow he was.

Next, he persuaded the board that now was the time to launch a global vision alongside further expansion at home. Oates waxed particularly enthusiastic about expanding in continental Europe although not without opposition. Alison Reed, who became finance director in 2001 but was then merely a member of Oates's team, bravely pointed out on several occasions that financially Europe had been a disaster. Only the Boulevard Haussmann store in Paris made serious profits – the rest either broke even or lost money. But for once Oates abandoned his cool calculating persona and talked passionately about his vision. As head of the international division, he knew that to expand overseas was to expand his personal empire. It was also a way of signalling to his colleagues and the outside world that he was a man of vision, of scope, of the world. If his plans had worked out, and M&S had become the UK's first truly global retailer, it would have been impossible for the non-executive directors to turn him down as the next chairman, however much they disliked him.

On the Sunday before the half-year results on Tuesday 4 November 1997, the *Sunday Times* splashed the business section with a story that Marks & Spencer was set to announce a £2bn expansion programme spread over three years. The plan included 'a big expansion of its retail space in Britain, extensive new product development and large growth in overseas sales as M&S makes a big push towards turning itself into a global retailer'. In amongst the optimism of that first article lay a clue for investors about the problems that lay ahead. It read: 'Observers believe the company's investment will slow the pace of profits growth in the short term ...'

Whoever had helped the *Sunday Times* with its story had wanted to get such a warning out into the marketplace. And as usual the market took the hint and the shares slowly began to fall. By Christmas they were back below 600p.

The expansion plan was formally announced the following Tuesday and, as with the Littlewoods deal, the daily financial press gave the move the thumbs up. Global expansion was all the rage and the writers of the highly respected Lex column on the *Financial Times* bought the company line wholeheartedly. 'Global retailers are in conspicuously short supply,' they wrote. 'And there is certainly no precedent for a high volume, focused department store succeeding. Yet M&S's confidence in going down this route is not misplaced. It has a powerful brand with proven international potential ... Patience, of course, is something investors will now be called on to display. The price of a step change in ambition will be a higher risk profile, and another year or two of subdued earnings growth. Only then will the rewards start coming through.'

It was a mark of the widespread admiration for Marks & Spencer that seasoned journalists and retail analysts could embrace the idea that M&S could be the first British retailer ever successfully to 'go global'. This move towards global expansion came at a time when the international business was doing relatively well. In 1997 the international division had made operating profits of £104m, but performance was patchy. While the Pacific Rim was booming, in America the return on sales rarely pushed above 3 per cent and neither Brooks Brothers nor Kings had provided the platform for expansion originally hoped for by Rayner. Profits from continental Europe too had been variable, yet Oates, the director in charge of international business, favoured more stores, particularly in Germany.

The day of the announcement saw Greenbury waxing uncharacteristically enthusiastic about Germany: 'There are 20 to 25 sites in Germany alone we would like to have tomorrow. My guess is it will take us five years to get them. That is still fast.'

Oates also played a more prominent role than usual at that conference, talking in almost proprietorial tones about the global strategy. 'To some extent we are breaking new ground,' he said. 'I don't think there is another retailer like us, and none attempting to do what we are now doing. We are pioneers.' He went on to outline plans to open branches in the Middle East, Latin America, India, China, Europe and Australia. Oates, hitherto a focused finance man, also took it upon himself to talk about fashion trends. 'People want to make the same fashion statements wherever you go,' said Oates. 'Velvet blouses and bootleg trousers are among this year's most popular items.' He did not say those items used cheap, synthetic fabric or that the blouses came in garish colours in direct contravention of Simon Marks's edict to avoid 'garish and tawdry merchandise'.

Greenbury and the other directors realised that to expand overseas was to expand Oates's power base. But despite his reputation for controlling everything, Greenbury did not hold Oates back. Perhaps Greenbury felt that if Oates was busy opening new stores abroad he would not be so desperate for the top job. Or perhaps it was more Machiavellian than that.

Whatever his motives, Greenbury was nervous about the overseas push. He had entrenched reservations about the Continent. His long years in clothing had made him something of an expert in the logistical nightmares of catering for different markets with different tastes. 'A Spanish woman in winter wears a lot of olive greens, oranges and yellows; in France it is very classical, all navy blue, flannel grey and some black often trimmed in red, white and yellow,' he explained. 'In summer the Spanish wear a lot of white and cream, something you do not see much of here. The French love natural fibres, the Germans like different fabrics and colours again. If you don't get these variations right then you don't sell the goods.' Sizing in different countries where women varied not only in height but also in shape was another problem with which M&S continually grappled. So for him not only to agree to expand so aggressively on the Continent, but to be quoted so enthusiastically, seemed strange. But perhaps by then he was too preoccupied with other matters to muster his opposition.

The third leg of the expansion plan was increased investment in the food business, which would carry more commodity lines such as flour, sugar, dried pasta and rice and would also embark upon a costly programme of installing delicatessen counters, fresh meat counters and bakeries in more outlets. It was one of those high-cost measures Greenbury disliked in principle, but Mike Taylor, the divisional director in charge of foods, persuaded him there was no alternative if M&S was to keep up with the competition. Even Asda was providing a delicatessen counter; how could M&S, the quality leader, not do so? Although highly successful, the food market share seemed stuck at 5 per cent, according to Baker Street figures, and although quality remained well ahead of the supermarkets' so did prices. Tesco, Asda and Safeway were catching up in the growth market of convenience foods. 'I still felt the soups, the chocolate mousse and the smoked salmon ring were worth making the extra journey for,' said one working mother. 'But by 1997 I found I could get so much at Tesco and Safeway that I made the effort to go to M&S less and less often.'

The final plank in Oates's grand design to enhance shareholder value was a big share buyback, something that would have taken the company into debt – making the balance sheet more efficient was the fashionable phrase – and enhanced earnings per share.

But Greenbury refused to countenance the idea. Innately cautious, and quite rightly so, considering what followed, he felt the company was taking enough risks as it was in its expansion drive, and the very last thing it needed was a so-called 'more efficient balance sheet' loaded with debt.

He was also unwilling to contemplate a radical reshaping of the company by way of a full-scale merger or takeover. He had turned his back on such a merger with GUS in 1995, but another opportunity emerged in 1998 when David Webster, chairman of the Safeway supermarket group, put out feelers. Safeway had been bought from its American parent and built up by Webster, James Gulliver and Sir Alistair Grant, who had merged their Argyll Foods group with it. But now it found itself struggling to maintain market share against its bigger rivals such as Tesco. Webster felt the company had become vulnerable to predators, and to pre-empt them he sought a benign suitor. And so he put in a call to Greenbury, who, intrigued, went to tea with Webster one afternoon at Safeway's discreet Mayfair offices. At first hearing, Webster's logic sounded compelling.

Safeway had spent more than £4bn building large new modern stores in out-of-town centres, where there was sufficient space for some non-food items such as clothing and homeware. Meanwhile, as Webster put it to Greenbury, the M&S food business lacked scale and, although Greenbury had opened twenty-two out-of-town stores, it did not have enough footage outside city centres. Webster mapped out a plan where M&S would bid for Safeway and the combined group would be able to provide the customer with a comprehensive food offer including all the premium M&S products – plus clothing, where M&S still dominated with a 15 per cent market share.

Greenbury behaved with elaborate courtesy at the meeting and was sufficiently interested to arrange another, this time at Baker Street with Peter Salsbury and his financial directors, Keith Oates and Robert Colvill.

Webster believed that a bid from M&S would have taken Safeway shareholders out at a good price and ensured the company was in capable hands. Like Wolfson, he wanted a good home for the company he loved. Unlike Wolfson, Webster would have been quite willing to sacrifice the Safeway name for the sake of his shareholders. But once again, Greenbury and his team saw problems. They agreed with Webster, after visiting the big, bright newer stores, that they would convert well to the M&S style with a full range of food, but the smaller Safeway stores were run down and often in the wrong place. Yet Greenbury was concerned that such a takeover would turn M&S into a food retailer in an increasingly competitive trading climate where supermarket returns were no more than 5 to 6 per cent of sales. There was also an accounting concern – if M&S were to make a straight bid for Safeway it would have had to write off up to £3bn of goodwill.

At a meeting of all the managing directors and most of the non-executives, Colvill made a detailed presentation of the deal and all its implications. His conclusion recommended that the board did not pursue the deal. The board unanimously accepted his recommendation.

The story showed once again Greenbury's cautious nature as leader of an insular company that could not accommodate the idea of getting together with outsiders. Yet in the troubles that lay ahead it was the food business that bolstered the profits as margins in clothing shrank in the face of fierce competition. How different life might have been if the Safeway acquisition had come along earlier and M&S had opted for that instead of Littlewoods and the £2bn expansion plan. But Greenbury politely told Webster he could not devote any more time to the idea.

While Oates was concentrating on strategic moves, Greenbury was becoming more hands-on, focusing more closely on day-to-day trading and agonising over what to do about the succession.

There were straws in the wind as early as the spring of 1997 that M&S was losing its appeal to customers. Just before the 1996–97 results in May, the fashion press blew the whistle. 'Why does nobody talk about Marks & Spencer any more?' asked Grace Bradberry, the *Times'* Style magazine editor. 'Two years ago, the fashion world could talk of nothing else … Yet now there is silence. When did you last hear someone chic boast of finding the perfect shirt in Marks & Spencer? When did you last notice anything from the store in a glossy magazine?' Not only had M&S lost its fashion edge, she wrote, even the basics were losing their appeal. 'The "basics", which so recently had fashion editors swooning, no longer seem to have that nearly-Donna-Karan edge. And though there are a few high-fashion items in the collection they can be found in only a handful of stores. In short, the chain is returning to its suburban roots.'

Yet nobody in the business community, if they even read the piece, paid any attention to what they would have regarded as idle froth. Two days later, when pre-tax profits of £1.1bn were announced, the financial press was unanimous in its praise for the company, which appeared to be firing on all cylinders. City analysts worried about the lack of growth opportunities on the food side, but M&S was portrayed as a quality business with excellent management – one that would continue to justify its reputation as a blue chip stock and the core retailing share of many a private investor's portfolio. It was the most profitable retailer in the entire world, after WalMart – the giant American discount group. A dash of excitement was added by plans for further overseas expansion in Germany and the Far East plus the move into home shopping.

The Lex column in the *Financial Times* declared: 'Indeed, while many of its competitors are buffeted around in the squalls of consumer demand, M&S resembles nothing so much as the proverbial tanker – neither nimble nor daring, but ploughing remorselessly forward.' The shares fell back by 16p on the day of the results as investors sold stock, nervous about sterling's strength, which the company had warned would knock £20m from profits in the year to 1998. But the *Daily Telegraph*'s Questor investment column concluded: 'At 493p the shares are trading on 17 times expected earnings, a historically cheap rating for one of the best managed companies in the sector. A long term buy.'

The shares duly raced ahead, peaking that October at 664½p and valuing the company at £18.95bn. But from then on, things began to roll downhill.

The half-year results announced in November 1997 produced profits before tax of £452.3m, a shade below analysts' forecasts. Sales in September had been hit by the 'Princess Diana' effect, where a stunned nation had stayed away from the shops following her death in a car crash in Paris at the end of August; the food side's sales were down as supermarket groups caught up with high-margin chilled meals and strong sterling was causing a temporary problem with profits from the Continent. Analysts shaved £65m off their profit forecasts for the full year to 31 March 1998, which would be announced in May.

Tensions ran high in Baker Street for the next few months in an all-out effort to beat the previous year's profits of £1.1bn. The economic crisis in the Far East, which had started with the collapse of the Thai baht but which now engulfed the region, hit profits there. In Europe the timing of expansion could not have been worse. Sterling had put on a spurt, growing stronger and stronger and decimating profits across the channel. Within the company there had been pressure to maintain margins in the European stores – but this would have meant clothing there looking ridiculously expensive against the local competition. They decided instead to endure the pain of keeping prices competitive to hold market share. All told, overseas profits fell from £91.4m to £68m.

At home, clothing sales had held up, showing increases of between 5 and 10 per cent. But by the end of the 1998 financial year on 31 March only a few of the new Littlewoods stores were up and running and the costs of refurbishing them and the nearby M&S stores were beginning to hit the bottom line.

Greenbury's luck had not quite run out. Thanks to adroit tax management relating to a change in the timing in the way VAT was charged on credit-card sales, a VAT credit emerged of £53.2m, which partly compensated for the lack of earnings abroad. Some would argue that it should have been charged as an exceptional item. Even so, the full-year results announced in May showed group sales up by 5 per cent and pre-tax profit 6 per cent higher at £1.17bn. Overall sales had been helped by a 27 per cent jump from financial services, which had also increased operating profit by 18 per cent to £89.4m. Once again there was no specific breakdown of the food or home furnishing businesses. In the annual report, the chairman limited himself to commenting on the new product development and plans for in-store bakeries and delicatessen counters – a sure sign that profits had not been as good as hoped.

In his statement, Greenbury also admitted for the first time that the offering of M&S stores differed vastly. 'There is no longer a typical Marks & Spencer store. Outlets vary enormously in size and each is laid out and merchandised for a specific purpose – from a departmental store of 150,000 square feet serving a wide area such as at Newcastle to a sandwich shop in the City of London,' he wrote.

M&S often had to make tough decisions about what to sell where. Take the example of men's navy blue suits – one of the most popular lines in menswear. Keeping a full range of sizes in every store that offered menswear became too costly and caused a welter of complaints from men who felt that if a suit was on display it should be available. So the decision was made to stock navy suits only in stores in a certain category, but to make sure that they were available in every size in those stores.

As for the future the City only needed to look at the last paragraph of Greenbury's statement to see trouble ahead: 'The group has entered a period of bold investment which will inevitably affect our profits over the next 18 months. However, we have always prudently managed our cash resources and, more important, taken the long-term view when growing your business. I am therefore confident that when the current expansion programme is completed we will remain as we are today, the most profitable retailer in Europe.'

One design change in the 1998 annual report, published in June, signalled that the company ethos was changing. The credo 'Quality, Value and Service Worldwide', which had been emblazoned on the front of every annual report since the mid 1980s, had been relegated to a small box at the bottom of the back cover. It was a fascinating example of indirect communication. When challenged, neither Greenbury nor any other director said they had even noticed, yet somebody must have approved its relegation. By the time the 1999 annual report appeared, it had disappeared altogether and it remained absent in 2000 and 2001.

In July 1998 nobody outside the company had any inkling of the war against time Greenbury and his managing directors were waging to keep profits growing. As one analyst later said with 20/20 hindsight: 'Rick had put on lots of new stores but he had juiced the rest of the business. And by then he had just about got every last drop.' Return on sales overall was up to 14 per cent, on clothing it was nearer 18 per cent.

At its simplest, Greenbury and his colleagues pushed the business too hard, something he would admit only much later. A little at a time, they sacrificed the founding family principles of value, quality and service in the dash for profits. In doing so they had jeopardised what the City calls 'quality of earnings' for greater quantity. Greenbury loathed the City, yet beneath the bluster he feared its power and yearned for its approval. The same was true of the press. 'Rick really used to work for those glowing headlines,' commented one director. Those close to him felt he was determined to show all those university educated public schoolboys in the City just how well he could do. Ironically, in so doing he danced to their tune of higher profits today while leaving tomorrow to take care of itself.

Even though they grumbled about him behind his back, none of his managing directors tried to stop him; on the contrary they aided and abetted him every step of the way. Whatever criticisms they had, the tradition of sycophancy was so ingrained that none would ever reach the chairman's ears.

The non-executives, led by the newer recruits Brian Baldock and Sir Michael Perry, both battlescarred veterans of big-company life, made attempts to sound a note of caution, but to little avail. 'Rick would never really listen to us,' said Perry after he retired in 2001. In 1997, the non-executives persuaded Greenbury to commission a survey of customer attitudes. They asked David Norgrove, Rayner's recruit from Whitehall, to conduct the survey. Norgrove had just been appointed as director of strategic planning and his remit was to analyse the business, look at where the money was being spent and where the best returns were. He investigated customer attitudes to service levels, quality, availability of items and market share. He also took a long hard look at how customers perceived the company – and if that perception was changing.

The survey showed a serious decline in the way the hitherto devoted customers viewed their favourite retailer. The first waver in devotion appeared following the *World in Action* programme in 1996 made by Martyn Gregory, the same journalist who made the 'dirty tricks' programme about British Airways and a self-styled scourge of big business. The programme claimed that one of M&S's suppliers had used child labour in its factories in Morocco, something that was later disproved, and that it had labelled garments made in Morocco as 'Made in the UK'. M&S won its libel action against Granada Television on the grounds that it had not known of the mislabelling. Yet from then on the absolute trust of the public was shaken.

Norgrove's report showed that customers had become less satisfied with the service. They noticed the dwindling number of sales staff on the floor, that it was more difficult to get the items they wanted in the right size or colour. M&S was failing Simon Marks's decree of having the right garments in the right place at the right time. And customers were beginning to shop elsewhere. And, added the report, too much money was going on new stores and not enough on the increasingly shabby more established shops.

Norgrove presented his report in April 1998 to Greenbury and the executive directors at a time when sales were showing double-digit growth and the company looked set fair for another record year.

Greenbury was not impressed. He thanked Norgrove for his work, but found its conclusions hard to stomach. He refused to let him present the report at a full board meeting, something that hurt Norgrove deeply. Even four years later he looked pained when reminded of it. When any of the non-executive directors tackled Greenbury privately on the matter – backed up as ever by complaints from their wives about how M&S was slipping – the answer was always 'Look at the profits'.

The misgivings of Alan Smith and some of his fellow directors back in the mid 1980s were being borne out in reality. Greenbury had proved a talented, instinctive merchant, but he was a poor strategist. With the exception of pushing the M&S move out of town, his vision was sclerotic. M&S had become so mired in its own history that when in September 1998 it was asked to make a 1990s contribution for a time capsule to be buried in the Business Design Centre in Islington, it contributed nothing more imaginative than a selection of knickers.

Yet at the same time Greenbury had begun to throw out – or to allow others to throw out – the heritage. It was evident to the footsoldiers in the provincial stores just what was happening. 'There was hardly any backup behind the scenes and the principles were going out the window,' said one store manager, who recalled his horror on being ordered to put the price up on a line of dresses that had gone particularly well. 'Simon Marks would have blown a fuse. In the old days if a line went well, you moved heaven and earth with your suppliers to get more – you never, ever put the price up. But Rick did.'

One senior selector told how Greenbury cut back on running trials of clothing lines – something viewed as essential by previous chairmen. 'It could be expensive to trial an item, particularly if it did not go well, and Rick started to say we should have the confidence and know-how to buy the right thing,' she said.

Paul Smith, in charge of Far East operations, ceased to send his trainee staff to the UK to see how it was done. 'The conditions in UK stores got so bad we stopped sending people because they were picking up the wrong message,' he said.

While Greenbury concentrated on squeezing profits out of the company he ignored the changing world outside. His attitude to technology was one example. 'Rick would boast that he did not have a PC and did not want to learn how to use one,' the head of one M&S supplier remembered. This at a time when Lord Hanson had been sending messages via his personal computer for five years, and when Sir Stanley Kalms, chairman of Dixons and avowed technophobe, had his PC programmed so that at the press of one key he could call up the latest sales figures from his shops. To some, Greenbury's refusal to embrace technology for his own use may have seemed an endearing eccentricity. To others it signalled that here was a man no longer open to the changes in the modern world. He had long since ceased to ask his young managers what was new; perhaps he didn't want to know. And he continued to pour scorn on the competition, be it in food or clothing. One friend recalled almost pulling him round a new Tesco to make him aware of what it was doing. But Greenbury refused to show any interest.

He was also finding managing Britain's biggest retailer increasingly difficult. It was as if he had created a monster too large to be managed by one man in the way that his hero Lord Marks had. And finding someone capable of taking over from him seemed as remote as ever.

While they recognised the need for change, the non-executives came to the conclusion after Baldock's review of 1997 that none of the four potential candidates to take over as chief executive, Keith Oates, Andrew Stone, Peter Salsbury and Guy McCracken, had yet sufficiently distinguished himself to be the obvious heir apparent.

That August there was an additional complication. Andrew Stone had been made a working peer in the Queen's birthday honours list. The honours had been recommended by a mixture of Tony Blair's new government and John Major's departing one. Stone, and for that matter Peter Salsbury, were both left-wingers and the relationship between Stone's wife Wendy and the prominent Labour MP Harriet Harman was thought to be instrumental in securing the honour for Stone. When the list of Labour working peers was reported, Stone's name appeared alongside that of David Sainsbury, chairman of Sainsbury's, and George Simpson, managing director of General Electric Company. To those with only a hazy knowledge of Marks & Spencer it could have looked as if Stone, whose joint managing director status was not always made clear, was on a par with them.

The announcement irked Greenbury as much as it delighted Stone. 'Rick was very upset,' said one friend. 'Anyone in charge of a public company would be galled to see one of his juniors get a peerage while he was still a knight.' Greenbury naturally affected otherwise and offered his congratulations but developed a fondness for recounting Rayner's opinion that 'working peerages didn't count'.

The salt in the wound was John Sainsbury's peerage. At the time the supermarket group was losing market share to Tesco and Asda while M&S had been powering ahead.

As a Tory supporter, Greenbury knew that the 1997 honours were his last chance and he must have nurtured some hopes that, despite the furore over the Greenbury Report, Major would reward his efforts on corporate governance. Now those hopes had turned to ashes, ashes made more bitter by Stone's lack of tact in celebrating his honour.

'Andrew became impossible. Suddenly there was a flurry of notes, all on House of Lords paper. It was very trying,' said one executive. 'And he would tell endless anecdotes about his life in the Lords, which could be very amusing, but it was tactless.'

There was a dispute over the company notepaper, which traditionally listed directors with peerages before those with knightoods, and thus would have put Stone at the head. The rule was abandoned.

Yet just as irksome as Stone's behaviour was its consequence – by accepting the peerage he had effectively ruled himself out of the succession race and the number of contestants was down to three. If the non-executives still distrusted Oates, then they had to choose either Peter Salsbury or Guy McCracken. But McCracken had not shown himself to be tough or hard-headed enough to lead the company. That left Peter Salsbury as the only possible anti-Oates candidate. Yet while the non-executive directors remained set against Oates, they were still far from convinced that at that stage Salsbury had sufficient experience or talent to be chief executive.

Thus, by the time the spring ranges appeared in the stores in March 1998,

Greenbury had swopped his managing directors round. The non-executives had suggested that if he wanted to prove that Salsbury was the most capable, he should put him in the most onerous job in the business – that of running clothing. In any case, Greenbury had decided that if Stone was going to spend time supporting the Labour government in the House of Lords he could not run an international business such as clothing. To the consternation of those who worked under him, Stone was asked to leave clothing to head foods, where there was less international travel. Guy McCracken, who had been head of food, was made managing director responsible for personnel, store operations, distribution and information technology – Salsbury's old job.

The stress on Greenbury began to show in his relationships with the media, the City and most of all with his colleagues in Baker Street, who increasingly avoided any contentious subjects. One was even quoted in the *Telegraph* as saying they 'didn't know whether to give him Valium or Viagra to help him through the day'.

The biannual results conferences for the City and the press often produced flashpoints for his anger. The City analysts would be summoned at 9.30 a.m. to the main conference room on the ground floor of Baker Street, the financial press a couple of hours later. The press would then stay to drinks and a buffet lunch with the directors along the corridor in what was known as the Marble Hall.

It was part of the culture of arrogance that the City and press were expected to make the pilgrimage to Baker Street. Most other companies had for years held such meetings in hotels near the City such as the Savoy or Howard, for the convenience of their guests. M&S and Shell were the last two to hold out against such compromise (and Shell, at least, with its headquarters in the Strand, was more conveniently placed). But M&S had never known failure and could see no reason to court anyone. 'M&S was a company that never wanted to see its shareholders or any outsiders. The attitude was defensive and Greenbury tended to answer all the questions,' said one analyst.

Despite having received some sympathetic coverage in his days as chief executive, Greenbury, bloodied by the aftermath of the Greenbury Report, already had a reputation for his open contempt of both the press and the stockbrokers' analysts. The institutions that actually owned the shares he could just about tolerate, but few others. When he became chairman he attempted to see the analysts in small groups, but because there were so many – about forty covering the retail sector – he found it impossible to talk to them all and those excluded would ring and complain, so he decided to see none of them.

He limited himself to seeing the main shareholders, most of whom would be expected to visit him at Baker Street, although he made exceptions for the Pru and the Scottish Life offices.

So the results conferences were the only occasions when the analysts got to see him – or any director apart from Oates – and they soon realised how easy he was to rile. 'Greenbury baiting' became something of a sport. 'We used to take bets on how long it would be before he would lose it,' recounted one young analyst. 'He would start off calmly and then gradually his face would go redder and redder and then suddenly he would explode. His favourite phrase was "I have never heard such absolute rubbish in all my life".'

The press would have similar experiences despite the efforts of John Stanley, head of corporate affairs, and his team to school him and supply questions they thought might be asked. In the main, Greenbury would glance through them and declare that he could handle the answers.

At the May announcement of the 1997 results, the audience was so impressed by the company hitting profits of more than £1bn that there were few critical questions to unsettle him in the formal proceedings. Surprisingly, in the light of the *Observer* article on Oates only seven weeks before, nobody asked about the succession. But during the drinks afterwards, when Greenbury was surrounded by a group of journalists, he was taken by surprise when Kate Rankine, a *Daily Telegraph* City page reporter who went on to become deputy City editor, bravely popped the questions. When did he plan to retire? Who might take over from him?

Greenbury blew a fuse and berated Rankine for even asking the questions. 'Do you honestly think that I would ever, ever tell you the answer to that? Why should I talk to a member of the press about it?' she later reported him as saying. Greenbury's view was that the question was unprofessional because Rankine knew that under City rules such sensitive information had to be released through the Stock Exchange. Yet someone of his experience should have realised that journalists often ask unanswerable questions just to gauge the reaction – and he had been wrongfooted.

Not only was he worried sick about the issue, he simply did not know the answer as Baldock was still sounding out the executive directors. Even so, he should have expected the question and he should have been prepared for it by Stanley and his many minions. A more relaxed chairman would simply have smiled and told Rankine the information would be released through the proper channels when the time was right.

But Greenbury made his contempt for the press in general and her as a woman clear. 'He humiliated her in front of her peers,' said one M&S director who witnessed the outburst. 'I knew from the expression on her face that there was going to be trouble.'

Greenbury later referred to her as 'a silly little girl' but he had made the fatal mistake of underestimating his opponent. Buoyed up by six years of unbroken success, he was prevented by his insularity and strange streak of unworldliness from understanding that, whatever he thought of her, Rankine worked not only for a national newspaper, but the one with arguably the most respected financial coverage next to the *Financial Times*. Rankine's report the following day stuck strictly to reporting the results, including the 16p fall in the shares to 593p, and Greenbury probably thought no more about it. But he was to discover the meaning of the phrase 'hell hath no fury like a woman scorned' two years later in April 1999, when in the *Telegraph* Saturday magazine Rankine's wrath exploded in one of the most damaging articles ever written about M&S.

Rankine was not alone in suffering abuse from the embattled Greenbury, who increasingly took out his pen to fight his and M&S's corner in confrontations with Fleet Street.

In July 1998 the *Sunday Times* published an article about the companies that were sponsoring the Millennium Dome. The article pointed out that three of the dome's biggest sponsors, BT, British Airways and Marks & Spencer, were or had been clients of GPC Market Access, the lobbying company that employed Peter Mandelson's former aide Derek Draper. The piece implied that the sponsoring companies might derive some benefit and pointed out that both Tesco, also a sponsor, and M&S would gain from the government's expected decision not to bring in a tax on supermarket car parks. Greenbury was understandably irritated, particularly as M&S, with only twenty-two edge-of-town stores, would hardly derive huge advantage from this. Only a few months before, he had sat on the right of John Witherow, editor of the *Sunday Times* and his host, at a private lunch with the chancellor of the exchequer, Gordon Brown. He could so easily have lifted the phone and had a quiet word. Instead a blaze of vitriol winged its way on to Witherow's desk, something that so antagonised him he directed his journalists to 'get Greenbury'.

Unfortunately such 'Rickograms' had been landing on journalists' desks for at least three years and were a continuing source of worry to his colleagues. The rule was that Greenbury had to pass everything through Stanley or one of the non-executive directors, but increasingly he either refused to make their suggested amendments or he simply sent the letters without consultation.

In mid September the *Investors Chronicle* carried a critical but balanced article about Marks & Spencer. In response, Greenbury sent the female editor, Ceri Jones, a letter, which she ran on 9 October and headlined 'Fierce riposte from M&S's Mr Grumpy':

Dear Sir,
What a load of old tosh. I have read some pretty inept criticism of our business, but yours of 18 September takes the biscuit. If making pre-tax profit of approximately £1bn is being in a quagmire, as you put it, then every other retailer would like to be in that position with us, bearing in mind that we are still by far and away the most profitable retailer both in the UK and continental Europe.

We are not trying to re-position ourselves, merely taking advantage of the opportunity we had to buy nearly 1 million feet of prime selling space which may well not produce results in the short term, but will certainly do so in the medium to long term. Incidentally, this Littlewoods acquisition was greeted with enthusiasm by the City, and people like yourself, who presumably thought we could convert the space overnight.

As far as our entry into the clothing catalogue is concerned, we had been studying the market for some two years, and this seemed as good a time as any to enter, albeit on a long-term basis.

Of course I readily accept that we should have been unique and forecast the collapse of the Far East economies and the effects of the ever-increasing strength of the pound in continental Europe. But along with all the other hindsight commentators, including yourself, we did not do so.

Regarding your bear points, all retailers' clothing sales across the country have collapsed in recent months, but we are still doing better than national figures. On the food side we have chosen to maintain margins rather than discount, which again in the long run will be to our benefit. You say that we have not become a bad business overnight, but two pages of contemptuous criticism does not support that statement.

One final point: it is reading articles like your own and being slagged off by journalists and analysts every day in various newspapers that makes me irritable, or as you put it, grumpy. You should try it day in, day out, before criticising others. I am glad to say that my family, my friends and my peers in business do not agree with you, which is some consolation.

The *Investors Chronicle* printed the letter, which had been sent against the advice of John Stanley, in full. It is the kind of letter advisors recommend writing, then consigning to the wastepaper bin. The fact that Greenbury sent it, and at a time when he knew his first-half results were going to show a downturn, demonstrated how much pressure he was under. As arguably the rudest and least grammatical letter ever sent by a chairman of a public company to an editor, it represented the clearest bear signal yet.

During the next few months Greenbury could have done with some friends in the press and the City. Instead, he had created a battalion of enemies whose fascination with M&S was set to escalate. In 1996 mentions of M&S in the UK press had been running at an average of 408 a month, in 1997 they rose to 568 a month. By 1998, as the fates dealt their hand, they suddenly shot up to more than 1,000 a month.

The *Investors Chronicle*'s critique of the company was perfectly timed. The heat was now well and truly on. From April to July clothing sales were up by 5 per cent. Andrew Stone's swansong ranges hit the spot for customers more often than not. Then came the thunderbolt. Apparently out of the blue, sales in the second three months of the year – August to October – instead of going up went down – an increase of 5–10 per cent had been budgeted; instead they dropped by nearly 1 per cent.

No one either inside M&S or outside had predicted this – in fact, the buying departments had massively overbought, mainly in the infamous grey. The downturn in sales rippled across the whole of the clothing sector. It hit M&S hardest and affected Next, with its smaller well-displayed formats, least.

By September – the end of the first half of the financial year – it was clear to those running the company that M&S not only faced reporting its first profit fall for six years but that there was no sign of recovery ahead. The effect on morale at the top of the company – people who had known nothing but success – was devastating. Greenbury became more autocratic than ever.

He had been increasingly irritated by the low profits from the smallest eighty stores, which carried a mixture of food and clothing. One weekend, after wrestling with the problem, he decided to slash the variety of clothing items on sale, cutting out all but the most basic goods and removing childrenswear from those branches. At the regular EDM that Monday he told his managing directors of his decision and instructed Salsbury to implement it. When Salsbury demurred, Greenbury refused to discuss the matter. 'I will brook no argument,' he is reported to have said.

Nothing stayed a secret for long in Baker Street and when other directors discovered what had happened they were horrified. 'I told Peter he must take it to the board, but he said Rick had forbidden him to discuss it,' said one non-executive. In the end nobody had the courage to take on Greenbury and the range of goods was duly cut back in eighty stores – much to the consternation of the customers. Among several protests, the Buxton store sent in a petition signed by more than 1,000 customers pleading for the return of a wider range of clothing. The policy remained until after Greenbury had gone.

On Tuesday 3 November the world woke up to discover that Marks & Spencer had suffered a 23 per cent fall in half-year profits to £348m – the first profits setback since the brief dip of 1992 and one that was quickly seen as the most serious since the Second World War. At the press conference to present the results Greenbury largely blamed the sudden drop in clothing sales in September and October, declaring: 'We are all in shock at the moment. It is a bloodbath in clothing. National sales have been in the red for five of the past seven weeks.' There was, he said, no sign of any recovery in the second half.

Baldock and the non-executives had made sure he would not be caught out on the succession issue again and gave him a carefully worded script. In short, it said the matter was under review and that the non-executives were in charge. No announcement on the matter was imminent.

Yet two days later, on Thursday 5 November, Peggy Hollinger of the *Financial Times* ran an authoritative story that Peter Salsbury had emerged as the favoured candidate after a review of all directors. Greenbury was expected to step down as chief executive the following May, but stay on as chairman until 2001.

She was spot on, which was not surprising as her sources were close to the M&S hierarchy. Indeed, Greenbury and Jacomb, after a series of intense discussions, had decided on just who would take new roles in a recast M&S

boardroom and that Oates would be made to exit stage left. But such news was not intended for public consumption for months.

In a letter to Greenbury dated 29 October, five days before the interim results, Jacomb sketched out how he thought the management should be changed. The appointment of the new chief executive, Peter Salsbury, would be announced immediately, along with the date of the changeover, which would be either after the annual results the following May, during the annual meeting in July or following the interims the following October. Stone would then become deputy chairman with Oates shuffled off into retirement.

Jacomb knew it was important that Greenbury's new job should be defined in writing, well aware of City concerns about former chief executives moving up to be non-executive chairmen. The worry was they would constantly try to steer from the back seat and not give freedom to their successors to make changes and stamp their own indentities on their organisations.

Greenbury responded in writing on the eve of the results, welcoming Jacomb's overall plan although wanting to delay the actual split of the roles, though not the announcement, to the end of 1999 or even early 2000. He pointed out that chief executives could become good chairmen whatever the City's worries, and cited the transfer of power from Sir Brian Pitman to Peter Ellwood at Lloyds TSB. Lastly, he pointed out that Sir Ralph Robins thought he ought to remain executive chairman with a chief executive working to him, along the lines of what prevailed at Robins' company, Rolls-Royce. Given the workload of any chairman of M&S and the terms of reference he expected to have, the job could not possibly be 'non-executive'.

Whatever the differences, the two men were aware of one thing – the need to handle Oates carefully. Jacomb insisted that he be told first that he was not going to get the top job and that terms be rapidly agreed for his retirement. 'The negotiation on this will be sensitive,' he wrote. 'However, I think that as [Oates] will clearly be unwilling to work under [Salsbury] and since he will want to ensure no adverse publicity for himself, all this may fall into place quite quickly.' The Prudential chairman thought self-preservation would compel Oates to respond rationally to his disappointment – and that he would soon organise a new high-profile job for himself. Given his track record, every headhunter in the City of London would surely be beating a path to his door.

But back in his gloomy office with the dark murals, Oates digested the gist of Hollinger's article and began planning something quite different. Had he been unofficially tipped off about the discussions between Greenbury and the non-executives, or was he moving in advance to pre-empt the course of events that the *FT* was sketching out? Knowing the traditional and insular company culture as he did, such a bright intellect might have realised that any attempt to force the leadership issue was doomed. But by then Oates had been hustling for the top job for five years – he was a desperate man.

# CHAPTER TEN

# *Crisis*

Two days after the results, Greenbury boarded British Airways flight BA 139 to Bombay intent on a mixture of business and pleasure. Travelling with him were his personal assistant Nigel Robertson, the divisional director for textiles Jim Stocks, who was married to Greenbury's long-serving secretary Celia, and the M&S external public relations advisor Tony Good – the man who had advised M&S on how to handle the press following the Keith Oates Monaco tax story in the *Daily Mail*. The trip had been Good's idea and it was the second time he had taken Greenbury to India. Tall, with a deceptively diffident manner, Good was an old India hand who had done business there for thirty years and had enviable contacts within the business community. He felt that M&S could benefit from buying more goods from Indian companies, which combined the advantages of lower labour costs, high technology and a good understanding of English. He also felt India was a retail revolution about to happen and that Greenbury should consider opening a pilot store there.

As the four men settled themselves into the first-class cabin for the ten-hour flight they were in good spirits, looking forward to escaping the British winter for a few days doing business on the sub-continent. After the business meetings, Greenbury, Stocks and Robertson had arranged for their wives to join them with the plan that the six would fly off to Goa for a week of winter sun.

In his role of senior non-executive director, Brian Baldock spoke to Greenbury at Heathrow on the telephone at around 10 a.m. that Thursday to tie up some loose ends and wish him a good trip. Two hours later a hand-delivered letter from Oates appeared on his desk – and on that of every non-executive director – with a copy to the absent Greenbury. The letter, which had clearly been a long time in the writing, highlighted where Oates believed the company had gone wrong and accused the non-executive directors of not taking the problems seriously enough. The problems were far worse than they realised, he wrote, and it would take a dramatic change to put them right. He was, he continued, the right man to drive those changes through and therefore they should make him chief executive. The language of the letter was calm and measured. As one director put it: 'The form of the letter was not inflammatory, but the substance was explosive.' Oates may have intended it as a bid for power – but it turned out to be a professional suicide note.

To Baldock and the other non-executives, his decision to wait until Greenbury had left the country before delivering his views confirmed their view of his unsuitability for the top job. His supporters believed he was courageous to do what no other director dared. Yet Oates's supporters felt he was motivated not by ambition but by a sense of duty. 'Keith simply did not expect Greenbury to leave the country after such bad results – in fact he asked him to stay to talk to the big shareholders,' said one. 'He was convinced nobody at M&S but him realised the seriousness of the situation.'

Oates felt that the bad figures, accompanied by a profit warning for the rest of the year, gave him the ammunition he needed to show investors that change was imperative. While the company had been lifting its profits year after year, Oates had felt nobody would listen to him. Now at last the world could see the mess the company was in.

For most of his M&S career Oates had found the culture frustrating. Although he had been allowed to build up the financial services side with Colvill, he felt unappreciated. Other directors rarely visited Chester and they took little interest in how it worked. Each year when the time came to draft statements for the annual report, Greenbury would always need reminding to include a paragraph on financial services. Oates told friends of his frustration that so many of his ideas had fallen on stony ground. His experience at BT gave him the idea to take M&S into mobile telephony – with a St Michael branded phone on sale in every store – but Greenbury showed no interest and, therefore, neither did any of the other directors. Oates also found the sheer size of board meetings – never fewer than twenty strong including non-executives – discouraged decision making.

The structure of the board also mitigated against robust debate – as up to three directors covered the same area. In 1997 Clara Freeman had been director of personnel reporting to Salsbury as joint managing director responsible for personnel (among other things), who reported to Greenbury.

There was Barry Morris, director of food, who reported to Guy McCracken, the managing director in charge of food, who reported to Greenbury. Colvill reported to Oates on finance, who reported to Greenbury. It was a structure that dragged argument down like treacle and choked quick decisions. Oates proposed a much smaller main board with another tier of trading directors beneath.

After reading his copy of the letter, Baldock rang as many of the other non-executives as he could reach and faxed the letter to a stunned Greenbury in India. Jacomb also phoned him and advised him not to rush back but to continue his trip. Initially Greenbury agreed. On the Friday morning the group stuck to their schedule, visited a supplier, had lunch at the British High Commission and toured the premier retail areas of Bombay. That evening the party flew to Madras, spent Saturday visiting suppliers and had dinner in their hotel, where there was only one topic of conversation. The plan was to fly to Bangalore the next day. From there, a private jet would fly them to Ahmadabad in Gujarat, where Greenbury was due to speak at the opening of a denim supplier's new factory.

But Oates had another missile to fire and it exploded in the Sunday press that weekend. 'Open warfare is about to break out in the boardroom of Marks & Spencer,' began the story on the front page of the *Sunday Times* business section. 'Hostilities will be triggered by the decision of Keith Oates, the deputy chairman, to start lobbying the company's non-executive directors to pick him as chief executive when Sir Richard Greenbury splits his roles, probably next year.' The *Observer* and the *Sunday Telegraph* also carried the story.

At least two 'friends' of Oates had been briefing the *Sunday Times* that November – one laying out the Oates plan of action and its reasons to John Jay, the managing editor, business news, and the other pouring vitriol about Greenbury into the ear of Jay's deputy and business editor, Andrew Lorenz. Oates subsequently denied employing anyone to put his point of view across to the media, but, whatever their motives, several of Oates's outside supporters communicated his ambitions to the City and financial press. One was Sir Nicholas Lloyd, the former *Daily Express* editor, who had formed the PR company Brown Lloyd James with the former Thatcher aide Howell James. Another was Sam Johar, a dynamic Indian businessman who had built up his own headhunting business and lived near Oates in Monte Carlo. Johar had some good contacts among the financial press, through whom he channelled the Oates line. Although Oates always maintained they were simply good friends who believed in his abilities, it may have crossed Lloyd's mind that if he succeeded in raising Oates to power, at least part of the M&S public relations budget might come his way. Johar too could reasonably have expected some assignments to find new blood for the company, had Oates attained his goal.

Brian Hudspith, the internal deputy head of public relations, acquired early editions of the Sunday papers and when Good woke up in Madras that morning a fax of the press coverage was already waiting for him. At breakfast in the club room of the Sheraton Towers Good showed the cuttings to a horrified Greenbury. But for the moment he decided to continue the trip and the four men caught a plane to Bangalore, discussing on the journey what the next step regarding the Oates crisis should be. At Bangalore they checked into the Oberoi, where they spent much of the day in Greenbury's suite while he rang various directors including Baldock and Jacomb in their respective country homes. To Good's astonishment, Jacomb still advised Greenbury to continue with his trip. Good told him he must go back to London as soon as possible. Greenbury agreed, asking him to cancel the Bangalore trip and make his sincere apologies. Instead of taking the private jet to Ahmadabad as planned, they used it to fly back to Bombay from where they took the BA 138 overnight flight to London, arriving at Heathrow at 7.50 a.m. on Monday.

Oates's 'friends' had continued their weekend's work. The Greenbury entourage arrived at Heathrow to read in the *Financial Times* that Oates was proposing 'a dream ticket' of himself as chairman and Peter Salsbury as chief executive.

Oates had indeed approached Salsbury with this idea, but Salsbury, who until then had always maintained a veneer of loyalty to Greenbury, refused. In retrospect, his refusal was motivated more by his hopes for total power if he appeared to back his chairman. Oates's case was that, together, he and Salsbury would provide a winning combination of retailing experience and strategic vision – an argument with some logic to it. But it was too late.

On his return to Heathrow Greenbury avoided the rush hour traffic by taking the Heathrow Express to Paddington, from where he was chauffeured to his Marylebone flat. There Baldock, Jacomb, Stella Rimington and Sir Michael Perry were waiting for him. Shaken and angry, Greenbury wanted to go straight to Baker Street, where the routine Monday morning meeting of directors was due to take place, and organise a firing squad to deal with Oates immediately. But Jacomb, a lawyer by training, said execution without trial would be wrong.

He said that the decision to split the roles of chairman and chief executive needed to be brought forward, but 'due process' had to be observed. Together the group thrashed out a rough plan of action. An emergency nominations committee would be set up to interview every executive director once more on their views and personal ambitions. There were to be never fewer than three non-executives present at each interview. At the end of the week the non-executives would recommend their preferred candidate for chief executive.

The executive directors, who by then had gathered in Baker Street, were rung and told to delay their meeting by an hour. They were asked to wait for Greenbury and the others to arrive, at which time an emergency board meeting would be convened. The group then left Greenbury's flat and arrived to find Oates and the other directors tensely waiting for them in the boardroom, under the sombre gaze of all the former chairmen. Not since Simon Marks had fought to regain control of his company from William Chapman in 1915 had emotions run so high. The meeting was mercifully short.

Jacomb led the proceedings. He formally proposed setting up the emergency nominations committee to be chaired by Baldock. Jacomb also proposed that 'it was imperative that there now be a total embargo on any press contact by any member of the board during this process in view of the damaging leaks which have occurred recently'. The proposal was agreed by everyone present – including Oates.

Nothing of the sort happened. The review took three weeks rather than one to complete, while the newspapers continued to speculate on whether Peter Salsbury, Oates or even Chris Littmoden – the director in charge of America and another highly ambitious individual – might get the job. Meanwhile Oates courted his fellow directors as never before, somehow expecting them to forget his previous disdain and to ignore the fact that if he did become chief executive, and ultimately chairman, he would immediately shrink the board and most of them would be either out or demoted. A few, such as Paul Smith and Chris Littmoden, were invited to his office to be offered high-flying jobs in his new regime, while he mapped out a new era for M&S under his leadership. 'He seemed quite strange at the time – I had never heard him speak in such impassioned tones,' said one.

Oates also put himself about publicly. He believed fervently that the outside world – the City institutions and some of the press – backed him to bring about the much-needed change at M&S. The evening after the emergency board meeting Oates attended a party thrown by Greg Hutchings to celebrate fifteen years of unbroken success at his company Tomkins, the Rank Hovis McDougal to Smith & Wesson guns group. Hutchings loved to party and it was a jolly affair in one of the Inns of Court in Middle Temple with all the serving staff dressed in medieval costumes. Amid this scene one guest remembered Oates, a tall, dark, brooding figure in black, standing apart. 'For all the world he looked like a medieval baron plotting against his king,' he said. 'It was not hard to imagine him in medieval garb with a stiletto at his hip.'

As promised at the emergency meeting, each director was interviewed twice, or sometimes three times. Oates was seen by Baldock, Rimington and Perry, and during the second session he rounded on Baldock and accused him of speaking to the press improperly. According to one of the people in the room he told Baldock he had no right making statements to the press. Baldock responded that, in that particular instance, Greenbury had asked him to make a statement on behalf of the chairman.

Baldock then accused Oates of using a professional public relations consultant to promote himself for the chief executive role – and of turning the procedure into a quasi-election campaign.

Oates loftily dismissed the accusation as rubbish. Baldock said: 'So please explain to us the role of Sir Nicholas Lloyd.' Oates turned pale at the reference and rose to his feet. 'So that's the game, is it? That's the game you want to play,' he shouted. Those in the room recalled their alarm at his agitation. 'His eyes were wide and there was a vein in his neck throbbing, it was quite frightening,' recalled one. In time-honoured tradition, Oates's defence was to attack and he began to accuse the non-executives of neglecting their fiduciary duty. What about Greenbury's use of the private plane to watch Manchester United play? He cited one particular game in Milan. Baldock inquired how long Oates had known about these things.

'Oh years,' replied Oates.

'Then why have you waited until now to bring it up?' asked one of the others present. 'You have known about these things for a long time. Why now?'

Oates insisted that it was their fiduciary duty to investigate his allegations, which they did. As far as the football match was concerned, Greenbury was able to demonstrate that he had been visiting a big Italian supplier in the morning, and he and executives from the supplier had all gone to watch the football match in Milan in the evening – events within the bounds of normal business practice. But it was not just the chairman's use of private planes that concerned the non-executives – it was their frequent use by most of the directors.

All too often, they felt, an executive would glide up the M40 in his chauffeur-driven Mercedes to RAF Northolt, the airfield used by the Queen, to be spirited away in a small jet on a business trip that could have been taken for a fraction of the cost on a scheduled airline – even flying first class as they always did. In these cases directors would claim that the time saved by travelling on a private plane would offset the extra cost – but it was one of those grey areas where the truth was hard to pin down.

'In our view most of the directors used private planes a little more than they should have done – Oates included. We had warned Rick about it,' Baldock said later.

'There was no substance to the allegations he made against Rick, but it shows how desperate Oates had become,' concluded one of the other non-executives.

In the middle of the review Oates, who was fighting his corner in every way he knew how, accused the in-house public relations man Brian Hudspith, who was deputy to John Stanley, and Tony Good of promulgating pro-Salsbury stories. The press had billed Salsbury as Greenbury's man – more accurately, he was the only possible alternative to Oates.

Baldock asked to see them in his office and when they arrived they found the non-executive director Sir Ralph Robins and Clara Freeman also waiting for them. 'It had the air of the headmaster's study,' Good later recalled. Baldock told them that Oates believed them to be 'spinning' against him and encouraged them to take legal advice as he was threatening to issue writs against them. Astonished, Good and Hudspith categorically denied any such activity, but even so, Baldock asked Good not to talk to any more journalists and suggested that Hudspith take 'gardening leave' until the review had been concluded.

Press speculation continued as the non-executives cast their net wide. Lord MacLaurin, who had recently retired as chairman of Tesco, was tipped as a successor to Greenbury. The story had a firm foundation. MacLaurin was informally sounded out for the chairmanship and he devised a clear and radical plan of action, which he outlined to Baldock. First, he told him, he would take M&S back to its basics of underwear and knitwear but forget about outerwear. In the resulting free space he would put concessions selling branded designer goods – the route taken by Debenhams and Selfridges. But, while he toyed with the idea, MacLaurin did not seriously consider taking on the job. Although retired from Tesco, he saw working for M&S as too much of an emotional conflict.

Around the same time Dominic Rushe in the *Sunday Times* speculated that Allan Leighton of Asda had been approached for the job of chief executive – another true story. But Leighton dithered and by the time he became seriously interested Luc Vandevelde had become executive chairman and the lines of power blurred. Leighton's only interest had been in working as chief executive to a non-executive chairman.

The review of directors was completed on 19 November, but the press was still unsure of what the final decision would be. The non-executives gave themselves a few days to look at their findings and called a board meeting on 25 November to announce their choice.

Oates still clung to the belief that he would become chief executive. Four days before the board meeting he is reported to have rung Anna Mann, the doyenne of London-based headhunters, and told her there would soon be a lot of work for her at M&S, as he believed he would be given the top job at the board meeting.

'Are you sure?' she asked, incredulous.

'Absolutely,' he replied.

'Well, Keith,' she is reported to have said. 'I think it is even money that you will be fired.'

On 24 November the non-executives made their decision. Peter Salsbury would be the new chief executive while Greenbury would be non-executive chairman. Oates was to meet the firing squad after all.

That evening both Baldock and Jacomb tried to contact Oates on his mobile phone, at home and through his secretary, asking him to return to Baker Street. They wanted to break the news of his 'early retirement' to him the night before the meeting, so that he would not be in the building the following day. But Oates did not respond to their calls. One of Oates's friends recalled a phone call from him at around 10.30 p.m. Oates told him that

Jacomb had left a message saying he would be in the office until midnight. Oates still seemed to believe he would get the job.

'I told him, "Keith, people only hang around in their offices till midnight if they are going to fire you,"' he said.

And so it proved. Towards midnight Oates finally responded to the messages and a meeting was arranged with Baldock and Jacomb at 8.30 the following morning. The two men had a carefully prepared speech ready for him when he arrived. When they told him Salsbury was to be chief executive and that he, Oates, would be expected to take early retirement, he was stunned.

He remained calm, however, and when he returned with his solicitor at 10 a.m. to negotiate the terms of his settlement he seemed in full control and determined to extract every penny of what he felt was due to him. The board meeting was set for 2.30 p.m. and at 2.29 Oates was still refusing to accept the terms of the package proposed. Baldock's and Jacomb's worst fears were realised when he suddenly threatened to attend the board meeting. 'I am still a director, I am coming,' he said.

Baldock then requested a few moments alone with Oates's solicitor. He assured him that the offer on the table was final and he should advise his client of this. Finally, Oates accepted the package – which included a financial penalty if he ever said anything publicly about the events leading up to his departure from M&S – and returned to his own office to pack his things. A tired but relieved Baldock arrived at the board meeting half an hour late.

One of Oates's critics at M&S once described him as a mixture of Captain Queeg – the flawed captain of a minesweeper in the film *The Caine Mutiny* – and Walter Mitty – the great dreamer. He continued to keep his residence in Monaco and, despite a period of illness following the drama at M&S, he remained a non-executive director of Diageo, heading the audit committee. He stayed as a director of British Telecommunications until early 2001, when he resigned from that troubled company following a board reshuffle. He remained on the English Sports Council and became chairman of Quest – a culture and sports watchdog dreamed up by Chris Smith, the former culture minister. But as far as full-time heavyweight jobs went, essentially he was cast into the wilderness, although he continued to tell friends in Monaco such as Johar that the subsequent problems of M&S would have been less severe had he been at the helm. Yet one business associate who unsuccessfully put Oates forward for two high-ranking jobs remarked that he was viewed as a troublemaker. Two and a half years later Oates had not taken another executive post at a public company.

The non-executives chose Salsbury to lead Marks & Spencer because the majority of his colleagues backed him and said they could work with him. Except for a few people over whom he had trampled in the race for the top, his colleagues viewed him as essentially a competent 'nice guy'.

What M&S needed at that point was a man such as John Browne, who became chief executive of BP in 1995 and transformed it from a bureaucratic old-fashioned company into a modern dynamic force that adapted to the changing times in the oil industry. But M&S did not have a person of such exceptional calibre as Lord Browne in its ranks.

Aware of this, the non-executives had asked headhunters to put up some candidates from other companies in the UK, but, according to them, they did not discover an outstanding retailer who could work with the 'unique' M&S culture. They were swayed by what Baldock described as the history of transplants. 'All the early patients died because the body rejected the new heart,' he said.

They still believed the company needed Greenbury at the top – to give continuity after the troubles and because he was still the most able leader they had. Salsbury, they believed, was a safe pair of hands who had worked in most parts of the business.

To the outside world Salsbury was viewed as Greenbury's man, and he had certainly allowed the public relations machine to put forward that view in the press. But Greenbury's motives for supporting him were mixed. 'Greenbury wanted Salsbury because he thought he was a puppy he could control,' said one Oates supporter. Whether or not that is true, there was nobody else in the running apart from Oates at the time – and Greenbury believed they could form a partnership. Greenbury had seen his friend Sir Brian Pitman move up to be non-executive chairman of Lloyds TSB with great success and felt he could do something similar. He negotiated a salary of £450,000 a year, less than half the £969,000 he earned in his last year as chairman and chief executive but far more than that of most non-executive chairmen, proof, he later claimed, that his role was intended to be hands-on. And there was no suggestion that he might relinquish his vast office.

Until the roles of chairman and chief executive were divided between them, Greenbury and Salsbury had always got on well both at work and socially. Soon after the decision, Salsbury and his second wife Susan, another former M&S selector, had a convivial dinner with Rick and Siân in their cosy Marylebone flat. Afterwards Salsbury wrote a fulsome letter to Siân praising Greenbury for standing firm in the face of such great opposition. 'The pressure on Rick has been intolerable,' he wrote sympathetically. He also indicated he would need all the help he could get from Greenbury in his early days as chief executive. 'I shall need to lean on Rick for support,' he wrote.

Despite Greenbury's dominant personality, most of the non-executives genuinely believed that he would work well in a non-executive capacity with Salsbury. David Sieff felt he knew better. When he had been director in charge of personnel Salsbury had secretly negotiated for his job, he claimed, and failed to tell him he would be taking over from him. 'He stabbed me in the back more than once,' Sieff told colleagues. But the others, influenced by Salsbury supporters such as Clara Freeman and Jim Benfield, backed him. 'We had our misgivings about Peter, but we felt the team was absolutely behind him,' said Baldock. 'We were convinced that Rick would act as his mentor as a non-executive and help coach him.'

They were soon proved disastrously wrong. They had reckoned without Salsbury's deep-seated loathing of Greenbury, which until then he had skilfully disguised under a pleasant, quietly spoken exterior. But the moment he was made chief executive his attitude towards Greenbury changed. Gone was the obliging lieutenant. In his place was a new tyrant who barely spoke to his old general – and soon made his contempt and hatred of him clear to everyone. 'Peter changed dramatically from the day he was made chief executive,' recalled one non-executive director. 'None of us was prepared for his hatred of Rick, or the irrational behaviour that supported that hatred.'

Out in the stores customers continued to hold back and by Christmas everyone realised that the full-year results would be far worse than anticipated even a couple of months before. Christmas was always crucial to M&S. The company normally made up to 40 per cent of annual profits in the six weeks before Christmas. Food sales always tripled during that time. The buying departments had budgeted for sales continuing to be up by 8 per cent on the previous year, but in fact sales were down by 2 per cent. It was clear there would be a huge stock writeoff. The conversion of the former Littlewoods sites and the refurbishment of the existing M&S stores near by caused more disruption and loss of sales than anyone anticipated. The crisis in the Far East put the region into losses and returns on the Continent continued to be hit by the strength of sterling.

After Christmas, Greenbury and Siân headed for their favourite winter destination of Barbuda in the Caribbean, a tiny island where the only contact with the outside world was one phone line and a fax machine in the resort manager's office.

Back in London Salsbury and his team examined the latest trading figures and realised the company was not just heading for a profits fall to around £900m as they had thought before Christmas – it was going to be much, much worse than that. At the beginning of the financial year they had been optimistic enough to aim at 1999 profits of £1.5bn. Now Salsbury stared into the abyss and saw that M&S would be lucky to make £650m – little more than half the profits of the previous year. The non-executives were horrified – it was imperative for the company to issue a profits warning to the City before the news leaked out and rumours began flying. Worse still, without a warning, the company could be accused of misleading the market – a serious offence under the Financial Services Act.

Salsbury's first major task as chief executive was to draft that warning. He faxed a copy of the proposed release to Barbuda. When it arrived, Greenbury, who had never been able to stomach any negative comments about M&S, was furious. To his eyes it read like a blow-by-blow criticism of his regime. 'Roughly what it said was Marks & Spencer have got it wrong,' he told colleagues. 'We have lost touch with our customers, we have not had enough staff on the sales floor to cope with them, we bought the wrong goods. Our supply base is not competitive any more.'

Greenbury rang Salsbury. 'I think this statement is a disaster,' he said. He urged Salsbury to talk about the one-off cost of roughly £400m that was affecting the group. The £2bn investment programme had sucked cash out of the business, the stock writedowns would cost £150m and there had been a turnround overseas of close to £100m, he said.

To Greenbury's dismay Salsbury refused to leave out admissions of past mistakes. 'I don't agree with you. I am the chief executive now and that is what we are going to say,' he told Greenbury.

So the statement went out and the shares plummeted by 13 per cent in one day to 340p. Rather than diffusing investor and public anger, the admission of mistakes seemed to strike a chord with everyone who read it. It was as if the great British public saw the announcement and said, 'Yes, we knew dear old M&S had lost the plot.' Overnight it was not just OK to criticise M&S, it became de rigueur. The British customer had arrived at what Bob

Worcester, the chairman of the research group MORI, called 'a turning point' in public opinion. For so many years M&S could do no wrong, but from then on, M&S could do no right. St Michael had lost his wings. 'St Michael's spell has been broken,' declared one analyst, slashing his profit forecast from £800m to £650m.

The vast acres of grey that winter had not gone down well, even though Paris had decreed grey to be the fashionable colour. But the problems went far deeper than getting the colour wrong for one season – the decline in the quality of the goods was accelerating. The jumper that lost its shape after washing, the straggly hemlines, ceased to be one-off aberrations. Customers started talking to each other about it. MORI used an 'excellence model' to determine public and investor perception of companies, measuring various factors including public trust. In 1995, 89 per cent of the general public trusted Marks & Spencer. By 1999 that number had fallen to 61 per cent. The high-street friend customers had trusted to deliver quality and value with style had betrayed them. The brand was on the skids.

The late David Ogilvy, the grand old man of advertising who made his fortune by building Ogilvy and Mather into one of America's most success-ful companies, used to say that the one factor that increased sales of a product more than anything else was an improvement in that product. The reverse is also true.

Quality had slipped and customers also noticed the absence of value. M&S clothes were no longer the great bargains they had been in the early part of the decade. Next was beating M&S on its own territory, sourcing dis-cerningly from overseas and producing wearable, stylish clothes at prices competitive with M&S's. And it was so much more pleasant to shop at Next, or Gap. The shops were smaller, more inviting, the staff would help find the right size and there was mercifully less choice. You did not have to wander past mind-numbing rails and rails of trousers or blouses. And if you wanted really cheap, high-fashion clothes you went to Zara or Matalan, where former M&S manager Angus Monro had to fight off customers.

When Greenbury returned to London after his break in the sun he made his displeasure clear and the relationship between him and Salsbury crum-bled rapidly. The non-executives had given each man a clear written outline of his new duties, but neither of them could stick to his brief. After nearly a decade of power, Greenbury found an advisory role where his advice was not taken intolerable. Salsbury, who had for years secretly wanted to change the way M&S operated, flung off his Mr Nice Guy image and addressed his task with all the tact of a military dictator. At one point he had all the portraits of the previous chairmen taken down from the walls of the boardroom because 'I don't like them looking down on me'. But Andrew Stone managed to persuade him to put them back up.

Jacomb and Baldock spent long, difficult meetings with the two men, together and singly, struggling to bring them back to a position where they would talk to each other again – to little avail.

Greenbury disapproved of almost everything Salsbury did in those early months. He stuck to his view that M&S had had one bad season coinciding with a savage retail sales downturn and what in retrospect looked to be over-ambitious expansion plans. But there was nothing wrong with the underlying fabric of the business, or the people.

Salsbury's style of communication by email also made Greenbury (and some of the non-executives) uneasy. Modern technology held no fears for Salsbury and for the first few months they poured from his computer. 'He was like a kid in charge of a candy store,' remarked a colleague.

After he put out the profits warning on 16 January, Salsbury's next act was to announce a management cull of nearly a quarter of M&S's top managers – removing thirty-four senior executives including three main board directors: Derek Hayes, John Sacher and Chris Littmoden. Greenbury argued for a gentler approach. John Sacher was due to retire at the end of 1999, he told him, and, surely Derek Hayes was more competent than Benfield, Salsbury's closest friend with whom he jointly owned a house in Tuscany. But Salsbury refused to listen. 'I want them out now,' he said.

Chris Littmoden, who had supported Oates, was fired while in America and Freeman, as head of personnel, refused initially to pay the full cost of his moving back to the UK. He felt forced to threaten legal proceedings before a more generous severance package was negotiated.

But hardest hit were older executives, including several divisional directors who Salsbury felt were under performing. Several, such as Mike Taylor, the divisional director in charge of foods, had been close to Greenbury. Indeed, Greenbury had asked Taylor to stay an extra year after his retirement date to oversee the new delicatessen and bakery counters; Salsbury then summoned him and 'asked' him to go early. Jim Stocks, the husband of Greenbury's secretary Celia, was another to go within months of his official retirement date. 'Peter threw out a thousand years of experience,' Greenbury was later to say. Not only that, Salsbury carried out the culling with none of the concern for human relations for which the company was famous. Within the rank and file of M&S, Salsbury soon earned himself the nickname Pol Pot.

Marks & Spencer had been top heavy for decades. 'The problem was,' said Kim Winser, one of the brightest talents, who had made divisional director of womenswear at 37 and left in 2000 to revitalise the Pringle brand for the Hong Kong-based Kenneth Fang, 'M&S was wonderful at developing people. We would develop and train, develop and train but nobody ever left so there was a log-jam at the top.' That log-jam contained a lot of 'clones' who knew exactly how M&S did everything, but had long ago lost touch with the outside world.

The culling was needed, but it was handled brutally. Salsbury and Freeman behaved as though their years of what they used to call 'brutalisation in the boardroom' had also changed the new top team into brutes. Freeman, then in charge of personnel, was dubbed by one fellow director 'the worst personnel director we ever had'. By all accounts highly intelligent, she was deemed by David Sieff along with Salsbury to have 'no feel for people'. Some of those who went had been within months of retirement and their pension payments were affected by their leaving the company early. Others felt that procedures were not adhered to. There was great bitterness.

Worse, it was soon clear that there was more to come. There is a well-known business adage that if you take over a company in a hostile bid, you must fire all the people you need to within the first six weeks or you are in trouble.

Salsbury had effectively taken over M&S, but although his cuts might have seemed brutal to those on the receiving end they were not deep enough – indeed, one fellow director called his regime 'death by 1,000 cuts'. Salsbury had joined M&S as a graduate trainee and knew personally all the people he was firing. The culling was part of a reorganisation that split the company into UK retail, overseas and financial services. Salsbury described the new organisation as 'probably the biggest change in the way we set ourselves up to do business in many years'. Others had a different phrase for it – 'slash and burn'.

But he made some positive moves too. Salsbury promoted Freeman to head personnel and made Stone chief executive of UK retailing with his own separate subsidiary board of directors – alas, a board that Stone never convened. Another change was the setting up of a company-wide marketing department to be headed by Salsbury's friend James Benfield. Benfield had been at Salsbury's first wedding and celebrated his second, nursing him through his divorce between times. More than one non-executive director warned Salsbury that their relationship was too cosy. What raised eyebrows outside the company was that M&S did not already have a marketing department – but then Simon Marks had not believed in marketing.

Within weeks of Salsbury taking over there was a brief wave of optimism. Many, both inside and outside, were relieved that Greenbury was no longer in charge and most knew that change, though painful, was necessary and wanted to give Salsbury a chance. The press and City too held off briefly as Salsbury made himself available to both groups in a series of interviews and visits. The shares recovered towards 400p. On 16 January Peggy Hollinger wrote a not unflattering piece on Salsbury in the *Financial Times* making him sound pretty punchy. In it he took responsibility for the collapse in profits. 'I suspect our buying stance was considerably more aggressive than most,' he said in a statement that wildly understated the excessive ordering of over-optimistic selectors.

One of the key roles of the marketing department was to take some of the power away from the 'buying fiefdoms', which in turn would mean less bureaucracy. The buying department was to be split up into several smaller units – again to take away some of its power.

'This is not shifting deckchairs,' insisted Salsbury to Hollinger. 'It is about taking a more customer-focused approach by giving more power to the selling side of the business.' The buyers would no longer be allowed to dictate which ranges a particular store would take – that responsibility would move to the new marketing department, he told her.

In March, Salsbury announced the second phase of the restructuring with another 200 job cuts among more junior executives in buying and store development – signalling to everyone in head office that nobody had a secure job any more. Many of those left were told to re-apply for their jobs.

Then, in May, he took the axe to the stores. One in eight store management jobs were to go and staff were to be shaken up as never before. Supervisors were either sacked or demoted and more staff were transferred from administration to dealing with customer needs. By now Salsbury had employed a number of outside advisors. Morgan Stanley Dean Witter were brought in and their senior corporate financier John Studzinski, known as

Studs, gave a talk to top management outlining what he saw as the main problems. Salsbury also appointed the management consultants LEK to prepare a strategic review.

His many new enemies soon began circulating stories that his drinking was out of control. A sociable company man, Salsbury had always enjoyed carousing late into the night with suppliers and colleagues and his powers of recuperation the following morning were legendary. But however much he drank, and however many times colleagues noted his shaking hands in the mornings, it did not stop a relentless pace of work.

On Saturday 24 April the *Daily Telegraph* published the fateful article by Kate Rankine in the colour magazine. Headlined 'The battle of Baker Street', it took the lid off life at M&S head office and shone a merciless searchlight on the inward-looking culture and hierarchical structure headed by Greenbury 'the autocrat'. The piece analysed the succession row blow by blow. Rankine also revealed that she had received her own Rickogram a year before, in April 1998, in response to an article about the power struggle at the top. Greenbury had written: 'First and foremost, the board itself, including six very powerful non-executive directors will eventually decide at the appropriate time, who succeeds me. Insiders, outsiders, the press or the City will not be involved, or their views given any consideration ...' The letter went on: 'Nobody is in "pole position" or for that matter "out of the race". Nor is there a power struggle. We work as a team.'

It says something for the collective paranoia at Marks & Spencer that several people at high level believed Rankine's article was almost solely responsible for the company's subsequent downfall and lack of ability to recover.

Its publication certainly declared open season on Marks & Spencer for the rest of the press. David Norgrove, then director of strategic planning, summed it up this way: 'There was a crystallisation of people's concerns that had been building up over a period. It suddenly became acceptable to criticise weaknesses in a way it had not been before. There was a time when you would ask a focus group to criticise Marks & Spencer and they would say: "No, we can't do that, it would be like criticising the Queen or my grandmother." The mishandling of the discussions we had with our suppliers about overseas production, the battle for succession, a poor season in terms of the product we bought plus the disruption from Littlewoods, made it suddenly acceptable for people to criticise M&S.'

And then came the terrible full-year results that were announced on 18 May, realising everyone's worst fears. Pre-tax profits for the year to March had collapsed from £1.2bn to £634.6m, although overall turnover was pretty much unaltered at £8.22bn compared with £8.24bn, helped by financial services, where sales leapt from £274.8m to £348.6m. Overseas operations came in with losses of £14.6m compared with a profit of £66.9m. UK retail sales fell by 4 per cent on a like-for-like basis, that is stripping out any increase from the larger selling space, and UK retail profits dropped from £871.5m to £479m.

Despite their estrangement Greenbury had in April asked Salsbury to show him the following year's operating plan and the two men met to discuss it with Stone, Freeman, Colvill and McCracken. Greenbury was instantly critical of the proposed increased spending on advertising and marketing at such a difficult time. 'We could make £850m this year [to March 1999],' he said, 'but if you follow this plan you will be lucky to make £750m.'

But the balance of power had shifted. Where six months before everyone would have meekly agreed with Greenbury, now they all backed Salsbury. Angrily Greenbury complained that far from discussing the plan with him, as a chief executive should with a chairman, Salsbury had presented it to him as a *fait accompli.*

'That is the way it is,' said Salsbury. There was an embarrassed silence and Greenbury left the room.

From then on Salsbury and Greenbury rarely spoke, and Salsbury took pains to isolate him from others. Greenbury discovered that one of the consultants had been ordered by Salsbury not to speak to him under any circumstances. Baldock and Jacomb would be asked to convey messages from Salsbury to Greenbury. Greenbury was at his wits' end – he had never dreamed that the man whom he had promoted as the right person to lead M&S would turn on him with such vehemence. He told Jacomb and Baldock the arrangement was not working. For his part, Salsbury complained that Greenbury could not let go, that he wanted to interfere at every point.

Two hurdles now loomed. The first was the strategic review conference in mid June, when the directors would hole up in a luxury country house hotel and discuss the future. This time the management consultants LEK, along with other firms, were preparing a discussion document. Greenbury, who was supposed to chair the conference, realised that nobody had discussed it with him and asked to be briefed. David Norgrove was given the task of talking to him, but the meeting did not last long.

Even more difficult was the annual meeting on 15 July when the board would have to face shareholders. As the date approached everyone became worried about Greenbury chairing the meeting – not least Greenbury. He took advice from a few trusted friends – Clinton Silver, Sir Brian Pitman at Lloyds TSB, Sir Christopher Hogg, by then at Reuters. Then, just before he and Siân were due to fly to Venice in early June, he had lunch with Good in a small dining room on Baker Street's seventh floor.

After the Oates affair Baldock had brought in the City based PR firm Brunswick, built up by Alan Parker to be arguably the most influential firm in the business. Baldock had seen Parker in operation at Guinness and he liked what he saw. Good had never been reinstated but he remained friends with Greenbury, who sought his advice on the way forward. Good opened the conversation by saying he would not wish to see unpleasant things happening to Greenbury at the annual meeting. Greenbury retorted that unpleasant things were happening to him all the time.

Good made it clear, in his gentle but firm way, that if Greenbury were to chair the meeting, which would be bristling with furious shareholders, analysts and journalists, he would have to eat substantial dollops of humble pie. He showed Greenbury a draft of a speech he had prepared that included the following statement: 'What I want to say to you today is that if I am guilty of any of the things of which I stand accused, then I want to offer you my most humble and sincere apologies.' It continued with a quote from Robert Burns. 'O wad some pow'r the giftie gie us, to see oursels as others see us!' adding, 'Unfortunately I do not have that power and I cannot judge myself. All I can say is that everything I have ever done in my 47 years with the company was because I genuinely believed it to be in the best interests of the company.'

Good advised him to then hand the meeting over to Peter Salsbury and not take any further part. The potential for Greenbury exploding under questioning was too great to be risked. If that happened, said Good, the press would be appalling and he would be forced to resign by the institutions. Greenbury read the letter carefully. His only comment was, 'I don't think I can do the Scottish accent.' To Good's surprise Greenbury shook his hand warmly and thanked him for the advice.

The following week he flew to Venice where, enjoying the delights of the

Cipriani and walking along the canals, he and Siân talked of little else. By the end of the week he had made up his mind. 'I can't go on working with Peter,' he told her. 'I think I should resign at the annual meeting.' Meanwhile Baldock and Jacomb had one more discussion with Salsbury, who repeated that working with Greenbury was proving impossible. Greenbury returned on the Friday evening to be met by his driver with a holdall containing a 700-page strategic review put together by LEK and the other consultants. He got through the first fifty pages of the synopsis and despaired. In a nutshell the message was that M&S had been too obsessed with the product and had not paid sufficient attention to the brand. It was a message that went directly against the credo he had learned from Simon Marks – that if you get the product right, then the brand will follow.

Over the weekend Greenbury rang Jacomb twice to vent his feelings. Jacomb suggested they both meet with Salsbury in Greenbury's office on the Monday morning.

At that meeting Greenbury told them of his decision to announce his retirement at the annual meeting. Jacomb pointed out that, as he disagreed so profoundly with the review document, it would be a mistake for him to chair the strategic review conference to discuss it, which was scheduled for the end of June at Hartwell House, a country house hotel near Aylesbury, and if he was not chairing the meeting as expected, the press would realise there was a crisis. There was a pause while Jacomb gathered his courage. 'We think,' he said, 'it would be best if we convened a special board meeting and you retired immediately.'

Almost relieved, Greenbury agreed. 'Fine, let's cut clean now,' he replied. 'The future of the business is not with me. It's better if I go now.' His chairmanship was over. Calmly he told the two men of his deep regret that he would not stay until he was 65 or beyond like his predecessors and he made a final impassioned request – that he should have his portrait painted, to hang alongside those of all the previous chairmen in the boardroom. Jacomb willingly gave him the undertaking that the company would honour that tradition. Jacomb never dreamed that Salsbury's dislike of Greenbury ran so deep that he would later refuse to have the portrait hung anywhere in Baker Street.

The announcement of Greenbury's departure went out the following day, 22 June. 'Sir Richard has made a terrific contribution to Marks & Spencer and to retailing over the years,' Sir Martin Jacomb told callers. 'He has always had the interest of the business at heart, however difficult the issue, and this is a big decision by a big man.'

Salsbury could not be gracious, even in victory. 'What we are doing has moved away from his methodology and thought processes; decisions were reached without him being able to have an input,' he said. 'The executive directors needed active impetus from the top that Rick was unable to provide.'

Greenbury and Salsbury have not spoken to each other since.

Like Margaret Thatcher, Greenbury is an example of the classic leader who hung on too long. Surrounded by weak people who pretended at all times to agree with him, he was eventually pushed out by those he believed were his loyal lieutenants. The parallels with him and Thatcher were clear. Both possessed of towering egos, they had rallied the troops in times of crisis and then allowed themselves to be diverted, seduced by the perfume of power. They both failed to nurture a worthy successor, or to bring in new blood. Their increasingly irrational behaviour was tolerated by their acolytes, who had found them inspiring on the way up, as long as the formula produced success. For Thatcher, the catalyst for her removal was the poll tax, for Greenbury it was the profits collapse and the attempted coup by Keith Oates. Both were great leaders whose tragedy was that they failed entirely to appreciate the impact of their own personalities on those around them. They both tended to shoot messengers bearing bad news and so the bad news ceased to reach them – until it was too late.

# CHAPTER ELEVEN

# Hello, Philip

S ales continued to decline. At the annual meeting on 15 July 1999 Brian
Baldock, then acting chairman, told shareholders that clothing sales
for the first fifteen weeks of the financial year had fallen by 10 per cent
with food sales 3.4 per cent lower. Even including the newly converted Littlewoods stores, total sales dropped by 6 per cent. By then, though, it was
evident that the entire British retailing sector – with the exception of Next
and Matalan – was in trouble. In the words of leading retail analyst Sundeep
Bahanda at Deutsche Bank: '1999 was a year to forget for the UK clothing
sector. The biggest losers were the mid-market players and the winners the
speciality clothing stores and value players.' By the end of the year the stock-
market value of 'mid-market player' Storehouse had fallen 61 per cent to
£226m; Arcadia, the old Burton group, was down by a half to £168m; Debenhams was down 47 per cent to £714m and M&S was 40 per cent lower at
£7bn, a pale shadow of the £19bn valuation achieved in the heady days of
October 1997, when M&S was by far and away Britain's top retailer by
market value. The July annual meeting was surprisingly good humoured in
the light of the sliding share price.

The first year of the new millennium was to be one of the most action
packed in the company's history. Freed of the constraints of his former
chairman Peter Salsbury went to work with renewed vigour. There is a well-
known joke in business circles about the new Russian president who asks his
predecessor for advice and in return is given two letters and told: 'When you
are in a tight spot, open the first.' The tight spot arrives after a few months
and the president opens the first letter. 'Blame me,' it says. He follows the
instruction and everything goes well until the next crisis. He opens the
second letter: 'Sit down and write two letters.'

During the summer and autumn of 1999 Salsbury vigorously adopted
first-letter mode. In Baker Street he set about demolishing many symbols of

the old regime. He dismantled the directors' servery, scrapped the silver salvers, threw out the dainty bone china with its gold-rimmed cups, toned down the plush dining rooms on the seventh floor and dispensed with the white-gloved waiters. From then on the lunchrooms became more modest in style, and available to any executive who needed to entertain visitors for a business lunch.

The old restaurant for clerical and junior workers in a nearby building was scrapped and a brand-new stainless-steel and salad-style communal restaurant opened on the first floor, designed to feed everyone in head office. From then on, refreshments delivered to offices came in earthenware cups. Melamine and gilt trays replaced the silver and the old-style waiters gave way to friendly waitresses. Even so, the tray still came laden with a plate of luxury biscuits and a choice of tea and coffee – so whichever was not drunk was simply thrown away.

Salsbury dispensed with the services of the company doctor, George Remington, because he 'lacked managerial abilities' and slimmed down the medical and other employee-welfare areas. Out went the hairdressing salons and free chiropody. Many of the medical services that had been free of charge or heavily subsidised were still available, but now they had to be paid for at commercial rates. Advised by Baldock, he even broke with M&S tradition in the appointment of a headhunting firm to find Greenbury's successor, choosing the more creative and entrepreneurial Whitehead Mann, headed by Anna Mann, rather than the establishment firm Spencer Stewart.

A left-winger in his youth and graduate of the London School of Economics, Salsbury displayed revolutionary fervour in his actions. The hierarchy must go, he declared, as he instructed directors to enter the building from the front with all the other workers. He wanted a flatter management structure, he said, more equality. Then he moved into Greenbury's old office and had it redecorated to his own taste.

The message from Baker Street via the Brunswick public relations machine for the next few months was unremitting – the woes of the company could all be laid at Greenbury's feet. It had been his constant interference in minor matters, his grandiosity, autocratic style and love of hierarchy that had brought the company down. If only he had not terrorised the entire board and wasted time choosing the colour of the loo walls, everything would have been all right.

Yet it was all hypocrisy. The divisional directors and many executives recalled that none of the managing directors had dared to jeopardise their jobs by standing up to Greenbury. 'They were all sycophants,' said one, 'sycophants to a man.' Salsbury, in particular, appeared to approve of everything his old boss did until he became chief executive: 'Peter managed to make Rick think he was right behind him.'

At the end of September Alan McWalter was appointed from Woolworth to replace Benfield as marketing director. What is more, he created a bigger, grander marketing department with new powers for him to manage. Marketing would take over many of the decisions of the buying departments in deciding just what the customer wanted.

Salsbury then embarked on his second boardroom sort-out. He fired his old friend James Benfield along with Lord Stone, who, after enjoying a brief honeymoon period with Salsbury during which he was elevated to head of UK retail, complained that he had found working for his new boss even more difficult than working under Greenbury. Salsbury, he grumbled, interfered at every turn and would not let him get on with the job – Salsbury complained that Stone could not manage. Whatever the reasons, Stone was out after thirty-three years. Benfield had been with the company twenty-nine years.

The two men enjoyed the last of the two-year-salary payouts – leaving a matter of weeks before all directors and executives were put on one-year contracts. Salsbury scrapped Guy McCracken's position of managing director for overseas operations, effectively demoting him (he stayed only a few months longer), and put himself in charge of UK operations – a sure sign of his growing fears for the future. David Norgrove was given the job of developing new business ideas.

Of the sixteen executive directors who sat on the board when Salsbury took charge, only eight remained. So much for Greenbury being the only autocrat in M&S. The six non-executives, including Baldock, now enjoying the title of interim chairman, still backed him, although with increasing misgivings.

Salsbury's next move was to put the Kings supermarket group in the United States up for sale, though he maintained that he was 'unequivocally committed' to keeping Brooks Brothers.

Soon afterwards, the non-executives persuaded the board to accept outside credit cards. Robert Colvill, who had taken over as chairman of financial services and reported directly to Salsbury after Oates's unceremonious exit, reluctantly agreed, although he accurately predicted that sales would not increase as a result. It would cost the company dear, both in charges to the credit-card companies and in lost business from M&S's own store card. But, like the fitting rooms that didn't reduce the garment-return rate, it was something the public demanded. M&S succumbed to the will of the customer just a month after the John Lewis Partnership, the other last bastion against the banks' plastic, threw in the towel.

Salsbury next took an axe to the British clothing manufacturers, most famously giving William Baird, a supplier of thirty years' standing, six months' notice. He and many of the board had realised that the 'unique relationship' with British manufacturers had long ceased to give M&S a competitive advantage – rather the reverse; it had become a millstone. When Salsbury went to break the bad news to chief executive David Suddens in October 1999, Suddens pleaded with him to delay the decision. He told him that Coats Viyella, another large M&S supplier then chaired by Sir Harry Djanogly, was poised to merge its clothing subsidiaries with Baird. If successful, the deal would lead to the enlarged group creating much greater manufacturing capacity overseas, which surely would be just what M&S wanted. Salsbury agreed to think about it overnight, but rang the next day to say his decision was final. Consequently the deal with Coats never took place and at the end of 1999 the group announced losses of £93.5m. Baird was forced to lay off 4,500 UK staff as it closed sixteen factories.

The move sent shock waves through the British textile industry and led to Baird suing M&S for £53.6m. Greenbury, who had been personal friends with Baird's former chairman Sir Donald Parr, was furious and agreed to testify in court about the basis of trust on which business with Baird and other major suppliers had been historically conducted, but to no avail. Baird pursued the case all the way to the House of Lords but in July 2001 their Lordships decided not to give Baird leave to appeal against the ruling by the Court of Appeal the previous February. The Lords said that Baird's case 'had no real prospect of success'. The company spent £1m on legal fees and undisclosed M&S costs; Suddens resigned as chief executive not long after.

In the winter of 1999 M&S's major UK suppliers were summoned to a conference and informed that far more product would have to come from overseas. Over the next two years, Dewhirst, Desmonds and Courtaulds closed UK factories and relocated their activities in North Africa, Thailand, Indonesia and China. Down the line at M&S, Salsbury slimmed and reorganised the buying teams to such an extent that few of the old relationships between individuals, the essence of the old M&S supply chain, existed. He aggressively set about finding new sources of supply.

By the time of the half-year results in November, Salsbury had destroyed the spirit of the company and the trust of its suppliers and staff. The sense of pride in being part of retailing's top team and working for a company that cared for its employees had gone. 'Peter and Clara sat up in Rick's old office for days at a time mentally masturbating,' said one director who was shown the door by the new regime. 'And when they had finished they ripped the heart out of the business.'

Salsbury appeared to relish destroying the old shibboleths, but like the Communists he had so admired in his youth, he had little idea what to put in their place. His lack of leadership soon showed. 'Peter had absolutely no vision for the future,' said another director. 'In a situation like that he needed to map out the future. He needed to say: "This is were we are going. It will take three years; here are the steps we need to achieve that; there will be pain along the way but it will be worth it – are you with me?" But there was none of that. When we asked about the future, all Peter could talk about was survival.'

By the second restructuring there were few smiling faces. Everyone was scared of losing his or her job; people's motivation had vanished. The company that for half a century had been a role model for the treatment of staff had disappeared. Those who turned to the top for guidance and inspiration found nothing but a frightened man who had no feel for those he was supposed to lead. Like busy fools, Salsbury and his new team rushed around changing, consulting and revamping to little purpose. Lack of confidence cascaded down from Salsbury and Freeman at the top, throughout the organisation to the humblest part-time checkout assistant.

Out there on the sales floor it showed. Customer satisfaction, which had begun to slide in 1998, now went into freefall. Staff became downright surly and extraordinary events took place. Items that had previously been a fixture in the food shops became scarce. The complaint of one woman shopper as she stood in front of the chilled cabinet in the food hall of the Moorgate branch in the City of London was typical. As she searched vainly for a packet of smoked bacon amid the array of unsmoked packs she turned to the woman next to her and declared: 'I don't believe it. This keeps happening and I keep telling the manager. I might as well go to my local Co-op.' Another scoured the shelves for her favourite meringue cases. When asked where the cases were a checkout girl replied dourly: 'I don't know. You will have to ask somebody on the sales floor.' 'But there is nobody on the sales floor,' the customer replied.

In clothing, those who spotted an item they liked often found their size was missing – and unlike in Next or Gap there was no one to help them. Of course it could be ordered – and couriered to your home for a fee – but while that suited a few, most people wanted to walk out of the store with their garments. Public trust disintegrated. The survey by research group MORI showing that, whereas 89 per cent of the British public trusted M&S in 1995, by December 1999 that figure had fallen to 61 per cent was a verdict even more eloquent than the collapsing share price.

The much-trumpeted autumn ranges failed to hit the spot. Between 1996 and 1998 M&S had lost market share, particularly among the young, who defected to high-fashion shops such as H&M, Zara and Matalan. In the thick of those turbulent uncertain days, in an attempt to woo back the young, selectors had gone overboard for lower-priced supposedly higher-fashion clothes. The young 'she' quickly perceived such ranges as poor imitations and continued to stay away, while her mother took one look, stocked up on knickers and tights and took her credit cards off to other shops on the high street.

And there were no shortage of competing shops to service her. M&S had not been alone in expanding the amount of floor space – many others had done the same. During 1999 UK retailers had added 3.5 per cent shopping space against a background of slower growth in clothing spending than in other sectors such as sports, furniture or pharmaceuticals. There was too much shopping space chasing the same number of customers, who also now expected lower prices. Price deflation – with which the electrical retailers had long come to live – hit clothing extra hard. The result was that in 1999 retail clothing shares underperformed the general retail sector by 15 per cent and the whole stock market by a massive 45 per cent. Yet amid this misery Matalan's shares almost trebled, valuing the company at £1.1bn as the public flocked to the discount chain, and Next's stock-market value increased by 9 per cent to £2bn.

M&S was doing almost as badly as its less blue chip rivals such as Arcadia and Debenhams – all mired in the mid-market. Half-year profits for the 1999–2000 financial year, announced on 2 November, fell by 58 per cent to £114.4m on sales down from £3.8bn to £3.7bn. For the first time in its history

M&S's market share in clothing was falling. Salsbury admitted losing market share of as much as two percentage points in clothing. Verdict, the retail research consultancy, showed M&S market share down from 13.4 per cent in 1997 to 11 per cent in 1999. Arcadia was the biggest beneficiary, up from 6.2 per cent to 8.2 per cent, with Next close behind, up from 3.9 to 4.5 per cent over the same period.

Salsbury flippantly pointed to the demise of leggings and tunics as a fashion. 'Leggings and tunics lasted for so long as the thing to wear that we took our eye off the ball,' he said, blaming a modest segment of the trouser market for the company's downfall. He also admitted to his shareholders that M&S would never be able to return to its former glories, with pre-tax profits of more than £1bn, with the business as it was then constituted.

For a few brief weeks after Greenbury's departure in June 1999, the non-executives continued to stand by Salsbury. They recognised that the business needed fewer people at the top, that the power of the buyers, with their over-cosy relationships with the UK suppliers, had to be smashed, that more overseas sourcing was vital for M&S to be competitive. Salsbury, they thought, had the right ideas. But, as they quickly discovered, he tried to do everything at once – and he was a lousy communicator. He fired employees and suppliers alike with ill grace and little acknowledgement of their past efforts. At the same time Salsbury was piling on the costs by bringing in armies of consultants and engaging a new advertising agency to create a new and expensive campaign. At a time when Next cut back on its marketing budget, Marks & Spencer (having only recently set up a marketing department) was jacking up its spending.

While Salsbury's scythe cut through the organisation the non-executives dallied over choosing another chairman. Baldock enjoyed his role of interim chairman and many believe he would have liked to make it permanent – if it had stayed a non-executive role. Sir Michael Perry, a former Unilever chairman, also aspired to the chairmanship – but again in a non-executive capacity. So while these two corporate veterans jockeyed for position, the search process undertaken by the headhunter Whitehead Mann continued slowly under the name of thoroughness. More than a hundred names from America and Europe were sifted through. Finally, in November, it was realised that top talent was not interested in a non-executive job where share options were not allowed – and that M&S needed a more hands-on chairman to support Salsbury. The board duly put out a statement with the half-year results in November saying that the company had decided to look for a full-time executive to be chairman. The news shook investors' nerves even more than the terrible figures. If ever there was a vote of no confidence in Salsbury, that was it.

Just before Christmas, six months after Greenbury's departure, Salsbury embarked on his third restructuring. He split the company into seven business units, each of which would be 'profit accountable'. There would be yet more customer focus.

The share price sank toward 250p – against 370p when Greenbury retired – and then came the stock-market rumours. Somebody was planning the unthinkable – a hostile takeover of Britain's best-known, if no longer best-loved, retailer. Worse still, that somebody was Philip Green – the self-styled hit-and-run merchant of the retail sector. Green, an old friend of Tony Berry of Blue Arrow infamy, had started out in the 1970s trading in jeans and gone on to run the small quoted clothing company Amber Day in the 1980s, with initial success. But profits collapsed after he injected the What Every Woman Wants chain into it, and he was ousted in 1992 with a £1m payout. In 1995 he bounced back to buy Olympus Sports from Sears, the Selfridges-to-shoes empire so painstakingly built up by Sir Charles Clore. He made a cool £38m profit when he sold it and moved his residence to Monte Carlo near his friends, the secretive Barclay twins, owners of *The Scotsman*. Not long afterwards, the Barclays backed his successful bid for the whole of Sears, a takeover that made him another fortune as he 'knocked out' the parts to various buyers. Although liked for his sense of humour and admired for his financial brain, Green was viewed with suspicion and remained on the fringes of the business establishment.

Strangely, Green gained what he hoped would be a critical entrée into M&S through Sir David Sieff, the last remaining family board member and by 1999 a non-executive. Sieff chaired the British Retail Consortium and had met Green while trying to persuade him to join the lobby group. Despite Green's buccaneering style, a sharp contrast to Sieff's cultured urbanity, the two men hit it off. Green told him he would like to meet Baldock as the acting chairman – so Sieff tried to broker an introduction.

But Baldock would have none of it. He guessed immediately what Green's intentions were and refused to meet, particularly as Green would not divulge the subject matter for the conversation. Baldock took the view that any meeting, however apparently casual, would be seen as 'formal discussions', a view he asked Sieff to pass on. Never short on chutzpah, Green rang Baldock direct and attempted to flatter him into a meeting. It was, Baldock recalled, a 'we are both important men in business – we should get together' type of conversation. But Baldock still refused to meet him, much to Green's annoyance. Baldock spoke plainly. If Green wanted to talk takeovers, he said, Green would have to put his ideas down on paper.

Then in mid December, when Green began to consult bankers about putting up the finance for what would be a £10bn bid, the rumours that he was about to pounce exploded in the press, pushing the share price from 248p to 312p in one day.

Baldock, who knew a thing or two about hostile bids from the days when Guinness made its fateful play for Distillers, had already formed a defence committee. Led by the investment bank Morgan Stanley, the Queen's stockbroker Cazenove and the PR company Brunswick, the group did its homework. Baldock ordered a close watch on Green's activities and served notices under Section 212 of the Companies Act on him and those associated with him, with the aim of flushing out any secret build-up of share purchases through nominee accounts.

Green recognised that M&S could not be broken up in Sears fashion and would need to be managed for the long term to yield the profits needed to justify a takeover. He put together a killer team of people who, although in existing jobs, agreed to leave if a bid succeeded. Allan Leighton, who with Archie Norman had transformed Asda, was Green's first choice to lead the turnaround. To work with him he persuaded Terry Green (no relation), who had led the revival in Debenhams' fortunes, to head the clothing business. As the head of the finance team he selected Richard North, then finance director of Bass – where embarrassingly Sir Michael Perry was deputy chairman. The pièce de résistance was Rupert Hambro, the urbane and well-connected investment banker. Hambro, Green decided, would be chairman, if the bid succeeded.

It says much for Green's confidence and his powers of persuasion that he was able to put in place such a turbocharged team. It also says much about the nature of the grip that Marks & Spencer exercised on the hearts of the nation, and the power of the brand, that such highly rated executives were ready to give up top jobs in an attempt to resurrect the fallen icon.

Green's bid plan was codenamed Project Mushroom. A consortium of international bankers led by the Lara Croft of loan syndication Robin

Saunders of the German group West LB, agreed to put up the loan finance. It would have been one of the most heroic fundraisings the City of London had ever seen. Yet the feisty Saunders, fresh from having raised more than £1bn for Bernie Ecclestone, the Formula One boss, was able to corral her banking colleagues into line. For investment banking advice Green turned to Sir Laurie Magnus, the baronet who had acted for him at Amber Day in its heyday. Magnus introduced Green to his current employer, the American investment bank Donaldson Luftkin & Jenrette, which after initial talks about the plan agreed to become the lead financial advisor. Merrill Lynch, the giant American securities firm known in the US as the 'thundering herd', was also brought in to lend financial muscle.

But not everyone at Donaldson Luftkin & Jenrette was happy about acting for Green. Directors of the New York office commissioned Kroll Associates, the world's best-known corporate detective agency, to draw up a report on him. And although Kroll unearthed no evidence that Green had ever been involved in any wrongdoing, its sleuths did link him to a number of unsavoury characters, something that was said to have worried Martin Smith, the chairman of DLJ in London, and his opposite numbers at Merrill Lynch.

Another concern was the financial terms of the deal as proposed by Green. His basic plan to sell off M&S's overseas businesses and give the UK clothing some style and pizazz sounded good. He wanted to put non-competing products into shops that were no longer profitable, while continuing to sell the M&S standard ranges. The last thing he wanted was to put stores up for sale and have rivals such as Next and The Gap move in.

But in return for putting it all together, Green wanted a bigger chunk of the cake than the advisors thought the City would wear. 'The financial terms were so hopelessly greedy, his own take so enormous,' said one advisor. 'He wanted to be creator, owner and driver.'

On top of that, Green's irascibility and lack of finesse did not go down well at DLJ, particularly when Margaret Young, a key member of the team, returned to the office in floods of tears following a difficult meeting with him.

In the first week of February 2000, top executives at DLJ in London and New York reluctantly decided they could not act for Green. Coincidentally, another storm had blown up the previous month when he responded to M&S's Section 212 notices with the news that his wife, Christina, had bought

9.5 million shares, a purchase that cost her about £23m. An M&S advisor at Morgan Stanley briefed the Sunday press accordingly. Although Green had sought approval for the purchase from the Takeover Panel and had acted properly in every way, the ensuing press reaction was hostile. An over-zealous news editor at the *Sunday Times* insisted on inserting the phrase 'insider dealing' in the headline and the first paragraph of the story, despite being warned of the potential libel. Green responded by suing the news-paper, winning an out-of-court settlement, but by then the damage was done. He had become a hostage to his past reputation.

The idea of such an adventurer gaining control of Marks & Spencer pro-duced a frenzy of press coverage. In January there were no fewer than 1,735 mentions of M&S in the UK press.

The week of 7 February, Martin Smith in his role as chairman of Donald-son Luftkin & Jenrette went to see Green in his office and broke the news that the investment bank was no longer prepared to act for him in his pro-posed bid for M&S. According to a member of the bid team, Green pleaded, cajoled and lost his temper – but to no avail. When Smith walked out of the meeting, the deal of Green's dreams was dead.

Never a man to stay down for long, Green bounced back and with the same team minus North and Hambro approached Alan Smith, the former M&S director who had spent a couple of years at Kingfisher before taking the chair at Storehouse, which owned both BHS and Mothercare. Green bought BHS from Alan Smith for £200m. It was a nibble compared with the mouthful that would have been M&S and left Smith as chairman of Mothercare.

From then on both companies recovered strongly. In May 2001, BHS showed a profits leap from £12.5m to £31.5m while Mothercare produced profits of £10.2m compared with a loss of £6.1m.

At M&S the delight and relief at escaping Green's clutches was short lived. On 14 February, St Valentine's Day, Kim Winser, who would have made a far tougher first female executive director than Freeman, resigned. The former head of women's casualwear, Winser had been elevated to divi-sional director of corporate marketing in the most recent restructuring, earning her the sobriquet 'custodian of the M&S brand'. But she had received an offer so tempting she could not refuse. One of Winser's Far East suppliers, Kenneth Fang, who had built up one of the biggest Far East knitwear groups, had bought the Pringle knitwear company and asked her to head it and restore it to profitability. A measure of her loss to M&S was that within twelve months she had revitalised the Pringle brand and transformed those Perry Como trademark diamond-pattern sweaters into must-have fashion items for the likes of Jamie Oliver and David Beckham. At that point the new guard at M&S began throwing money at her to persuade her to return – without success.

Winser was the first of the real talent to leave voluntarily. Nigel Robertson and Roger Whiteside, both former Greenbury personal assistants, were not far behind. Both had been promoted by Salsbury to be joint divisional directors of food when Mike Taylor left in the first cull. They made a dynamic team but Salsbury's seven-way split of December 1999 separated them. Whiteside was left in sole charge of food while Robertson became head of change – or Change Tsar as he was instantly dubbed by the press. Salsbury was stunned and furious when in March 2000 they both quit to set up their own on-line food delivery business – an idea they had put unsuccessfully to M&S. They were given a week to tidy their offices and go.

Within a few months they had teamed up with Waitrose, which bought 40 per cent of their business L M Solutions for £35m and lent expertise and personnel. They renamed the business Ocado and brought in BOC to advise on the logistics side. A 300,000 square-foot warehouse was built near Hatfield in preparation for the launch in autumn 2001.

At every level throughout M&S, the talented people began to be poached by the competition. 'Everyone is miserable; the CVs are all on the street,' commented one senior selector.

Into this affray stepped Luc Vandevelde, a cool, cultured Belgian who spoke five languages and pressed his own olive oil. Appointed executive chairman on 25 January 2000, he took up his new post at the end of February after moving his family from Paris to a small company flat in London.

Green, who was still stalking the company at that time said: 'They need a striker and they have hired a goalie.'

Vandevelde seemed as different from Greenbury as it was possible to be. At 48, he was fourteen years younger, with a relaxed charm and a mental agility in sharp contrast to either Greenbury or Salsbury. Yet like Greenbury he was a driven man. And also like him, Vandevelde had been forced by fate to forgo a university education to help a parent. His father, an entrepreneurial merchant, had been killed in a car accident when Vandevelde was 14, leaving his mother ill-provided for with six children. They lived in the small town of Halen in Belgium. Vandevelde left school at 18 and trained to be an accountant, paying his early salary straight into his mother's bank account. 'The sheer fact that I have had to fight against people who have two, three, four or five years more education than I had, made me fight just a little more,' he told Amanda Hall of the *Sunday Telegraph* at the time of his appointment. It was an elegant echo of Greenbury's comment about more highly educated colleagues: 'They may have gone to university, but I have learned all I needed in the university of life.'

Vandevelde had joined Kraft in his early twenties, restructuring the group's manufacturing and working in America as well as on the Continent, where he masterminded the group's acquisition of Jacobs Suchard in 1990. After joining the French supermarket group Promodes in 1995 as chairman, he transformed it into one of the best-performing food retailers in France, before negotiating a merger with its bigger rival Carrefour. In the combined group, named Carreprom, Vandevelde would have been number two – and clearly he preferred to be number one.

Choosing Vandevelde had been an arduous process. By Christmas 1999 the non-executives had whittled their list of possible chairmen from the first trawl of 100 candidates down to three. One was Jurgen Hintz, a Dutch high-flying former Procter & Gamble director who went on to be head of the packaging group CarnaudMetalbox and then Caradon, the industrial conglomerate; another was Sir Peter Davis, then chief executive of the Prudential (where, embarrassingly, Jacomb was chairman) and the other, Vandevelde. At that point Jacomb had to stand aside from the decision making.

Prophets are often not recognised in their own country, and so it was with Davis. A former Sainsbury executive who had risen to director level, he had left in 1986 after realising he would not make it to the top while members of the Sainsbury family still dominated. He joined Reed International, which he slimmed down and revitalised before becoming chief executive of the Pru, where initially he made the mistake of appearing in its television advertisements, but went on successfully to expand the business and launched Egg, the internet bank. Hugely energetic, Davis, who sat on the board of the Royal Opera House as well as holding a clutch of non-executive posts, had been looking around for the next big job and an informal conversation with Anna Mann about Marks & Spencer put him in the running. He knew most of the non-executives there from the corporate circuit, but his subsequent interviews with them did not go too well. 'Peter seemed to be more concerned about Peter Davis than Marks & Spencer,' said one. 'The other candidates on the shortlist did enormous amounts of home-work and put forward analytical papers on strategic mapping, but he did not.'

The reality was that Davis, who also sat on the board of Boots as a non-executive, already knew a great deal about food and general retailing in the UK. Although clothing would have been a new field for him, he would have hit the ground running, whereas Vandevelde, who had little knowl-edge of the British market or clothing, could barely walk. But the non-executives – certainly Brian Baldock and Sir Michael Perry – preferred to take their chances with, so far as Britain was concerned, an unknown. In early February, just as Vandevelde was organising his move to London, Davis moved back as chief executive to his old firm Sainsbury, where the family had allowed performance to slip. It was the right job for him, but a loss for Marks & Spencer. 'It was a pity we didn't go for Peter,' said one director who had voted for Davis. 'He would have been far better than Luc. He knew how to handle staff and suppliers. He would have given a sense of leadership.'

Vandevelde brought with him a good brain and an outsider's view. At a time when globalisation was a byword for success, his international aura appealed to the company. His objective, well-presented analysis impressed the non-executives and won over Salsbury, who, despite his closeness to Freeman, was finding life at the top lonely and hard.

Vandevelde had the luxury of a strong negotiating position as Carreprom would have delivered him juicy bonuses. So M&S provided them, welcom-ing him with a £2.2m 'golden hello' and a package that could, if things went well, earn him up to £1.3m a year and £10.4m in shares over five years.

And so, after eight months of thrashing around, M&S had an executive chairman – against all the corporate governance dictats of the day – and a so-called chief executive in Peter Salsbury, who found his role somewhat diminished.

Vandevelde had admired Marks & Spencer from afar for years – and even used it as a management model in his previous career. He had no idea of the scale of the challenge he was undertaking, as he was later to admit. Nothing could have prepared him for the mayhem and demoralisation within the company. He could well have thought the group was simply experiencing a trading downturn that a bit of sorting out would put right. From such a beginning things could only get better – and he would emerge not only a hero – but a rich hero.

Christmas 1999 trading was terrible. Like-for-like sales were down 5.3 per cent and sales of clothing and footwear fell by almost 8 per cent. To rub salt into the wounds, Next's chairman David Jones admitted Christmas sales had been below expectations – but, even so, they were up by 6 per cent on a like-for-like basis. Salsbury announced a 'price repositioning', which meant cutting prices and profit margins along with them.

Vandevelde arrived at M&S and said what everyone wanted to hear. He thought Salsbury was terrific, and he looked forward to making M&S even more international. The world was their oyster was the implication. The City analysts loved him and the journalists were impressed. The shares, having fallen initially on news of his appointment, recovered to 260p by the end of February 2000.

By this time the American management consultant AT Kearney, Inter-brand, plus six other consultants had been beavering away at Baker Street for the best part of a year at an estimated cost of £2m a month. The final bill came to more than £40m. When Bob Willet, of Andersen Consulting (now renamed Accenture), who was managing director of Littlewoods' lacklustre high-street stores and had presided over the profits collapse at the old Gateway chain, was appointed to oversee the work of the other eight consultants, the process threatened to descend into farce.

In March the recommendations of the consultants began to emerge as action. To many fanfares M&S announced an overhaul of its brand. 'St Michael' would be minimised on the labels and those shiny emerald green bags consigned to history. Instead there would be matt apple-green bags in a trendy design for clothing. Food bags would have the same design, but in matt lime green. Analysts could not resist some caustic comments about the quality of the contents counting rather more than the bag itself.

Springtime also saw the launch of the new Autograph range – a collection by top designers aimed at those who bought the premium smoked salmon, rocket salad and tarte au citron from the food halls but never went near the clothes. Designers such as Betty Jackson, Katharine Hamnett and Julien Macdonald said they were thrilled to be involved. 'I'm really proud of the collection,' gushed Jackson. 'The quality is fantastic and the prices are amazing.'

The fashion press loved it and initially sales went so well in the first sixteen stores that seven more were added. Separated from the main selling space by partitions, the whole ambience of Autograph signalled a different kind of clothing. There were well-lit individual fitting rooms, wooden coat-hangers and young funky sales assistants in androgynous uniforms.

But the initial promise was not to be fulfilled. The clothes sold quite well but sometimes came back on grounds of quality. And there was low-key grumbling that if one was paying so much more for a designer garment, surely it should not need to have an M&S label in it. For most well-heeled women who bought their food and underwear at M&S, Autograph went against the grain. 'I just don't feel right paying £80 for a sweater, when I know I can get one for £35 in the next department,' commented one. By 2001 Autograph had made no money and proved to be little more than a conver-sation point.

David Norgrove was put in charge of developing new ventures. His brief was to invest in start-up companies and take M&S into the dotcom era. One such was an investment in Confetti.com, a company started by James Ben-field, his former colleague. Other investments included Splendour.com and the ill-fated Talkcast, a multimedia company. There was also an experiment with 'new concept' lingerie shops in Europe following the success of the Salon Rose range of daring underwear designed by Agent Provocateur, and made by Coats Viyella. More importantly, Norgrove was to examine ways that M&S could profit from its technical expertise. For decades M&S tech-nologists gave away their developments to suppliers without any patent pro-tection. When that technology was copied M&S margins suffered. Norgrove realised that the pioneers were often the ones with arrows in their back. He wanted to change that.

On 23 May 2000, in the midst of this frenetic activity, Luc Vandevelde slashed the dividend for the first time in Marks & Spencer's history and announced a fall in full-year profits to £517m against £628m. There were no 'one-off' costs to blame this time and the full-year dividend was cut from 14.4p to 9p. Vandevelde also announced another boardroom restructuring – the fourth since Salsbury's appointment as chief executive fifteen months before. Out of the door went clothing directors Joe Rowe and Roger Aldridge. Barry Morris opted to take demotion from the main board to 'business unit director for womenswear' rather than sacrifice some of his final pension.

Despite the mayhem, Cool Hand Luc, as he had now become known, oozed confidence about the future. 'If I don't deliver in two years' time, then I won't be sitting here in two years' time. Within a year, you will see signs of a recovery,' he said. It was a statement he would later regret.

Once more he declared his support for Peter Salsbury, standing side by side with him for a photograph. 'If he was not here, I don't think I would be either,' he said.

Few believed him. In the *Daily Telegraph*, Kate Rankine quoted M&S insiders as saying: 'Nobody can believe that Peter and Clara Freeman are staying.'

At the July annual meeting, Vandevelde wowed the private shareholders with his Gallic charm and apparent ability to relate to them. Media obsession with M&S appeared boundless. During 1999 the average monthly mentions in the UK press had risen to 1,262, peaking at 1,715 in November, after the results. By June there were two television programmes underway, one by the BBC's *Money Programme* team, another by an independent television company, Blakeway, for Channel Four. The Motley Fool, an internet chat room for shareholders in quoted companies, carried 6,000 messages on the M&S site, which was started in late 1998. By 2001 it was up to 7,000 messages – at least three times as many as those for rival retailers, though less than those for beleaguered technology stocks.

A brief respite came in June when the secretive Dutch-owned retailer C&A pulled out of the UK, closing 130 stores at a cost of 5,000 jobs. The closures were to be effective by the end of the year. The move highlighted the depressed state of the UK clothing market and temporarily made the problems at M&S seem just part of the retail downturn. The relief at M&S was palpable – others were in trouble too. Retail analysts wrote screeds on how younger customers wanted super-cheap, high-fashion clothes from Matalan, Zara and H&M, while older working women – in increasingly powerful positions – were now daring to be stylish at work. They celebrated their financial emancipation by turning up to work in Dolce & Gabbana, Jasper Conran or Max Mara.

For those in the middle such as M&S and Arcadia, trading remained dire. The Gap, too, announced a sharp downturn in profits.

Meanwhile, Salsbury decided to turn the screws on the remaining UK suppliers, 'asking' them to accept cuts in their margin. Coats Viyella, now chaired by Sir Harry Djanogly, the man who had been trying to negotiate the merger of Coats's clothing interests with William Baird when M&S withdrew its custom, decided to turn the tables. In an unprecedented move, the company stopped supplying M&S with almost immediate effect. Vandevelde later claimed the move had cost the retailer at least £6m of lost knitwear sales and threatened, but never embarked on, legal action.

Vandevelde had seen enough of Salsbury in action. He switched headhunters from Whitehead Mann, hiring Jill Ader of Egon Zehnder International to find a new chief executive.

Part of the Salsbury revolution had been to spend vast sums of money on advertising and marketing. During 1999 and 2000 – as Next and others slashed their marketing spending – marketing costs had soared from less than 1 per cent of sales to 3 per cent. Alan McWalter, along with the advertising company Rainey Kelly Campbell Roalfe/Y&R, had come up with a series of high-profile television and poster advertisements designed to grab consumer attention.

The first in the series – which became known as 'the fat lady ad' – showed size-16 model Amy Davis rushing up a hill in Somerset, throwing her clothes off in the morning mist until she reached the top, where she threw up her arms and shouted triumphantly: 'I'm normal.'

Launched in early September, the ad got lots of attention – and consumers hated it. Various groups of women protested: the naked female body reminded Jewish women of the Holocaust; it offended Muslim women who believed in covering up; and it antagonised the rest of the female population under 50, most of whom spent their lives trying to look svelte. Did M&S think they all had bottoms that big – and if they had, did they want everyone to know? Fifty per cent of M&S customers might be size 14 or over, but the other half were size 12 or under. In the midst of their panicky desperation, both McWalter and the agency had forgotten the very basic point – one that the departed Andrew Stone and Kim Winser understood all too well – that buying clothes is aspirational. As Nigella Lawson pointed out, writing in the *Observer*, 'The fashion magazines that women buy are the ones with semi-starved waifs on the cover.' If ever there was a signal that the new management at M&S had lost the plot, the fat lady ad was it.

Apparently unnoticed by Salsbury, Freeman or Vandevelde despite the welter of informed comment from the research group Verdict and other retail analysts, designer brands had gripped the imagination and wallet of the newly rich modern woman. As Lawson continued: 'Only those who have

228

no interest in fashion (in other words, those unlikely to be spending much on clothes in the first place) would dream of buying their clothes there any more. The label is king. And St Michael, unlike St Laurent, doesn't count as a designer tag.'

Shopping at M&S was simply no longer cool, she added. 'And the reason it isn't cool is because the contemporary ethos – average wage notwithstanding – is one of conspicuous consumption.'

Along with the ads – the rest of the series were less appalling if unmemorable – went the disastrous slogan 'exclusively for everyone'. It was plain to see M&S was flailing around trying to be all things to all people. At the same time as Amy was romping up the hill in the morning mist, size 10 'It girl' Tara Palmer Tomkinson was modelling the new M&S Salon Rose lingerie. Tara, as everyone knew, shopped mainly in Brompton Road for designer labels such as Versace, Fendi and Gucci.

So much customer research had been done by the consultants that nobody at M&S any longer had a clue who they were aiming at. Asked by an analyst who the core customer was in autumn 2000, Alan McWalter replied that, in his view, there was no such thing. There were, he declared, eleven different types of M&S customer.

The analyst shuddered. Later she told a friend: 'As he said the word eleven, that scene in the film *Titanic* where they realise the boat is definitely going down, flashed through my mind.'

By the time September was halfway through it was clear to Vandevelde and the non-executives that the autumn sales were going to be even worse than those in the spring. It was time for Peter Salsbury to sit down and write two letters.

But before he could do so, the news leaked out that Roger Holmes, the heir apparent to Sir Geoff Mulcahy, head of the Woolworth to B&Q group Kingfisher, had been poached to head UK retailing at M&S. If he did well, the job of chief executive would clearly be his.

A hurried statement on 18 September announced the departure not just of Salsbury but of Freeman and McCracken too. They took just a year's salary each, amounting to a total £1.2m – although options and other perks doubled that figure. Behind them they left just one main-board director who had been there at the time of Keith Oates's attempted coup nearly two years before. Robert Colvill, the irreproachably polite finance director, was the lone survivor. The reality was that no one apart from him and his deputy

Alison Reed knew enough about the complexity of the M&S finances or the financial services arm to risk doing without him.

Salsbury left, relieved to be out of the firing line but a sad and disappointed man. 'I failed to deliver,' he told colleagues. Yet in one way Salsbury had succeeded in what he set out to do. Painfully, slowly, the culture was beginning to change. The rout of the old guard was complete. He left a company stripped of its old identity, but with little idea of what the new one might be.

In October 2000 a new 'concept store' in Kensington was opened, refurbished at great expense. Bright and shiny, the store's creamy interior and chrome fittings gleamed and twinkled in the bright, bright lights. But where was the product? The vast interior had been broken up into small 'lifestyle' areas à la Next, which meant that finding what they were looking for became more of an initiative test than most shoppers wanted. When a desired item was eventually tracked down, chances were it was not available in the right size. Revamping Kensington and two other concept stores had cost a staggering £70 per square foot and involved shutting the doors for several weeks. Twenty-two less ambitious 'concept stores' were rolled out across the country at an average cost of £27 a square foot. Once again they looked good but failed to provide enough product. Many went to look, few stayed to shop.

Holmes's departure from Kingfisher, where he had been expected to take over eventually from the chairman Sir Geoff Mulcahy, had created such a storm that he was prevented from joining M&S until January. An infuriated Mulcahy insisted Holmes take 'gardening leave' but that did not prevent him from watching, analysing and having the occasional informal meeting with people at or connected with his new employer.

The half-year results in November could have been worse, showing pre-tax profits falling just 5 per cent from £193m to £183m, but the trading figures for the previous five weeks were awful. Like-for-like sales of clothing and gifts had plunged by 17 per cent in the five weeks to 4 November. Trading had deteriorated badly since the previous half-year to September, when sales had been down only 2.8 per cent.

The run-up to Christmas 2000 was even worse than the previous year's. Worse still, the opposition was knocking M&S dead. Matalan had become the undisputed darling of the stock market – and of the discerning bargain hunter as well as the lower-income shoppers. The shares had soared from

59p on flotation to 800p. Annual profits at £55m in 2000 were still a fraction of those at M&S but that did not stop tabloids such as the *Daily Mail* comparing their products on the fashion pages. On 4 December a double-page spread showed five similar outfits – one each from M&S and Matalan – giving the relative ratings and an appraisal. Matalan won every time on price while the comments on the M&S offerings verged on the derisory.

Next continued to increase sales and profits. In the four months before Christmas, Next sales rose by 6 per cent. Arcadia began to recover and even Laura Ashley, for so long the basket case of the industry, made a profit. It may have been just £1.7m, but it compared with losses of £7m the previous year and the press welcomed the company back to the land of the living with pages of glowing coverage. At M&S, Vandevelde launched an internal 'fighting back' campaign. Large green posters appeared in the staff quarters of all stores, with an accusing Kitchener-type finger pointing, asking what 'You' were doing to bring customers back. In the run-up to Christmas all directors and senior executives were drafted to work for a day in the store nearest to where they lived, helping customers to pack or stacking shelves. The idea was to put them in touch with the grass roots and to lift the morale of the staff. It may have done so, but in trading terms Christmas was proving to be yet another episode of dashed hopes and broken dreams. When the figures emerged for the sixteen weeks to 20 January 2001, like-for-like sales were 5 per cent lower than for the previous Christmas. The patient was still in a critical condition.

CHAPTER TWELVE

# *New beginnings*

For an ambitious 40-year-old looking for a place in the history books, reviving Britain's most high-profile corporate casualty presented a mouthwatering challenge. Peter Salsbury's successor, Roger Holmes, with his squeaky-clean boy-next-door looks, may not have struck the M&S rank and file as the man to lead Marks & Spencer out of its difficulties. 'Isn't he young?' was the initial reaction of staff in the stores when he first started wandering around wearing a friendly little name badge with just 'Roger' on it. But appearances can be deceptive. Holmes started his career at McKinsey, a leading management consultancy, the Jesuits of global capitalism, and went on to join Kingfisher, where he ran Woolworth and was credited with revitalising B&Q, the do-it-yourself chain. In his McKinsey days, Holmes had looked up to Archie Norman (another McKinsey 'graduate') and had watched his former colleague with admiration, first in his role as finance director of Kingfisher and later as he turned round the fortunes of the Asda supermarket group in the mid 1990s. Holmes followed Norman to Kingfisher. Although well versed in the do-it-yourself market, he had little experience of clothing or food retailing or of financial services. But his McKinsey training had given him the ability to find and use talented people – and to borrow former colleagues' good ideas without a blush.

Enter George Davies, the 'groovy grandpa of fashion' best known for creating the Next chain in the 1980s and as the mastermind behind the George range of clothes for Asda in the 1990s. The man who had recruited Davies to Asda had been Archie Norman.

Davies opened the first Next shop in 1982 and by 1988 it had become a household name credited with changing the way women shopped. Next had also taken over the mail order company Grattan, and at one point was making profits of £90m. Then, just before Christmas 1988, Davies was ousted by the head of Grattan, David Jones, supported by the rest of the board, who accused him of reckless debt-funded over-expansion and autocratic behaviour. Davies was shattered – and for many years he and Jones regarded each other with mutual loathing.

An engaging Liverpudlian who enjoyed being compared to a British bulldog, Davies soon bounced back, joining Asda where, by 1999, the cheap but stylish George clothing range had grabbed 2.5 per cent of the UK clothing market. The range catered for men, women and children and took up 13 per cent of Asda's selling space, generating £600m of sales. But after ten successful if tempestuous years – Davies fell out with his new bosses at WalMart, the giant American retailer, which had taken over Asda in late 1999. Both Archie Norman and Allan Leighton, Asda's chief executive, had quit and WalMart's management style did not prove to be to Davies's taste. He let it be known he was looking for a new challenge.

John Jay of the *Sunday Times* wrote a piece in his Agenda column of 29 October suggesting that one way out of M&S's difficulties would be to hire Davies. 'He may not know much about how to run a big business, as his period at Next shows, but he is one of the great instinctive retailers and might just be the man to turn the sentiment of customers and investors,' he wrote. 'Hiring Davies might seem high risk, but M&S needs to be bold to pull itself out from its spiral of decline.'

The piece was pure serendipity. At the time Jay had no inkling that M&S – along with many other businesses including Tesco and the property company British Land – were pursuing Davies. Holmes asked his old boss at McKinsey, Michael Mire, to forge the initial introduction and when the call came Davies was instantly intrigued. M&S had been his role model in his early career at Littlewoods and at Next he had aspired to many of its values as well as poaching some of its staff. At the height of Next's success in 1988 he had even talked of overtaking it, saying that if Next could grow at 25 per cent compound for ten years, it would be 50 per cent bigger than M&S. 'It's tough, but it's possible,' he said.

Keen to meet M&S's new broom, but intent on total secrecy, Davies sent one of his own drivers to pick up Holmes in London to take him to 'The Barn', his operational nerve centre in the grounds of his Cotswolds farmhouse, for a clandestine meeting.

The two men hit it off straight away, much as Norman and Davies had done a decade before. What had been scheduled as a brief chat lasted for several hours as the cool, analytical Holmes and the fiery, creative Davies discussed how they might combine their talents.

Out of that first meeting came the idea that Davies could create a sub-brand for M&S aimed at fashion-conscious women – a range of clothes that, as Holmes put it, 'would have all the authority of the George Davies name as the creator'. Davies was enthused by the idea, but he had no wish to join M&S as a director. 'I had done that at Hepworth [which became Next] and Asda. I did not want to be involved in managing another company's people again,' he said. Later, the lawyers thrashed out a deal where Davies would become a dedicated supplier, using his own people and his own suppliers – most of them in Italy, Turkey and the Far East – although a few in Leicestershire and Nottinghamshire.

At Asda, all the warehousing and distribution had been done by the supermarket chain. This time, Davies wanted total control – the clothes and accessories would be delivered by his organisation direct to the M&S stores. There they would be displayed in a separate area fitted out by Davies's designers. Even the hangers, in a different colour of transparent plastic for formal wear, casual wear, sleepwear and sportswear, would be designed by him.

For Davies, who found the bureaucracy of big business stifling, the deal had the attraction of giving him total autonomy without the need to worry about renting and running retail properties. The price for such autonomy was high – Davies put up £12m of his own money to get the show up and running – but the rewards for success would be high too. At 59, he had finally negotiated, in the words of the old Leonard Cohen song, 'the deal that was so high and wild he would never have to deal another'. The range would account for 10 per cent of the women's clothing and cover 250,000 square feet spread over ninety stores.

The details of Davies's three-and-a-half year contract took months to sort out – particularly as Tesco was still courting him at the time. When the news finally hit the press on 2 February, the shares jumped 16p on the day to 240p – well off the low of 186p the previous December. The man whose shops had so threatened M&S in the 1980s was riding to the rescue of his old role model and adversary. In April, the new venture gained a brand name, Per Una – Italian for 'for one woman' – suitably continental to fit the times. Unlike the George brand at Asda, it would be wholly owned by Davies. He would supply M&S exclusively in the UK, but if successful, the brand could ultimately be sold overseas through other retailers. The Per Una brand promised both the fashion and flexibility of Zara alongside the value and quality of M&S. The launch was scheduled for autumn 2001.

Holmes meanwhile took a long, cool, McKinsey-style look at Marks & Spencer. He appraised the five restructurings, the myriad initiatives, the advertising and marketing campaigns, the confused and demoralised staff. And he held up his hand and shouted: 'STOP!'

Somewhere within Michael House there used to hang a cartoon. It showed a bulbous-nosed company chairman sitting in front of a graph showing sales in vertiginous decline. A small and humble minion was pictured in the foreground, timidly making a suggestion. 'Well, chairman, we've tried everything else, how about trying to get the product right?' It could have been created for Holmes.

He finally moved into his office at Baker Street in January 2001, just as a report from the performance monitoring consultant Oak Administration revealed Marks & Spencer as the company that had destroyed more shareholder value than any other FTSE 100 company in the previous three years. The report showed that M&S's total shareholder return had fallen by more than 67 per cent between December 1997 and December 2000.

Holmes got to work. 'I was very struck by how inwardly focused the company had remained through the period of change. They had been through all this de-layering but they were still all looking backwards,' he said. 'Nobody seemed to be asking how many customers coming into the stores were actually experiencing a difference.'

Holmes talked to real customers. He recruited them in pairs and walked with them round the stores. They varied from M&S loyalists – the ones who said: 'I can't see what all the fuss is about' – to furious critics, who felt angry and betrayed. His conclusion was: 'We needed to get back to a passion for product.' The story had come full circle. As Simon Marks often said: 'Good goods will sell arse upwards.'

Holmes's challenge was to restore profitability in clothing and claw back market share. Verdict, a retail research firm, estimated the M&S market share had fallen from 13 per cent to 10.5 per cent between 1996 and the end of 2000. M&S's own figures showed the decline was from 15 per cent to 12 per cent but the message was still the same. Verdict had Next up to 5.2 per cent, Matalan with 1.9 per cent and Arcadia up at 8.1 per cent. George at Asda had 2.6 per cent while the department stores had made impressive inroads with their share rising from 3.8 per cent to 5.4 per cent.

Holmes devised a simple strategy to revitalise women's clothing sales. Davies would be given his head in the creation of a fashionable range for younger people. The rest of the M&S clothing talent would be galvanised to target the core customer – women from 35 to 50. 'We need to produce classic clothes that are not boring – classics with a twist,' he told colleagues. To that end he recruited Yasmin Yusuf, the designer behind the Warehouse shops, and fired Barry Morris, who had been kicked off the board in one of the Salsbury restructurings but had held on to his job as head of clothing. By a quirk of fate, as Davies was joining M&S, Brian Godbold, the design director during the heyday of the mid 90s when M&S had received so many fashion plaudits, was recruited to work on the George brand at Asda.

In early spring 2001 Holmes called the suppliers together – Dewhirst, Desmonds and Courtaulds Textiles, by then owned by Sara Lee of America and told them they needed to regain a sense of pride and focus on the product. 'Aspirational quality' became the eerily familiar new buzzword along the endless corridors.

In the food business Holmes put renewed energy behind innovation. The new range of microwavable 'steam cuisine' was protected by patent, but the 'passion for the product' had still to return to the senior executives. Until Greenbury's departure, the directors would sample all new food lines either in the company dining room or at home at the weekend. Yet after the presentation of the annual results in May 2001, one main board director admitted to a journalist that he had never tried a steam cuisine dish, even though they had been in the stores for several weeks.

Holmes also wanted customers all over the country, in smaller stores as well as bigger, to feel they were in a modern environment. His plan was that by the end of 2001, two-thirds of M&S stores would have a new look – not at £70 a square foot, nor at £27 a square foot, but at £14 a square foot. The refits would be quick and effective – lighter colours, new tills, better lighting.

On the Continent and in the United States, Holmes did his homework. Europe was losing £34m a year, Brooks Brothers and Kings had absorbed more than £1bn of investment yet yielded tiny returns. He made the decision that only an outsider free of the emotional baggage of the past could make – they had to go.

On 30 March M&S announced its sixth restructuring in little more than two years. In the UK the direct catalogue business – a pale attempt to compete with Next Directory – was closed. In the United States, Brooks Brothers and Kings went up for sale. As for the thirty-eight European stores which between them were losing £34m a year, they would be closed or sold. At a stroke Vandevelde and Holmes put an end to Rayner's vision in America and Lord Sieff's continental aspirations. Twenty-five years of expansion had come to an abrupt end – at a loss of 4,400 jobs.

The moves – strangely in accordance with Philip Green's plans for M&S had he succeeded in taking it over – met with approval from analysts and other retailers. 'It is absolutely the right thing,' said the chairman of another big retail chain. 'Their foreign stores have always been a disaster – they had no understanding of local markets.'

The City was not so sure about plans to raise £1.4bn from the sale and leasebacks of the UK freehold sites, many of which had been painstakingly put together by Simon Marks and his property guru Arthur Giffard. City institutions had seen retailers such as Burton and Ratner go that route before – with little long-term benefit. Why should M&S destroy the competitive advantage of low-cost property? The answer, it seemed, was so that it could hand back £2 billion to disgruntled shareholders in the hope of giving some impetus to the share price.

It was a ploy that seemed to work, helped by optimism about the Holmes/Davies double act. As the FTSE index of the leading 100 shares fell by 11 per cent in the first seven months of 2001, Marks & Spencer shares rose by 35 per cent from 186p to 251p, making it the best performing FTSE share over that period.

The City debate was soon drowned out by the howls of protest over the continental closure proposals. Holmes and Vandevelde had reckoned without the French trade unionists. Closing an M&S store in Britain had always provoked opposition from local customers and petitions, which occasionally ended up in the House of Lords. But closing thirty-eight stores in France, Spain, Germany and Holland resulted in a fully orchestrated demonstration of angry trade unionists marching up and down Baker Street in the full glare of British media attention. Between 30 March and 10 April there were sixty mentions of M&S in the *Financial Times* alone. Vandevelde's office was deluged with furious letters – even from Holland, where there were just two stores. M&S customers abroad also showed extraordinary emotion about the closures. Where would they get their marmalade, their smoked salmon, their knickers? Within M&S the view was that if those same customers had spent more money buying a wider range of goods the closures might not have been necessary.

Most of the outrage focused on the lack of consultation with the local staff before the closures were announced. But as a UK public company M&S's first legal duty was to shareholders. Pulling out of Europe was price-sensitive information that needed to be reported to the Stock Exchange first – failure to do so would have been a breach of the Financial Services Act. Even so, those who knew about these things said it could have been handled more cleverly. Surely Luc Vandevelde, a Belgian who had worked for years in France, should have known how to get this right? After all, he was being paid enough, as the press pointed out increasingly often.

Vandevelde, who had just notched up his first year with M&S, was about to pocket a £704,000 bonus at a time when every other bonus in the company had been scrapped. His bonus had been negotiated when he joined the company, but that did not prevent a wave of hostile emotion, not only from the trade unionists, but also from the rank and file at Baker Street. Why should they have to sacrifice their bonuses if the man at the top did not?

Resentment boiled over when the *Guardian* received a series of internal papers showing the dire state of trading. In-house profit projections for the year had fallen to £430m, the bottom end of analysts' expectations and £59m below the prediction three months previously. Return on capital had fallen from 17.5 per cent to 15.2 per cent, while costs were rising. Profits per square foot in the clothing departments were less than half, from £18.90 to £9.40.

David Norgrove's new-ventures experiment had officially lost £13m – although some analysts put it at nearer £40m – and was to be closed, while the new lingerie shops had failed to find favour with continental women and had lost nearly £1m.

The leaker had also told the *Guardian* of the fury of long-serving M&S staff at the salaries being offered to new blood such as Yasmin Yusuf and Michèle Jobling, the former Liberty chief executive, who had been brought in to head childrenswear.

The *Guardian* article proved too much for Vandevelde (or was it the non-executives?) and at the end of April he agreed to defer his bonus for a year.

A brief lull followed before the annual results to March 2001 were announced on 22 May. At the press conference, held nearer the City at

Brunswick's presentation theatre, the atmosphere was surprisingly relaxed as journalists sipped cranberry juice and nibbled the best of M&S party snacks.

Vandevelde and Holmes, sporting different versions of the new washable men's suit, mounted the dais with Colvill. Norgrove and Alison Reed – who was due to take over from Colvill as finance director in 2002 – and a number of M&S staff sat towards the back of the auditorium. In a sense, the *Guardian* had done the company a favour. Pre-tax profits for the year came in just 7 per cent lower at £481m on sales of £8.1bn, down from £8.2bn the previous year. If, however, the exceptional charges of the store closures in Europe and various other initiatives were added in, profits had fallen to £145.5m. As if in relief, the shares moved up a couple of pence to 259p. Whichever profit figure observers chose, it was a far cry from the £1.2bn announced just three years before in 1998.

Vandevelde admitted that, contrary to his earlier predictions, there would be no clear recovery by the time he had been with the company for two years. There might, however, be 'pockets of recovery'. The three directors, striving to look relaxed, refused to comment on current trading. The leaker had done it for them. The *Guardian*'s internal figures had showed womenswear clothing sales down by 15 per cent in the first seven weeks of the new financial year.

The day after the results, on 23 May 2001, the memorial service took place for Marcus Sieff in the West London Synagogue in Upper Berkeley Steet, a ten-minute stroll from 'The Arch'. In almost every way, it was a memorial service for the old Marks & Spencer. Many of the people gathered under the vaulted ceilings and stained glass no longer worked for or supplied the company that had for so long been the focus of their lives. Most of them still shopped for food at M&S; some still shopped for clothes, but often with a sense of disappointment.

Sir Richard Greenbury and his wife Siân arrived a full ten minutes before the service was due to begin at 5 p.m., Greenbury's white head towering above everyone else. Luc Vandevelde squeezed into a rare single seat on the opposite side of the synagogue with just a couple of minutes to spare. Family, close friends, lords and ladies took their places in the reserved seats. As well as the Sieff family there were Sachers, Susmans, Lerners and Markses. There were Lord and Lady Wolfson of Sunningdale, Harry Woolf, the Lord Chief Justice, and Lady Woolf, and Lord Feldman. There were many past directors, distant and not so distant. Lord Stone and James Benfield attended but Salsbury did not. Apart from Vandevelde and Colvill there were no current main board directors – Roger Holmes had headed for the airport a couple of hours before. Of the non-executive directors only Sir Martin Jacomb, who had joined in 1991 and knew Sieff, was there. Lord Haskins, Sir David Alliance and Peter Wolff represented suppliers past and present, while from the arts world came Dame Vivien Duffield and Edward Fox.

Many memories in the assembled company stretched back as far as Simon Marks, but the man they had come to remember was his nephew Marcus – and how his personality shone through the service. The tributes from David Susman, a director under Sieff, and John Hunt, manager of the Reading store for much of his career and a man whom Sieff rang every single week, were moving and humorous. The uncrowned prince of British Jewry, Lord (Jacob) Rothschild, quoted *Hamlet* and talked much of Sieff's contribution to Israel and his 'beloved Marks & Spencer'.

His son David Sieff, whose retirement had been announced the day before, told a wickedly funny story about how his father, his brother Michael Sieff and Bob Fox, the impresario, behaved so outrageously while watching a horror film that they were asked to leave the cinema. All those who paid tribute spoke of his appetite for life, his love of women and his tireless work for M&S and for peace in the Middle East. Nobody said 'Thank God he got Alzheimer's before the crisis hit M&S,' but many thought it. Listening to the tributes, it was as if M&S were still in its heyday, the undisputed king of the high street.

Amanda Sieff, Marcus's daughter, all but stole the show with her spirited rendering of the famous speech from *Henry V* launching into: 'Once more unto the breach, dear friends, once more or close the wall up with our English dead,' with spine-tingling vigour. Her sister Daniela read an excerpt from *The Prophet* by Kahlil Gibran and Simon Sieff, a grandson, took for his text the poem 'Death is Nothing at All'.

Jonathan Sieff, the grandson with the biggest helping of his grandfather's charm and raw energy, mounted the dais to read from A. P. Stanley:

He has achieved success who has lived well, laughed often and loved much.
Who has gained the respect of intelligent men and the love of little children.

Who has filled his niche and accomplished his task.
Who has left the world better than he found it.
Who has never lacked appreciation for earthly beauty nor failed to
    express it.
Who has looked for the best in others and given the best he had.
Whose life was an inspiration and whose memory is a benediction.

As one mourner whispered in the middle of the service, it was the end of an era. And as the music of Verdi's 'Chorus of the Hebrew Slaves' from *Nabucco* swelled, so the questions came and they were as much about Simon Marks as his nephew. Could the catastrophe have been avoided? If so, how? Would Simon Marks have done any better than the professional managers that followed Sieff?

Sceptics would say Marks would never have coped with the modern world, with the increased competition and the maturity of the market. But just as he had noticed Woolworth's encroachment, he would have noticed the new competition catching up and the move to out-of-town shopping. His edgy second-generation immigrant insecurity would have kept him alert to change.

Marks would never have let the return on sales go above 10 per cent, nor allowed the kind of 'tawdry' goods that began to proliferate in the stores into *his* Marks & Spencer. The company might have stayed relatively small – he believed 250 stores was about the maximum it could support – and he would have eschewed breakneck expansion or overseas adventures. Profits would have grown more slowly and he would almost certainly have antagonised the City – although he would have kept a controlling shareholding. But he would have stuck to his maxim – product, people and property. The company would have been smaller but it would have been in better shape and with its reputation intact.

Perhaps the most promising sign that a new era was beginning was the news of the move from Baker Street to a gleaming new development at Paddington Basin and a building that would house 2,000 people rather than the 3,000-odd at the old headquarters. Holmes had made his feelings about those long corridors and closed doors clear in his first interview with Kate Rankine of the *Telegraph*.

As long as the nerve centre of the company remained at Baker Street, too much of the old culture would endure. There had been efforts at modernisation. The old dark reception area was opened up and the lighting improved. The cumbersome dingy furniture was replaced by stylish modern seating and trendy banquettes in blues and pinks and purples. But the queue to the elegant women on the reception desk was still chanelled through the same kind of control system used at the exchange counters in M&S stores. And on several of the tables in the waiting area were signs that read: 'All pass holders are requested to wait in the reception area until collection by their host'. It smacked of the old M&S command-and-control culture.

Upstairs on the first floor, the commissionaire who guarded the directors' corridor had long gone. Vandevelde scrapped the blue regal carpet and had the original herringbone wooden flooring sanded to give a more modern feel. Even so, the herringbone pattern held memories of school for many, while the corridor stretched in front of the beholder almost to infinity. The lights may have been brighter, the decor lighter, but it still smacked of Kafka.

Vandevelde, still under the influence of Peter Salsbury's slash-and-burn policies, had the portraits of the former chairmen removed from the boardroom, replaced by blown-up fashion shots from the marketing department. But the portraits remained a contentious issue. Sir Martin Jacomb as senior non-executive had promised Greenbury on his retirement that his picture would hang in the boardroom alongside those of his predecessors. Yet Salsbury, in Stalinesque mode, had sworn that Greenbury's portrait would never be hung with the others. It was as if he was trying to airbrush his mentor out of M&S history. It seemed that the only diplomatic thing to do was to remove the pictures of all the previous chairmen. Vandevelde must have felt ambivalent about having his immediate predecessor's portrait hanging in the headquarters. He had joined in the 'let's blame Rick for everything' campaign and no doubt felt it would be hypocritical to hang the portrait when there had been so much ill feeling towards Greenbury.

In May 2001 Vandevelde, with the agreement of most of the non-executives, decided that the way round this tricky problem was to return all the portraits to the families of the subjects. At this, Sir David Sieff, who was on the point of retirement, ran out of patience and wrote a strongly worded letter to Vandevelde protesting at the idea that the portraits of the men who had built M&S into a national institution were going to be removed from the headquarters of that institution. 'I told them you could not rewrite history,' he said. After a stormy board meeting during which Sir Michael Perry and Sir Ralph Robins, two of the older non-executives, objected vigorously to the portraits leaving the building, a compromise was agreed. The portraits of Michael Marks, Simon Marks and Israel Sieff would be hung somewhere in the headquarters, but not in the boardroom. The portrait of Teddy would go to his widow, Lois, that of Marcus Sieff to David. As Derek Rayner's mother and sister had both died, his was to go to his old friend Alistair Sampson, the antique dealer with whom he shared rooms at Cambridge along with Geoffrey Howe. Greenbury's recently completed portrait by Richard Foster, showing him in kindly mood, would go back to him to hang in his Berkshire home. It was an astonishing exercise in petty-mindedness.

Months before, Vandevelde had ordered the walls of Greenbury's office to be demolished so that there was no visible trace of the space he occupied. The area where once his word spelled life or death for a jumper neckline was converted into an open-plan office for secretarial and administration workers.

But apart from Norgrove, who kept open the door to his grey monk's cell of an office, the directors kept their doors closed. No one standing outside could guess at the nature of the antique furniture, the fine pictures or the number of windows within.

Middle management still walked in fear of the summons to the personnel office. One selector, highly rated by the old regime, was told she had no chance of promotion because the more senior positions had been earmarked for fresh blood.

If in the summer of 2001 there was a sign that something had changed fundamentally, it was in the nature of the people you met in the corridor on the long trek from Zone A to Zone D. Where in 1998 there had been closed-faced men in suits and deferential women in skirts, there were now young funky people with spiky hair wearing jeans and chinos. They looked relaxed and open to new ideas – unburdened by the past. M&S was not the only company for which they had worked, it might not be the only one for which they would work in the future.

The sound of laughter could even be heard as this new breed of M&S employee chatted together in groups and headed for the café. Perhaps some were laughing about the fate of Matalan, whose shares had plunged following warnings of lower profit margins and the dramatic ousting of the chief executive Angus Monro by the controlling shareholders. Or maybe they were marvelling at the success of Zara, whose owners had just become the richest people in Spain after the flotation of their holding company Inditex. The shares had soared from the offer price to value the company at £7bn – virtually the same as the market value of M&S.

In the cult movie *Annie Hall*, Woody Allen declared mournfully that 'a relationship is like a shark, if it stops moving it is dead'. Retailing is no different. Sometime in the second half of the 1990s, Marks & Spencer stopped moving. The thinking of the people at the top had ossified. All the events that took place between November 1998 and May 2001 were effectively a series of resuscitation attempts. By the time of the annual meeting in July, the eyelids were beginning to flutter, there was a faint flush returning to the cheeks, but at that stage, the patient was still on life support.

# Bibliography

Bookbinder, Paul, *Simon Marks, Retail Revolutionary*, London, George Weidenfeld and Nicolson, 1993.

Bower, Joseph and Matthews, John, 'Marks & Spencer: Sir Richard Greenbury's Quiet Revolution', discussion paper, Harvard Business School, August 1994.

Briggs, Asa, *Marks & Spencer 1884–1984, A Centenary History*, London, Octopus Books, 1984.

*Directors' Remuneration: Report of a Study Group chaired by Sir Richard Greenbury* (Greenbury Report), London, Gee Publishing, 1995.

Harris, Christine with Bower, Joseph L., 'Marks and Spencer, Ltd.', discussion paper, Harvard Business School, 1975, revised January 1977.

Lewis, David and Bridger, Darren, *The Soul of the New Consumer*, London, Nicholas Brealey Publishing, 2001.

Montgomery, Cynthia A., 'Marks and Spencer', discussion paper, Harvard Business School, May 1991.

Owen, Geoffrey, *From Empire to Europe*, London, HarperCollins, 1999.

Rees, Goronwy, *St Michael: A History of Marks & Spencer*, London, Pan Books, 1985.

Sieff, Israel, *The Memoirs of Israel Sieff*, London, George Weidenfeld and Nicolson, 1985.

Sieff, Marcus, *Don't Ask the Price: The Memoirs of the President of Marks & Spencer*, London, George Weidenfeld & Nicolson, 1987.

# APPENDICES

# Marks and Spencer profits
# from 1927 (flotation)

| | Pre-tax profits | Sales | Number of UK stores |
|---|---|---|---|
| 1927 | £74, 938 12s 6d | £1.3m | 135 |
| 1930 | £335,174 16s 9d | £3.6m | |
| 1935 | £1,086,597 14s 2d | £11.4m | |
| | £m | £m | |
| 1940 | 2.4 | 27.03 | 234 |
| 1945 | 1.9 | 18.1 | |
| 1950 | 4.6 | 52.6 | |
| 1955 | 9.2 | 108.4 | |
| 1960 | 17.6 | 148.0 | |
| 1965 | 27.5 | 219.8 | |
| 1970 | 43.7 | 360.9 | 245 |
| 1975 | 81.8 | 721.9 | 252 |
| 1980 | 173.6 | 1,667.9 | 252 |
| 1985 | 303.4 | 3,213.0 | 265 |
| 1990 | 604.2 | 5,608.1 | 272 |
| 1995 | 924.3 | 6,806.5 | 283 |
| 1996 | 965.8 | 7,211.3 | 284 |
| 1997 | 1,102,0 | 7,841.9 | 286 |
| 1998 | 1,168.0 | 8,343.3 | 294 |
| 1999 | 628.4 | 8,224.0 | 294 |
| 2000 | 557.2 | 8,195.5 | 300 |
| 2001 | 480.9 | 8,075.7 | 303 |

# Company comparisons

## Clothing market shares, 1996–2000, %

| | 1996 | 1997 | 1998 | 1999 | 2000 |
|---|---|---|---|---|---|
| **Specialists** | | | | | |
| Marks & Spencer | 13.0 | 13.4 | 13.0 | 11.4 | 10.5 |
| Arcadia | 6.0 | 6.2 | 6.4 | 7.2 | 8.1 |
| Next | 3.4 | 3.9 | 3.9 | 4.4 | 5.2 |
| C&A | 2.0 | 2.0 | 1.9 | 1.8 | 2.0 |
| BHS | 2.5 | 2.4 | 2.4 | 2.2 | 2.1 |
| Sears | 2.4 | 2.4 | 2.0 | | |
| Matalan | 0.7 | 0.8 | 1.0 | 1.3 | 1.9 |
| New Look | 1.1 | 1.4 | 1.5 | 1.6 | 1.7 |
| Littlewoods | 1.7 | 1.5 | 1.2 | 1.1 | 1.2 |
| River Island | 1.3 | 1.2 | 1.1 | 1.2 | 1.2 |
| Gap | 0.6 | 0.6 | 0.8 | 0.9 | 1.1 |
| Etam | 0.9 | 0.8 | 0.7 | 0.8 | 0.8 |
| Monsoon | 0.4 | 0.5 | 0.5 | 0.6 | 0.6 |
| Oasis | 0.3 | 0.4 | 0.4 | 0.5 | 0.5 |
| Austin Reed | 0.3 | 0.3 | 0.5 | 0.5 | 0.5 |
| Other specialists | 25.8 | 25.5 | 25.4 | 27.3 | 27.3 |
| **All specialists** | **62.4** | **63.3** | **62.7** | **62.7** | **64.7** |
| | | | | | |
| **Grocers** | | | | | |
| George at Asda | 1.6 | 2.0 | 2.2 | 2.5 | 2.6 |
| Tesco | 0.9 | 0.9 | 1.0 | 1.1 | 1.2 |
| Sainsbury | 0.4 | 0.4 | 0.3 | 0.3 | 0.3 |
| Other grocers | 0.9 | 1.0 | 1.1 | 1.1 | 0.9 |
| **Sub-total** | **3.8** | **4.3** | **4.6** | **5.0** | **5.0** |

|  | 1996 | 1997 | 1998 | 1999 | 2000 |
|---|---|---|---|---|---|
| **Department stores** | | | | | |
| Debenhams | 3.7 | 3.8 | 3.8 | 3.8 | 3.9 |
| House of Fraser | 1.6 | 1.6 | 1.5 | 1.5 | 1.6 |
| John Lewis | 1.2 | 1.3 | 1.3 | 1.3 | 1.4 |
| Other department stores | 3.8 | 4.5 | 5.4 | 5.5 | 5.4 |
| **Sub-total** | **10.3** | **11.2** | **12** | **12.1** | **12.3** |
| **Mail Order** | **12.2** | **12.8** | **12.7** | **11.9** | **10.4** |
| **Other** | **11.3** | **8.4** | **8.0** | **8.3** | **7.6** |
| **Total** | **100.0** | **100.0** | **100.0** | **100.0** | **100.0** |

Source: Verdict Analysis

# Marks and Sieff family tree*

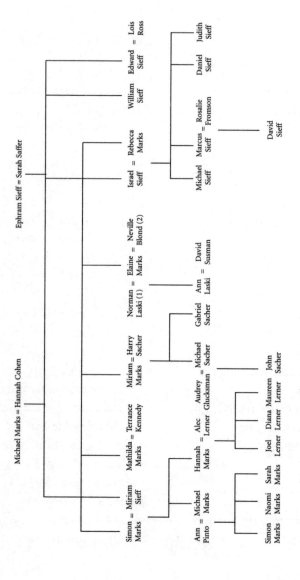

*Source: *Simon Marks, Retail Revolutionary* by Paul Bookbinder.

# *Index*